Indigenous Audibilities

Currents in Latin American & Iberian Music

Alejandro L. Madrid, Series Editor
Walter Aaron Clark, Founding Series Editor

Indigenous Audibilities

Music, Heritage, and Collections in the Americas

AMANDA MINKS

OXFORD

UNIVERSITY PRESS

OXFORD
UNIVERSITY PRESS

Oxford University Press is a department of the University of Oxford. It furthers
the University's objective of excellence in research, scholarship, and education
by publishing worldwide. Oxford is a registered trade mark of Oxford University
Press in the UK and certain other countries.

Published in the United States of America by Oxford University Press
198 Madison Avenue, New York, NY 10016, United States of America.

CIP data is on file at the Library of Congress

ISBN 978–0–19–753249–2 (pbk.)
ISBN 978–0–19–753248–5 (hbk.)

DOI: 10.1093/oso/9780197532485.001.0001

Paperback printed by Marquis Book Printing, Canada
Hardback printed by Bridgeport National Bindery, Inc., United States of America

To Sofía and Luis

Contents

Figures

About the Cover Image, *The Game*

The Game (1955, egg tempera on panel) is a painting by Emilio Amero, who was born in Ixtlahuaca, Mexico, in 1901 and died in Norman, Oklahoma, in 1976. Amero worked in various media throughout his life, not only as a modernist painter and muralist, but also as a photographer, cinematographer, and most extensively a lithographer. He began his career as a draftsman for the ethnographic drawing department at the Museo de Arqueología in Mexico City, under the direction of his friend and former classmate Rufino Tamayo, who later served as a mediator between the art scenes of New York City and Mexico City (to be discussed in Chapter 2). Reflecting on his early work, Amero said, "I copied the idols and other forms of preconquest people. Many of them looked like neighbors from my childhood in Ixtlahuaca."[1] Although Amero is not directly a subject of this book, his time working as an art professor at the University of Oklahoma (beginning in 1946) coincided with many of the institutional figures discussed in Chapter 1. His struggles within institutions in Mexico and the United States also parallel the stories throughout this book.

Painted in earthy tones with a golden hue, *The Game* portrays female figures with angular gestures as if in a stylized dance, but open to multiple interpretations. The seated figure on the right could be a street vendor or a mendicant. Some of Amero's characteristic visual elements here include sharp-edged pebbles and the flowing cloth of Indigenous textiles. Heads turned slightly, lips sealed, the two figures in the foreground look off toward the left of the painting, while an iguana positioned beneath the line of their gaze looks up at them. The straight, perfect corners of the brick wall contrast with the rugged terrain beneath the women's feet and with the distant landscape we glimpse on the right beyond the brick wall. Leaving the viewer with ample room for conjecture, *The Game* may evoke the indeterminacy

---

[1] Quoted in Phelan (2015: 2), from Joseph Taft, "Life Touched by Conversations with Emilio Amero," *Norman Transcript*, Norman, Oklahoma, 1976.

and interplay of the modern and the traditional, the rural and the urban, the visible and the audible, the present and the past.[2]

Credit: *The Game*, 1955 (egg tempera on panel), Amero, Emilio (1901–76) / Fred Jones Jr. Museum of Art, University of Oklahoma, USA / © Fred Jones Jr. Museum of Art / Gift of J. Wendell Andrews / Bridgeman Images.

---

[2] This note draws on information and ideas presented in Merida [1937] 1968, Phelan (2015), Zúñiga (2008), and the museum exhibit label written for *The Game* by Mark White, former curator of the Fred Jones, Jr., Museum of Art. My interpretation has also been shaped by conversations with Andrew Phelan, former director of the School of Art at the University of Oklahoma and a specialist in Amero's work.

Acknowledgments

Developing a multisited project over more than a decade requires many words of thanks. I gratefully acknowledge all the libraries and archives that opened their doors to me in person or provided access to digital collections. I conducted archival research at the Centro Nacional de las Artes (Mexico), the Instituto de Historia de Nicaragua y Centroamérica (Nicaragua), the Music Division and the American Folklife Center of the US Library of Congress, the Columbus Memorial Library of the Organization of American States, the Benson Latin American Collection of the University of Texas at Austin, the Western History Collections of the University of Oklahoma, the Oklahoma Historical Society, and the Oklahoma Department of Libraries. During the process of revision, I was finally able to travel to Chile and visited the historic sound archive which is now the Centro de Documentación e Investigación Musical in the Music Department, Faculty of Arts, of the Universidad de Chile. At various stages of research, I used digital collections based at the following institutions: the *Revista Musical Chilena* at the Universidad de Chile, the Memoria Chilena platform of the Biblioteca Nacional of Chile, the Museo Chileno de Arte Precolombino, the Fonoteca Nacional of Mexico, Oklahoma State University Library, and the Western History Collections of the University of Oklahoma. In addition to these institutions, I communicated with the American Philosophical Society and the New York Public Library for the Performing Arts to acquire scans of specific archival materials. I am responsible for the interpretations within this book, which do not reflect the positions of the institutions where I have conducted research.

At the University of Oklahoma Libraries, I am especially indebted to Lina Ortega (Sac and Fox), Todd Fuller, Barbara Laufersweiler, the interlibrary loan staff, and the staff of the digitization lab. Lina Ortega provided feedback on my Oklahoma-based chapter (Chapter 1) and has been a wise collaborator in Indigenous archiving projects. Dan Swan, Chris Aplin, and Josh Garrett-Davis also provided crucial feedback on Chapter 1. Conversations with Jerry Whistler Snow (Sac and Fox) helped me interpret Don Whistler's work and the broader family collections which Jerry organized and deposited in the Western History Collections. I am grateful to Laura Peterson and her family for permission to quote from the John Joseph Mathews (Osage) Collection in the OU Western History Collections.

In developing Chapter 2 through Mexico-based research, the staff of the Biblioteca de las Artes in the Centro Nacional de las Artes kindly facilitated my research visit back in 2012. I am grateful to the staff of the Fonoteca Nacional who engaged in Zoom and email conversations with me in the fall of 2020, including Mariela Salazar Hernández, Celene Eslava Rojas, Victor Manuel Heredia Arriaga, Leonora Manríquez Zepeda, María Teresa Ortiz Arellano, and María Margarita Sosa Suárez. Octavio Murillo Alvarez de la Cadena of the Instituto Nacional de los Pueblos Indígenas also contributed to the discussion.

I published parts of Chapter 2 in a Spanish-language article in *Latin American Caribbean and Ethnic Studies*, a 2022 special issue edited by Laura Giraudo and Emilio J. Gallardo Saborido.[3] I received valuable feedback from two anonymous reviewers as well as Laura Giraudo, Emilio J. Gallardo Saborido, and Kristina Nielsen. I am especially indebted to Laura Giraudo for sharing a digitized collection of materials related to Henrietta Yurchenco's 1940s work at the Inter-American Indian Institute. These materials are part of the Archivo Histórico del Instituto Indigenista Interamericano (AHIII), which was initially digitized under the management of the last director of the Institute, Guillermo Espinosa Velasco. Laura Giraudo has generously shared knowledge and materials in coordinating the Red Inter-Indi, a network of scholars interested in inter-American indigenismo, with which I am affiliated. I am also grateful to Henrietta Yurchenco's son, Dr. Peter Yurchenco, for permission to publish a photo of his mother, Henrietta Yurchenco. Many thanks to Jessica Gottfried Hesketh for sending me books from Mexico.

At the Library of Congress American Folklife Center, I am grateful to Nancy Groce for sharing her thoughts with me, and to Judith Gray for reading and providing invaluable feedback on the Introduction and Chapter 2. Also at the American Folklife Center, Todd Harvey helped with Lomax research and heroically tracked down early Chilean recordings deposited in the Library of Congress. Meeting James Wintle, a music reference librarian (also a vocalist and composer) in the Performing Arts Reading Room at the Library

---

[3] For the full citations of my previously published articles related to the topic of this book, see Minks (2014, 2020a, 2020b, 2022) in the references.

of Congress made for a great "archive story," to use Antoinette Burton's term. Chatting about Oklahoma connections, we discovered that we attended the same elementary school at the same time in a small town in southeastern Oklahoma.

My Nicaraguan research for Chapter 3 began and ended in the Benson Latin American Collection at the University of Texas at Austin. I am grateful to archivist Dylan Joy for his support, especially during the height of the pandemic when travel was impossible. I was incredibly fortunate to spend seven months in 2016 in residence at the Instituto de Historia de Nicaragua y Centroamérica (IHNCA) of the Universidad Centroamericana (UCA) in Managua, Nicaragua. I am grateful to the Fulbright Scholar Program for funding my residency and to the generosity of all the IHNCA personnel who facilitated my research and teaching. Many friends and colleagues from the UCA have remained in my thoughts and in my heart. In my "diplomado" seminar course on ethnomusicological research methods at the IHNCA, I learned a tremendous amount from my students, who included not only university students but also musicians, theater professionals, media makers, workers in the heritage sector, and veterans of the 1979 Revolution and the 1980s civil war. It is difficult to describe the thrill of presenting a historical song in class and suddenly have the students join in, singing along in harmony. It has been a great pleasure to continue communicating and collaborating with some of these amazing people.

Chapter 3 grew out of two previous articles, one published in English in *Latin American Caribbean and Ethnic Studies* (2014, Vol. 9, No. 3), and another published in Spanish in *Trans: Revista Transcultural de Música* (2020, Vol. 24), which was a special issue edited by Antonio Monte, Helga Zambrano, and myself. The 2014 article benefited from the feedback of Laura Graham, T. M. Scruggs, Jennifer Goett, and two anonymous reviewers. The 2020 article benefited from the feedback and editing of Antonio Monte as well as Iñigo Sánchez Fuarros. My research on Nicaraguan historical discourse has benefited greatly from ongoing conversations with Bernard Gordillo and Juan Pablo Gómez, both of whom provided invaluable feedback on Chapter 3.

It is a tribute to the strong institutionalization of music studies in Chile that I was able to carry out so much research for Chapter 4 before visiting Chile in person. Chilean composers' involvement in the inter-American networks of the 1940s led me to pursue Chile as a research topic, and contemporary Chilean scholars and librarians have created tremendous resources in the form of publications and digital collections. Daniel Party and José Manuel Izquierdo König provided feedback on an article I wrote about the Library of Congress letters between Charles Seeger and Domingo Santa Cruz (*Latin American Music Review* 2020, Vol. 4, No. 1), parts of which were incorporated into Chapter 4. I fleshed out Chapter 4 in the text of an online presentation for the Semana de Musicología at the Instituto de Música of the Pontificia Universidad Católica in 2021. I am grateful to José Manuel Izquierdo König, Daniel Party, and Alejandro Vera for inviting me to participate, and I learned from all the presentations and discussions. As I worked through early issues of the *Revista Musical Chilena* (via its seamless digital platform), Cristián Guerra Rojas answered deep historical questions promptly and thoroughly in his position as editor.

My visit to Chile in June of 2022 was crucial for refining my interpretations. Before traveling, my dear colleagues and neighbors in Oklahoma, Marcelo Rioseco and Carolina Ruedas, gave me a thorough orientation to Santiago and pandemic-era travel. My trip to Chile coincided with a conference on traditional and folkloric musics organized by Christian Spencer at the Universidad Mayor (Campus El Claustro), as well as the launch of a book and CD of Carlos Isamitt's work under the direction of Freddy Chávez at the Universidad Metropolitana de Ciencias de la Educación (UMCE). I benefited from rich conversations at both these events as well as other meetings outside them. In particular, I thank Christian Spencer, Gabriel Rammsy, Ignacio Ramos Rodillo, Héctor Pavez, Jacob Rekedal, Eileen Karmy, Martín Farías, Juan Carlos Poveda, Luis Achondo, and Daniel Party. I also thank the outstanding performers of Isamitt's music during the UMCE event which breathed new life into these works. Visiting Claudio Mercado at the Museo Chileno de Arte Precolombino enriched my understanding of the repatriation of Isabel Aretz's Chilean collections and Claudio's long-term work mediating collections and communities. At the sound archive in the Department of Music at the Universidad de Chile, Fernanda Vera and Rodrigo Torres took time out of their day for a long conversation about the twentieth-century founders of Chilean music research. I am eternally grateful to Freddy Chávez Cancino, the curator of Carlos Isamitt's family archive, for his ongoing support and feedback which shaped Chapter 4, and to Dionis Isamitt Danitz, the son of Carlos Isamitt, for sharing his memories and collections. The warmth and generosity extending from their collaboration surely follows in Carlos Isamitt's footsteps.

I am grateful for the feedback I received at presentations sponsored by the Society for Ethnomusicology, the American Anthropological Association, the Native American and Indigenous Studies Association, and the Central American Cultural Studies conference. I am also grateful for feedback on my invited lectures at Columbia University, the University of California at Berkeley, Reed College, the University of North Texas at Denton, the Universidad Centroamericana in Managua, the Pontificia Universidad Católica in Santiago, and the Universidad Metropolitana de Ciencias de Educación in Santiago. My 2013 presentation at Columbia was a collaboration with Alvaro Baca, and I especially benefited from follow-up conversations with Laura Graham and Rosemary Coombe.

Pulling together this multisited study has been no small challenge, and I could not have done it alone. Ana María Ochoa read the first full draft of the manuscript and generously shared her brilliant perspectives which helped me begin to see the forest and not only the trees; she also suggested using "Indigenous Audibilities" in the title. My Introduction benefited from the feedback of Kelly Tatro and Kim Marshall, as well as the Honors College Faculty Research Seminar, including Ben Alpers, Marie Dallam, Julia Ehrhardt, Dan Mains, Carolyn Morgan, and Sarah Tracy. Rodrigo Chocano's expertise in heritage discourses as well as the Seeger collections was a godsend. I am grateful to Andrés Amado for his quick responses to specialized questions. Lila Ellen Gray engaged in inspiring dialogue and helped me make decisions at various stages. Morgan Luker was a close fellow traveler and provided expert feedback on my book proposal as well as several presentations. Aaron Fox has been a steady interlocutor and source of encouragement. I am grateful to Anthony Seeger for dialogue about this work at various points, and to Kim Seeger for supporting the scholarly use of materials from the Seeger collections at the Library of Congress.

Many friends and colleagues at the University of Oklahoma have provided long-term inspiration, dialogue, and moral support. Though I cannot name them all, I want to especially recognize Amanda Cobb-Greetham (Chickasaw), Raina Heaton, Misha Klein, Joshua Nelson (Cherokee), Sean O'Neill, Laurel Smith, Sarah Tracy, and Dan Swan. Lots of critical thinking came out of long walks and talks with Kirsten Edwards, whom I miss greatly since she moved on. I thank Kim Wieser for permission to quote from her poem in the epilogue. Christina Giacona helped me wrap my head around some of the overlapping issues in our projects, and Danielle Herrington was a great resource for questions about the voice. I thank all my undergraduate students in the Honors College who patiently read draft excerpts of my book as part of their course readers, which enabled me to work through ideas in class. Two Honors research assistants—Grace Green and Crystal Neill—helped me organize materials. Kamryn Yanchick (Seminole/Mvskoke) was an inspiring partner on another project which helped inform this book. It is a privilege to work in an academic unit where research and teaching are supported as interconnected endeavors. Research for this project was funded by the University of Oklahoma Honors College, the Oklahoma Humanities Council, and the Fulbright Scholar Program. Additional financial support was provided from the Office of the Vice President for Research and Partnerships and the Office of the Provost, University of Oklahoma.

I deeply appreciate the efforts of Oxford University Press, especially the series editor Alejandro Madrid for his interest and support, my previous editor Suzanne Ryan, my current editor Norm Hirschky, and the entire production team. Two anonymous reviewers helped me clarify my approach and certain points of analysis. Despite the feedback I have received through formal and informal channels, some errors or misinterpretations may slip through the cracks of this work, for which I take full responsibility. I hope that some readers will grasp loose threads and weave new perspectives in the future.

Personal and intellectual histories sometimes intersect in unexpected ways, and layers of relationships run beneath the text of this book. I grew up hearing stories about Latin America told by my great-aunt, a Catholic Ursuline nun born in 1929 to poor white farmers living on the edge of the Navajo Nation in New Mexico. From childhood, she dreamed of working in Latin America. Soon after the Second Vatican Council, she was sent to Venezuela in 1966 and was living in Santiago, Chile, at the time of the 1973 military coup. These are complicated histories. I am grateful for the pathways opened to me, but I remain critically conscious of the legacies of colonialism and my own positioning within them. My ancestors were white farmers and ranchers who moved around the Southern Plains and Southwest United States in the early decades of the twentieth century, trying to make lives on cheap land which had been Indian land. Without conscious design, this work may be a partial response to those personal histories.

A word of heartfelt thanks must go to my loving family members, near and far, especially my dad and my siblings Laura, Joy, Aaron, and their families. My older sister Laura (who taught me to read, way back in our pretend school) read drafts and gave me pep talks. My mother passed away in the middle of this project, but her influence continues. Many thanks to Beth for sharing her joyful spark.

Finally, this work has been supported in myriad ways by my partner in life, and shaped by our conversations about history, politics, and indigeneity. *También agradezco a su familia por todo su apoyo y por compartir la magia de la comarca.* I count myself lucky to live with someone who could instantly interpret the abbreviations of a 1940s letter closing, "De usted Afmo. Atto. Amigo y S. S." This book is dedicated to our children Sofía and Luis, whose affectionate and attentive love makes me grateful every day.

A Note on Terminology and Abbreviations

Moving between heritage discourses in English and Spanish requires close attention to language and translation. In Spanish, *patrimonio* (patrimony) is the most commonly used term to convey a sense of heritage as it is usually understood in English—the collective culture or property that is passed from one generation to the next. *Patrimonio* is also an important legal term for nation-states and Indigenous peoples, among others whose rights to culture and resources are enshrined in legal documents. In addition to *patrimonio*, the terms *herencia* and *acervo* appear across case studies in this book. The Spanish word *herencia* can refer to material inheritance, to the process of transmission, or to physical and moral attributes passed from one generation to the next. *Acervo* can mean heritage, following a sense of wealth or treasure (material or cultural). Importantly, *acervo* can also mean "collection," moving from the abstract to the concrete in heritage management.

National and international institutions are notorious for the proliferation of acronyms that become second nature to insiders and part of the mystification of bureaucracy to outsiders. In this book, I use the following acronyms that were part of the everyday discourse and publications of the institutions I analyze:

III Inter-American Indian Institute / *Instituto Indigenista Interamericano*: founded 1940, headquarters in Mexico City with affiliated institutes throughout Latin America.

PAU Pan American Union / *Unión Panamericana*: founded 1890, headquarters in Washington, DC, integrated into the Organization of American States in 1948.

SEP Secretariat of Public Education / *Secretaría de Educación Pública*: founded 1921, Mexican federal agency headquartered in Mexico City.

WPA Works Progress Administration: established 1935, US federal agency headquartered in Washington, DC, renamed Work Projects Administration from 1939 to 1943.

Introduction

During the years when I began working on this book, I often huddled near the rows of metal bookshelves devoted to Native American and Latin American histories on the first floor of the University of Oklahoma main library. In that area, in the company of rotating exhibits of Native American art, was a collection of volumes titled *América Indígena*, Indigenous America, lined up inconspicuously on the first row of shelves, toward the bottom. This was the primary research publication of the Inter-American Indian Institute, founded in Pátzcuaro, Mexico, in April of 1940. In the first volume of *América Indígena*, the US Commissioner of the Bureau of Indian Affairs, John Collier, published an article (in Spanish) titled "New Concepts of Indigenous Unity." The article introduced the founding of the Inter-American Indian Institute and provided a long excerpt of a speech by D'Arcy McNickle given at the University of Oklahoma in July of 1940.[1] McNickle was one of the first Native Americans in the professional ranks of the Bureau of Indian Affairs, although he considered his primary vocation to be that of a writer, especially a novelist. He also loved music and had studied the violin earlier in life.[2]

McNickle had attended the founding congress of the Inter-American Indian Institute in Mexico and gave the speech in Oklahoma less than three months later to a diverse audience of Tribal leaders, government officials, academic specialists, and missionaries.[3] In his speech, McNickle insisted on the heterogeneity of Indigenous peoples while also asserting their commonalities, including colonial experiences, autochthonous forms of governance, and self-determination. The speech repudiated the notion that Indigenous peoples were disappearing and defended the strengthening

---

[1] Collier (1941).

[2] McNickle was an enrolled member of the Confederated Salish and Kootenai Tribes of the Flathead Reservation, where he grew up in Montana. His mother was Cree from Canada and his father was Irish (Parker 1994).

[3] Details about the conference were published in local newspapers such as the *El Reno Daily Tribune*, which placed the news article under the title "'Vanishing' Race Gaining Rapidly" (1941). Other speakers who were part of the formal program included Tribal leaders, "state writers," historians, and "Indian service anthropologists" who worked for the Bureau of Indian Affairs.

Indigenous Audibilities. Amanda Minks, Oxford University Press. © Oxford University Press 2024.
DOI: 10.1093/oso/9780197532485.003.0001

of Indigenous sovereignty in political and cultural terms. McNickle's speech, delivered in English at the University of Oklahoma, was translated to Spanish in Mexico City for the purpose of publication in *América Indígena*. This translated text then made its way back to the University of Oklahoma, first as part of the Department of Anthropology collections, then catalogued and shelved at the main library, where it came to share space with Native American art of Oklahoma and the Southwest United States (see Figure I.1).

Indigenous arts were encoded in the founding convention of the Inter-American Indian Institute, summarized in that first issue of *América Indígena* along with McNickle's speech. The convention included mandates for promoting autochthonous music, dance, and theater; protecting Indigenous arts and artisans; and organizing inter-American festivals of Indigenous arts.[4] In the 1940s a cluster of activities revolved around Indigenous music, which was tied to other arts through social and aesthetic relations, both in the institutional networks and in Indigenous communities.

During this period, discourses about Indigenous music and culture in the United States and in different countries of Latin America moved into closer dialogue than before. What can we learn when we try to listen to historical sources that document these interactions? What becomes audible and what remains inaudible, particularly in the context of the unequal relations stemming from colonialism? And how did these discourses contribute to ideas about heritage? Heritage has often been associated with received traditions and collective perceptions of the past, but it also entails claims of cultural identity, ownership, and belonging in the present. In listening to the archive, we may better understand the formation of discourses about heritage. These discourses include purist representations of national cultures, as well as the controlled recognition of cultural difference within the nation. Heritage discourse can also make counterhegemonic claims, thereby disrupting dominant structures of representation.[5]

In *Indigenous Audibilities*, I explore these histories through four case studies which involve intimate stories and multifaceted relations in and between the United States, Mexico, Nicaragua, and Chile. These histories involve various institutions, especially the US Works Progress

---

[4] "Editorial," *América Indígena* (1941: 6).
[5] García Canclini ([1990] 1995); Smith (2006); Trujillo (2008); Harrison (2013); Geismar (2015).

Figure I.1 Cover of *América Indígena*, 1947, Vol. 7, No. 4. This copy from the University of Oklahoma Libraries was originally part of the Anthropology Department subscriptions, demonstrating the networks between academics studying Indian affairs in Oklahoma and the Inter-American Indian Institute in Mexico. Apparent coffee stains show signs of use.

Administration, the Inter-American Indian Institute, and the Pan American Union. As Laura Giraudo has suggested, studying the undersides of institutions reveals the historical processes through which Indigenous peoples and cultures were folded into modern ethno-racial hierarchies.[6] This approach also reveals the participation of Indigenous actors in national and transnational institutions—often marginalized, but actively negotiating the power structures of their time.[7] As my case studies move from US Indian Territory to Mexico to Nicaragua and then to Chile in the southern cone, we will see that all of these sites were cross-cut by transnational networks, and in a sense they are all borderlands at the intersections of those networks. Alejandro Madrid has discussed the potential for using borderlands studies "to understand other contact zones and epistemological borders," while still recognizing the cultural specificity of geopolitical borderlands.[8] My approach is also resonant with Karl Jacoby's notion of "the borderlands between history and storytelling."[9]

The stories of this book serve to historicize theoretical paradigms in the overlapping disciplines of ethnomusicology, folklore, and anthropology. In the late nineteenth century, European concepts of folklore were adapted to new settings as independent nations in the Americas grappled with the cultural diversity of their populations. In the first half of the twentieth century, researchers across the Americas increasingly documented rural and ethnic cultures as a resource for defining national identities that were distinct from Europe. Some of these projects aimed to incorporate a broader range of the population into citizenship, and some made early attempts at decolonial interventions. In the late twentieth century, institutionalized discourses of folklore were largely converted to discourses of heritage and especially "intangible heritage." This new wave of heritage discourse aimed to bridge local, national, and global interests in culture but often reproduced many of the assumptions behind older discourses of folklore. To be sure, the transnational lines of influence were not necessarily continuous across time periods. Nevertheless, in the late twentieth century, national and regional histories of cultural policy came back into dialogue with the globalizing frameworks associated with the United Nations Educational, Scientific, and Cultural Organization (UNESCO), the World Intellectual Property

---

[6] Giraudo (2013). See also Giraudo and Martín-Sánchez (2011); Giraudo and Lewis (2012).
[7] Giraudo (2006); Giraudo and Martín-Sánchez (2016).
[8] Madrid (2011a: 8).
[9] Jacoby (2008: 6).

Organization (WIPO), and international human rights documents. The on-going contestations around cultural policies, old and new terms, and their meanings suggest that culture is still very much a site of political struggle.[10] Tracing the social networks and narratives of past discourses can deepen our understanding of struggles in the present day.

We need to turn to the archive with multiple critical sensibilities to re-cover not only cultural forms, but also the ways those forms were collected and ordered, by particular people working within their own social-historical contexts. The idea of "Indigenous audibilities" draws attention to listening as a key technique for representing Indigenous music and voices through various modes of inscription, including writing, composition, and sound recording. Listening and inscription do not create a transparent conduit to Indigenous culture, but I argue that the traces of Indigenous lives and voices are still embedded in archival collections. This is what makes archival collections powerful, and also what makes them precarious, because of the risk of recirculating sounds from ethnographic collections that were never intended to be shared.

This introductory chapter charts the conceptual areas that frame *Indigenous Audibilities*. First, I discuss concepts of records, recordings, and the effects of inscribing Indigenous music through various technologies. The inscription and reproduction of Indigenous music took place in artistic projects of composition as well as documentary projects of preservation, and I explore the relations between these modes of representation. Then, I consider how "archival thinking" can be reconceptualized through atten-tion to music, sound, and listening. This leads to thinking about institutions, networks, and power structures. Finally, I use Walter Benjamin's concept of historical constellations to provide a broader view of the deep histories that enabled the stories that unfold in the following chapters.

Records and Recordings

This book blurs the boundaries between the record as a sound disc and the record as archived knowledge. Mediation through archival collections

---

[10] Williams (1977); Coombe (1998: 24). Coombe (2009) discusses the varied use of the terms "folk-lore," "traditional knowledge," "traditional cultural expressions," and "cultural heritage" by the WIPO Intergovernmental Committee on Genetic Resources, Traditional Knowledge, and Folklore.

involves the creation of various kinds of "records" on paper, disc, tape, and more recently through digital codes. These records structure, and are structured by, the genres they contain and the formats through which they are preserved. The organization of archival records also depends on the actors, social relations, and power structures through which records were collected and deposited.[11] The archival principle of *respect des fonds* leads to the practice of maintaining the original order of the collection. However, when a collector has accumulated items in multiple formats, these may be separated into the institutional divisions that specialize in different formats, such as sound recordings, photographs, or manuscripts. Thus, for example, early Indigenous recordings made by the US Bureau of American Ethnology were transferred to the Archive of American Folk Song in the 1940s to be copied for preservation purposes, but the written documentation with the collection metadata did not always accompany them.[12]

Sound recordings have a particular status because of their technologies of reproduction, which require special equipment for discerning their contents. Jonathan Sterne's work demonstrates how technologies of reproduction shaped modern concepts of authenticity and originality.[13] The creation of copies, especially on a mass scale, concretized the idea of an original. We might say that a sound recording can never be an original performance, but it takes on the aura of original authenticity when it is very old or when it was recorded in a remote location, especially with Indigenous people. Record collectors and others tend to fetishize "first recordings" and the arcane details surrounding them, yet ideas of authenticity are constructed, not natural.[14] Furthermore, the multiplication of copies and their dissemination have deeper cultural histories beyond mechanical reproduction. Modern affective relations toward heritage show some continuity with older cultural practices such as the replication and fetishization of icons.[15]

I argue that practices of recording encompass written representations of musical and linguistic sound, including notation "by ear"—in other words, embodied practices of aural transcription connecting the ear and hand. As Lisa Gitelman has shown, the development of sound recording technology

---

[11] See Turner (2020).

[12] In his history of the Archive of American Folk Song, Peter Bartis notes that the Library of Congress recording laboratory, which provided duplication services, was established in 1939, but even in 1935 some Native American recordings were being transferred to the Archive of American Folk Song (Bartis 1982: 60, 97).

[13] Sterne (2003).

[14] See, e.g., Petrusich (2014) and Sullivan (2014).

[15] Rozental, Collins, and Ramsey (2016); Rozental (2017); Taussig (1993).

was bound up with the practices and ideologies of writing, and these relations continued in the ways recording technologies were operationalized in documentary research.[16] Though early proponents of ethnographic recording promoted the apparent objectivity of the recording machine, some documentarists continued to use aural transcription in the field. They made handwritten notes of music, text, and context as an accompaniment to their mechanical recordings and sometimes as a substitute when their machines were inoperable. The objectives of field research did not absolutely require the marketable commodity of the sound recording, as in commercial recording ventures. Even in histories of commercial recording, Sergio Ospina has highlighted the importance of written ledgers that contained clues to what was recorded in addition to resources for the recordists' communication during recording sessions, such as foreign language phrases.[17]

Indigenous peoples have played a special role in recording histories. In the last decade of the nineteenth century, the new reproductive technology of the phonograph was quickly adapted to the work of preserving Indigenous cultures. Documentarists understood the phonograph to be a scientific apparatus that would overcome bias in collecting the music and language of diverse cultural groups. It was especially useful for music because non–music specialists could make recordings during fieldwork and share them with music specialists at other times and places. Documentarists were motivated by the assumption that Indigenous peoples were on the path to disappearance, and that time was running out to capture their stories and songs for the purposes of science and history. Through phonographic documentation, many Indigenous peoples came into close contact with recording technologies before white Americans had access to recordings in their homes.[18] Some Indigenous people also made home recordings of their own music, and by the 1940s several Indigenous-directed commercial recording companies had been launched in the United States.[19]

Brian Hochman has argued that preservationist ideologies surrounding the study and collection of Indigenous cultures were fundamental to the meanings of new media in the twentieth century. He writes:

---

[16] Gitelman (1999).
[17] Ospina (2019: 116–117).
[18] Troutman (2009); Hochman (2014); Brady (1999).
[19] On Indigenous-directed commercial recordings in the United States, see Garrett-Davis (2021). On Native American home recordings in Oklahoma, see Aplin (2010: 205–212).

During the late 19th and early 20th centuries, encounters with race and cultural difference actually helped to construct the *authority* of new media technologies, both as socially intelligible inventions and as reliable archives of the real. Race produced media, in other words, even as media produced race.[20]

Dominant conceptions of what counted as true Indigenous culture were recorded and represented as "reliable archives of the real," shaping discourses of fidelity in recording. But documentarists could not make recordings of Indigenous music without some kind of cooperation from Indigenous singers and musicians. Indigenous people had input into what was recorded, and what was withheld.[21] Modern notions of authenticity in media emerged from interactions among recording machines, non-Indigenous recordists, and Indigenous people who participated in research and recordings.

Mechanical recording crystalized Indigenous orality in a material object, the sound record, which was also perceived as a record in a historical sense. In the words of David Samuels and his coauthors, sound recordings "promised to bring the fullness of performed vocal and sonic presence of the past to future generations, and as a technology of memory, sound recording was quickly incorporated into the idea of the archive."[22] I argue that the locus of authenticity, the key to unlocking the past, came to reside in those recordings and in the archives where they were held, rather than in the communities where they were recorded. Indigenous music was refigured in various ways in these discourses, sometimes as a symbol of national or regional heritage, other times as a relic of universal human history. Either way, Indigenous music was most often projected into the past, while contemporary Indigenous communities were kept on the margins or completely outside of the nation-state.

Representing Indigenous Music

In the early twentieth century, methods for recording Indigenous music also included practices of "art music" composition—in this context, music

---

[20] Hochman (2014: xxiii). For other theorizations of fidelity, see Sterne (2003, Chapter 5) and Bronfman (2016: 118–119).

[21] See Brady's discussion of Frances Densmore's fieldwork strategies, as well as her failures (Brady 1999: 90–93).

[22] Samuels, Meintjes, Ochoa, and Porcello (2010: 332).

that was written for European instruments such as the piano and violin. In practice, these compositions spanned a range of popular and elite genres and performance venues, and they sometimes involved Indigenous performers. This music tends to be called "*indigenista*" music in Latin America, and "Indianist" music in the United States. There is a long history of representing Indigenous music in European and Euro-American art music, usually drawing on imagined icons of exotic "others."[23] The stereotypical representation of indigeneity in art music continued in the twentieth century—flutes, drums, and ostinato rhythms. But in the Americas, some composers used transcriptions of Indigenous music in their compositions, and a few also conducted their own documentary research. In the 1940s, inter-American cultural workers often had a difficult time parsing the distinction between collections of Indigenous music (either sound recordings or transcriptions) and the representation of Indigenous music in art music compositions.

We can better understand the confusion around these musical discourses if we consider a lecture given by the US Indianist composer Charles Skilton to the Music Teachers National Association in 1918. Skilton was one of the composers whose works were recommended to the Inter-American Indian Institute in the 1940s, as I will discuss in Chapter 2. Skilton's 1918 lecture was titled "Realism in Indian Music"; he used "Indian music" to refer both to the music created in Indigenous communities and to the art music compositions that portrayed Indian music. For Skilton, using the "realistic method" in composition meant that "the characteristics of Indian music are strongly featured and set forth with such assistance from modern technic as shall render them most vivid and impressive, without destroying their individuality." He did not make a distinction between composers who had direct experience with Native music and those who relied on the transcriptions of others. Most strikingly, he called for a defense against European musical influence by stating: "We need a Monroe Doctrine in music."[24] Skilton's lecture did not mention Latin America explicitly (at least not in the printed version), but it is significant that in advocating for American music based on American sources, Skilton referenced a political

---

[23] Pisani (2005); Browner (1997, 1995); Born and Hesmondhalgh (2000). Wolkowicz (2022: 6) notes the shifting position of the "Other" in the creation of Latin American art music, and calls for interpreting this music in the context of a Western periphery.

[24] Skilton (1919: 108, 114).

mechanism that justified US intervention in Latin America. US nationalism slipped quickly into imperialism.

These compositional movements in the United States and in Latin America
should not be conflated; they emerged from different historical and cultural contexts and followed different trajectories. In the US context, as Tara
Browner has written, the links between Indigenous music documentation
and Indianist composition took off in the 1890s, and the vogue of Indianist
compositions peaked prior to 1920. Browner identifies three main groups of
Indianist composers in the United States:

> those who did their own collection and transcription of songs (Burton,
> Lieurance), those who used the transcriptions of others but made an effort
> to become acquainted with Native cultures (Farwell, Cadman, Beach), and
> those who saw the transcribed Native melodies as musical raw material,
> and to whom Native musics in their original context was not a primary ob-
> jective (MacDowell).[25]

Browner's study makes clear that conducting fieldwork did not necessarily
lead composers to challenge the prevailing ideologies of racial hierarchies.[26]
Indigenous music documentation was not a direct conduit to Indigenous
culture, but rather was shaped by white researchers' preconceptions and
misconceptions. Nevertheless, the collaborative work of Alice Fletcher and
Francis LaFlesche is an example that is difficult to categorize, given their
close relationship and LaFlesche's Omaha background. Many composers
drew on their transcriptions, and LaFlesche also worked on an opera using
Native texts.[27] Another area of complex cultural negotiation was the participation of Native musicians in Indianist performances. Native musicians
and radio hosts sometimes used Indianist performance idioms which could

[25] Browner (1995: 66).

[26] See, for example, Browner's discussion of Frederick Burton, who worked for the American
Museum of Natural History and the Chicago Field Museum and whose transcriptions became a
common source for Indianist compositions (Browner 1995: 62–64, 71).

[27] This was the unfinished or unperformed work titled "Da-o-ma," begun in 1910 by Charles
Wakefield Cadman, Francis LaFlesche, and Nelle Eberhart (Browner 1995: 93). On Francis LaFlesche
and Alice Fletcher, see also Mark (1988) and Ramsey (1992). To cite another exceptional case, the
composer Jack Frederick Kilpatrick grew up in Cherokee communities of Oklahoma and spent much
of his life studying Cherokee traditional culture in collaboration with his well-known Cherokee
wife, Anna Gritts Kilpatrick. Their documentation was a key source for Jack Frederick Kilpatrick's
compositions, which were often labeled "Indianist" within dominant discourses of the time (Giacona
forthcoming).

target Native as well as non-Native audiences.[28] In these examples, musical authenticity does not map neatly onto cultural heritage, again blurring the boundaries between an authentic Indigenous music and representations of Indigenous music or practices of Indigenous musicians.

In Latin America, the representation of Indigenous music had a more enduring impact in art music composition, given the greater prominence of indigeneity in the construction of many national identities in the region. Reviewing trends across time periods, Daniel Castro Pantoja has made a distinction between *indianista* music of the nineteenth century, *indigenista* music of the early twentieth century, and new *indianista* cultural movements of the late twentieth century.[29] Indianista music of the nineteenth century, like the parallel movement in literature, valorized Indigenous people of the distant past as symbolic patrimony, while Indigenous people of the present were subjugated and denigrated. Indigenista cultural movements of the early twentieth century coexisted and sometimes intersected with attempts to improve the conditions of Indigenous people and integrate them into national citizenship. Castro Pantoja rightly ties indigenista movements to projects of modernization and nation-building and points out that different movements overlapped in different time periods, so, for example, the romanticization of the distant past continued during the indigenista period. Whereas indigenista movements were directed primarily by non-Indigenous people in the first half of the twentieth century, the final decades of the twentieth century saw the emergence of new transnational movements of Indigenous rights and a new politicization of Indigenous culture directed by Indigenous actors. Not all times and places necessarily conform to this overarching analysis, but the distinctions draw attention to the variability of indigenista music.

Latin American composers used a variety of musical resources in indigenista compositions at different moments and sometimes even in the same work. According to Leonora Saavedra, the Mexican composer Carlos Chávez at times used stereotypical icons of Indigenous music that had emerged from European compositional practices, but he also drew specific Indigenous musical fragments from the documentary work of his contemporaries; these approaches came together in Chávez's *Sinfonía India*.[30]

---

[28] Troutman (2009); Green and Troutman (2000); Garrett-Davis (2020: 255).
[29] Castro Pantoja (2018: 254–256). See also Wolkowicz (2022: 23).
[30] Saavedra (2015a); see also Saavedra (2015b).

Bernard Gordillo has shown that the Nicaraguan composer Luis Delgadillo sometimes used European orientalist approaches to represent Indigenous music, but in other works he used Indigenous music transcriptions provided by a colleague in Guatemala and by Delgadillo's own research in Bolivia and Peru.[31]

Latin American ideologies of race were very different from the United States, with consequences for representations of Indigenous music and heritage. In many Latin American countries, individuals' education as well as their place and style of living were more determinant of racial categorization than phenotype or ancestry. Although Peru is not a focus of my book, it is an important reference point for understanding the variability of racial identification and cultural knowledge among indigenista composers and intellectuals. For example, the Peruvian composer Teodoro Valcárcel, who was most active in the 1920s and 1930s, had some Indigenous ancestry and composed songs with lyrics in Quechua and Aymara. Yet, in the words of Raúl Romero, "he was far from being a *provinciano* without musical education."[32] Valcárcel studied in Europe and premiered many of his works in Paris and Barcelona. Other Peruvian intellectuals in the Andean highlands used indigenismo strategically to support their claims of cultural authenticity, positioned against the Europhile culture of coastal Lima. At the same time, by making Indigenous culture an object of erudite analysis or creation, indigenistas positioned themselves above the Indian source communities and on the same level as Lima intellectuals.[33] Zoila Mendoza has argued that the rise of indigenista performance in highland Peru was not an exclusively elite project but rather emerged from cross-class and cross-ethnic interaction.[34] Joshua Tucker also points out the "musical traffic across social boundaries" which "made it difficult to separate Andean elite and popular spheres in the first place."[35]

The Peruvian case shows that simplistic dichotomies between elite/popular, white/nonwhite, and dominant/subordinate cannot capture the multiple hierarchies and cultural affiliations in different arenas of indigenismo and indigenista composition. The cross-cultural affiliations of art music composers should not excuse them from critiques, but a full analysis requires

---

[31] Gordillo (2019: 70–83).

[32] Romero (2017: 97). See also Wolkowicz (2022: 87–90).

[33] de la Cadena (2014). See also de la Cadena (2005) on *indigenista* networks more broadly.

[34] Mendoza (2008: 7).

[35] Tucker (2013: 46, 48). See also Rios's (2020) thorough analysis of folklorization and indigenismo in Bolivia.

attending to the cultural contexts and the methodologies that shaped their work, making some openings possible for ideological shifts, and foreclosing others.

US Indianist and Latin American indigenista compositions were subject to different frameworks of reception in US performances. Appropriation of Native American materials by white US composers usually did not put their whiteness into doubt. In contrast, Latin American composers and their music were often racialized as "Indian" by US audiences, even when they were not working with Indigenous thematic or sonic materials.[36] Many white US intellectuals and audiences considered Native American music in the United States to be defunct or in decline. They imagined Indigenous music of Latin America to be more vibrant and more authentic, a surviving resource for conceptualizing American heritage more broadly. These ideologies among US audiences were also projected onto Latin American art music. Carol Hess uses the concept of "Ur-classicism" to analyze the US reception of Carlos Chávez's *Sinfonía India* and *Sinfonía Antígona* in the 1930s. Hess writes that Ur-classicism "created conditions for absolute music that united the usable past of ancient America with the universal whole, all within the 'freshness' the tabula rasa promised."[37] In other words, these Pan American musical discourses promoted universal aesthetics that aimed to break from European trends in the "New World," while reconciling the ancient heritage of America and of Europe.

Hess brings to light a revealing review written by the avant-garde composer John Cage in 1942, following a symphonic concert in Chicago. In its entirety, Cage's review illustrates the differentiation between indigenista authenticity and Indianist artifice, as well as the overlapping spheres of Pan American performance. Cage was enraptured by Carlos Chávez's *Sinfonía India*, which, he said, "could easily become our Pan American Bolero." Cage perceived that Chávez was quoting Indian melodies directly, in contrast to Charles Wakefield Cadman, a US Indianist composer also featured in the concert. Cage wrote that Chávez's Sinfonía India "relies completely on musical elements which never call for literary explanations but speak in terms of rhythm and sound, to which everyone responds." Most significantly, Cage wrote: "Hearing this *Symphony* [by Chávez] for the first time one has

---

[36] Saavedra (2015a); Delpar (1992); Hess (2013a). Eduardo Herrera (2020: 58–59) reveals the tendency of US cultural actors and institutions to conceive of Latin American composers through an indigenista lens even in an avant-garde context of the 1960s.

[37] Hess (2013a: 48–49).

the feeling of remembering it. . . . The *Sinfonía India* is the land we all walk on, made audible."[38] Cage was conveying the felt relations among notions of memory, territory, and audibility which shaped inter-American discourses of the 1940s.

From Archival Thinking to Archival Listening

In the following chapters, I put narratives of social relations at the center of my archival explorations, which can be read as a counterpoint to broad media histories and to focused analyses of collected objects, recordings, or compositions. My social-historical method—listening, reading, and thinking beyond the archived object—opens up some of the concrete human experiences that are contained or represented by collections.[39] Archives are themselves fragments of lives and societies, selected and ordered through highly uneven and unequal processes.[40] Though historians commonly recognize the biased perspectives encoded in archives, there is more work to be done in examining the cultural processes of collection that create and contribute to archives.

To develop my case studies, I have read along the grain, and against the grain, of institutional archives. As Ann Stoler has argued, understanding the dominant structures of institutions is essential to uncover the voices of resistance through counterhegemonic analysis.[41] Reading along the grain of archives reveals the ideologies of institutional structures, while reading against the grain reveals the heterogeneous and disruptive forces within and around those structures.

Both practices require "archival thinking," a term Kirsten Weld has used to conceptualize a dual method of historical and political analysis. In her book *Paper Cadavers: The Archives of Dictatorship in Guatemala,* Weld writes:

> On the historical side, archival thinking requires us to look past the words on a document's page to examine the conditions of that document's production . . . On the political side, archival thinking demands that we see archives

---

[38] Cage (1942: 186), quoted in Hess (2013a: 79).

[39] I intend this "social-historical method" to be resonant with the Russian sociohistorical school of Bakhtin, Voloshinov, and Vygotsky, who focused on the analysis of heterogeneous voices and social hierarchies in discourse, communication, and cognition in the early twentieth century.

[40] Mbembe (2002: 20–21); Hamilton et al. (2002: 10).

[41] Stoler (2009).

not only as sources of data to be mined by researchers but also as more than the sum of their parts—as instruments of political action, implements of state formation ("technologies of rule"), institutions of liberal democratization, enablers of gaze and desire, and sites of social struggle.[42]

Weld analyzes rediscovered police archives from a particularly dark period when Guatemalan activists and bystanders were subject to extreme state repression and terror. The material bureaucracy of this repression did not allow much room for struggle, but its preservation later enabled a public reckoning and a recovery of the fates of missing people who were victims of state terror. The records of people who had been silenced became vehicles of testimony years after their death.

Archival thinking can also include *hearing* the enduring, conflictive sounds and voices in archives. Morgan Luker has coined the term "matrix listening" to convey focused attention to sound objects. Matrix listening involves "listening to" the multisensory materiality of the sound recording (including the matrix numbers on record labels) rather than "listening for" preconceived sounds or genres.[43] The scratchy playback of old and reduplicated sound recordings draws our attention to the materiality of a format (e.g., 78 RPM disc, or reel-to-reel tape) and to what we perceive as its "noise." Noise can also represent broader phenomena of cultural and technological mediation.[44] While noise may push us further from an originary source and its pristine aura, noise also becomes part of the aura of archival objects. This kind of noise is an aural corollary to "dust." In Carolyn Steedman's formulation, "dust" is the visceral texture of what is collected and catalogued in archives and still there after years of inattention. The dust, writes Steedman, "is about circularity, the impossibility of things disappearing, or going away, or being gone."[45]

Though music recordings are an obvious medium for the audibility of Indigenous culture, I do not bracket "Indigenous music" as an exclusive object in this book. I want to avoid reproducing the objectification and detachment of Indigenous music from the people whose ancestors' voices are embedded in archival collections. Indigenous cultural knowledge held in institutional

---

[42] Weld (2014: 13).
[43] Luker (2022).
[44] Novak (2011, 2013). See also Cardoso (2019) for a study of the contemporary governmental regimentation of noise in Brazil.
[45] Steedman (2002: 164).

collections must be approached with respectful care, collaboration with source communities, and often projects of repatriation.[46] I am engaged in these kinds of projects and they have informed my approach, but they are not the focus of this book. I did not try to listen to archived Indigenous recordings unless source communities had approved them for public consumption. Dylan Robinson has conceptualized the acquisitive and extractive nature of white settler listening positionalities as "hungry listening." These positionalities, he notes, are not reducible to race but require constant attention to and critique of the hegemonic structures of perception. "Listening itself," he writes, "may become an act of confirming ownership, rather than an act of hearing the agonism of exclusive and contested sovereignties."[47]

My analysis in this book focuses on the interactions of intellectuals as they developed national and international discourses about Indigenous music and folklore. In his book *Autoridad, Cuerpo, Nación: Batallas Culturales en Nicaragua (1930–1943)*, Juan Pablo Gómez has explained the importance of analyzing intellectual discourses of the past:

> Cultural and intellectual interventions . . . construct a discourse that legitimizes a mode of authority according to the cultural forms of a society. Such interventions are not limited to the contexts in which they operate. They leave legacies and cultural inheritances (*herencias*) that are sedimented in the social, which later generations take on in the task of struggle and dismantlement.[48]

The intellectual discourses of the past have ideological effects; studying them as a cultural and historical object reveals the contingency of power and the possibility of challenging inherited structures.

Most of the intellectuals directing institutional projects were not Indigenous, but I draw attention to the role of Indigenous intellectuals and others who pushed back against the dominant discourses of their time. In a critical historical analysis, Jorge Pavez Ojeda uses the term "ethnographic laboratories" to analyze the sites of interaction between scholars from the

---

[46] Gray (2015); Christen (2011); Christen and Anderson (2019); Minks, Swan, and Nelson (2018).
[47] Robinson (2020: 13).
[48] Gómez (2015: 15–16). "Las intervenciones culturales e intelectuales . . . construyen un discurso que legitima un modo de autoridad según sean las formas culturales de la sociedad. Dichas intervenciones no se limitan a los contextos en que operan. Dejan legados y herencias culturales que se sedimentan en el todo social y con las cuales las generaciones posteriores se ven en la tarea de luchar y desmontar."

North and from the South, and their interaction with Indigenous intellectuals who were collaborators and coauthors of classic anthropological works, whether or not they were recognized as such.[49] The collections and texts that resulted from these networks of interaction were coproductions with many layers of meaning, authorship, and power. For Pavez, the genealogies of jointly produced ethnographic laboratories are embedded in the materiality of the archive, and especially in particular collections. As a result, the archive is heteroglossic with divergent cultural claims and modes of authority.[50]

Voicing, listening, and writing have played a key role in the intellectual genealogies that shape the politics of knowledge and disciplinarity.[51] Ana María Ochoa's theorization of aurality opens up methodologies for listening to the multiplicity of voices and other sounds encoded in written texts and archival collections. In this sense, aurality encompasses the "immediate and mediated practices of listening/hearing that construct perceptions and understandings of nature, bodies, voices, and technologies in particular moments and places."[52] In the colonial and early national periods, listening to and writing about sound regimented the political and ontological definition of the person. However, the regimentation of voices was never complete, because, in Ochoa's words, "the uses of the *ear* in relation to the *voice* imbued the *technology of writing* with the traces and excesses of the acoustic."[53] I am especially interested in the traces of repressed voices that emerge in archival texts. Jacques Derrida's theorization of the archive emphasized the links between the physical archive and the psychic archive. Crucially, according to Derrida, when something is politically or psychologically repressed (as opposed to destroyed), it can reemerge.[54] I use the concept of trace loosely, not confined to Derrida's theories. In the historical narratives of this book, I draw attention to the traces of voices in archives without pinning them down.

Discourses around Indigenous archival collections have helped to sharpen analysis of the ethics of cross-cultural music circulation in the context of unequal access to intellectual and cultural property rights around the globe.[55]

---

[49] Pavez Ojeda (2015).

[50] See also Felipe Barros's (2013: 14, 40) conceptualization of a "musical ethnographic archive" and "ethnography in the archive," analyzing the ethnographic practices that created collections, as well as the practices of managing and interpreting those collections.

[51] Faudree (2013); Weidman (2014); Minks and Ochoa (2021).

[52] Minks and Ochoa (2021: 25); Ochoa (2014).

[53] Ochoa (2014: 7).

[54] Derrida (2002).

[55] See, e.g., Anderson and Geismar (2017); A. Fox (2013); Gray (2015, 2019); Francis et al. (2016); Reed (2019).

Tied together with the rapid pace of technological change is the modern fascination with old archival objects, their tactile dust in analog form and their audible noise that accumulates through reduplication and transfer from analog to digital formats. The nature of the archival encounter depends on the relations between the people whose sounds and voices were recorded, and the people who confront those records (aural and written) years later. The dust and noise can incite an emotional response for the historian or for anyone else enraptured by the proximity of things from another time and place. It may be that the value of collected items always depended on something unseen, an aura attributed to distance or spirituality or peculiarity.[56] But when there is a cultural and/or familial tie in the archival encounter, this is not just a fascination with history or difference. It is a reconnection with relatives and other kinds of close cultural relations.

Institutions, Networks, Power

As Michel Foucault suggested, archiving is a tool of power/knowledge production; metaphorically, the archive is "the law of what can be said."[57] Institutions and their classificatory systems put beings and things in particular kinds of order and render the world intelligible under particular regimes of power. Modern state power has tended to move beyond official state institutions to structure everyday conduct. Archives evolved from being part of the "curiosity cabinet" (a precursor to museum collections) to becoming an absorptive apparatus that encompasses the curiosity cabinet and structures everyday life.[58] Foucault's portrayals of institutions were often totalizing, with little space for the consciousness or intervention of historical actors. In contrast, I argue that the institutional networks in this book were heterogeneous, conflictive spaces where diverse personalities vied for their own agendas. Spaces of cultural policy and bureaucracy were shot through with multiple, intersecting ideologies of gender, race, indigeneity, class, and nation, which could be reconfigured with unexpected consequences. As Rodrigo Chocano has written in analyzing contemporary music and cultural policy, "humans operate within organizations in creative and strategic

---

[56] Pomian (1990); Benjamin ([1935] 1968).
[57] Foucault (1972: 129). González Echevarría ([1990] 1998) and Chamosa (2010: 16–22) discuss how projects of cultural collection in Latin America, as in Europe, were tied to legal regimes.
[58] Giannachi (2016: xix).

manners, transforming meanings within them that shape their actions and project outcomes."[59]

Álvaro Fernández Bravo has discussed the value of analyzing transnational networks in the 1940s, when new circuits of intellectual exchange developed within the Americas. In this framework, the concept of networks emphasizes intermediary positions, mobility, contingent alliances, and intermittent social formations beyond the hegemony of the nation-state. In the 1940s, transnational networks constituted new fields of knowledge, not only through connections but also through exclusions. In the Americas, musical and social scientific discourses were transformed in the 1930s and 1940s by the forced immigration of Spanish intellectuals from Franco's Spain and Jewish intellectuals from across Europe. In some historical studies, inter-American networks of the 1940s have been dismissed as one-sided agents of US hegemony, but recent scholarship has drawn out the heterogeneous and sometimes contradictory alliances forged within them.[60]

This book focuses on purportedly noncommercial institutions—the national and international organizations that sponsored research on Indigenous music and culture for purposes such as nation-building, scientific preservation, and cultural diplomacy. Yet this history involving state and international institutions should be read in dialogue with commercial music histories. Pablo Palomino notes the simultaneous development of "nationalist art music, folklore research, and urban commercial music" in Latin America in the 1930s.[61] These were not isolated from each other but often interacted. The realms of art music, folk music, and commercial music appeared to occupy different spheres in part because musicologists "based their own legitimacy on the ability to separate legitimate from illegitimate music."[62] As Eileen Karmy Bolton has shown in the Chilean context, upper-class composers denigrated musicians who made their living performing a wide range of music because commercial constraints purportedly limited

[59] Chocano (2019: 766). See also Chocano (2022, 2023).

[60] Fernández Bravo (2009: 118). Fernández Bravo notes the example of María Rosa Oliver, the Argentine writer and Communist sympathizer who worked under the auspices of the Office of Inter-American Affairs in Washington from 1942 to 1944, purportedly promoting US interests and at the same time meeting with leftist artists and intellectuals across Latin America, as well as Soviet diplomats in Washington. Other recent studies of the multifaceted relations in inter-American networks include Palomino (2020), Giraudo and Martín-Sánchez (2016), C. Fox (2013), and Pernet (2004, 2007).

[61] Palomino (2020: 16). See also Ochoa (2006). Dent (2009) provides a recent example of the dual processes of genre formation in commercial and folklorized realms.

[62] Palomino (2020: 16).

the creation of high art.[63] Many researchers and officials in inter-American institutions considered their work as a defensive response to the mass popularity of transnational genres such as jazz, boleros, and tangos.

Musicological diplomats also reacted to the stereotypical representation of Latin America in Hollywood, including a string of propagandistic films made with support from the US government in the early 1940s. As Juan Carlos Poveda has demonstrated, music played a key role in these films produced jointly by Disney and the Office of Inter-American Affairs, a wartime entity within the US federal government. Poveda's analysis suggests that music and dance appealed to audience emotion, represented the fusion of cultures under US hegemony, and provided a medium for the sexualization and exoticization of Latin American women. Moreover, the links between primitivist rhythm, the body, and sexuality shaped an idea of the Latin American as "festive, tropical, sensual, intense, savage, and exuberant."[64] These animated films (for *children*, Poveda emphasizes) reveal how US political and economic interests were wrapped up in white masculine desires for exotic sexuality.

Moving through varied networks, both commercial and documentary recording projects were presented as an exploration of new territories through difficult journeys, but these were not exactly the same kind of expeditions. Sergio Ospina's history of early Victor recording projects in Latin America reveals the important role of "recording scouts," as he calls them, who generally traveled from the United States to make recordings in Latin American cities. They had variable knowledge of Latin American music and often limited language skills, and the challenges of their journeys merited their use of the term "expedition." As I will show in Chapters 2 and 4, documentarists traveling within Latin American countries, or from one Latin American country to another, were seeking more remote, rural areas where the oldest musical traditions might be found. Ironically, many members of rural populations were moving in the opposite direction toward cities, but rural recordings made in situ were most valuable in the folkloric frame.[65]

---

[63] Karmy Bolton (2019); Karmy (2021a, 2021b).

[64] Poveda (2021: 139). See also Poveda (2019) and Hess (2017). Pernet (2007: 153) notes that despite musicologists' attempts to distance themselves from these cinematic representations, Disney used the Archive of American Folk Song for sources and guidance in their musical production.

[65] For example, in the early 1940s, Isabel Aretz left her home in Buenos Aires to make recordings of Andean music in Bolivia and Peru, as I discuss in Chapter 4, at the same time that Andean musicians were traveling from Bolivia to Buenos Aires to perform for an urban, European-oriented audience (Rios 2008).

Although commercial and documentary recordists had different objectives and aesthetic paradigms, musicians and audiences were often less concerned with the distinctions between them.

Race, gender, and class were powerful intersectional vectors that shaped the possibilities for intervening in institutions and official heritage. The gendered dimensions of heritage discourses are explicit in the words patrimony and *patrimonio* (in Spanish)—the most common term in the law and policy of heritage in Latin America. Stemming from the Latin root *pater*, patrimony ties a patriarchal familial origin to a broader sense of the shared culture of the nation, large or small. Nayive Ananías has discussed the notion of "private patrimony" in domestic spaces and social relations, which helps to reveal how gender and power run throughout "public patrimony" as well.[66] This notion is embedded in Derrida's genealogy of the archive, which is both a place and a law, the house of the archons, those who commanded, where the archic function is patriarchic.[67]

Though women tended to be marginalized in institutions of the Americas, a range of female recordists and researchers played key roles in collecting vernacular music in the early twentieth century.[68] Roshanak Kheshti points out that most of the music recordists under the US Works Progress Administration in the 1930s were white women. Field recording usually prescribed the objectivity of the recordist as a silent listener and observer whose trace, Kheshti argues, was inscribed in the recording along with the musician or singer. As a challenge to this practice, the Black American anthropologist Zora Neale Hurston used her own voice and body to participate in field recordings, a kind of "sonic infidelity" that "rejected the authority of the archive."[69]

Margaret Bruchac has noted the central role of Native American women in the documentation of Indigenous cultures, as they often served as sources for white anthropologists, either through direct collaboration or through the mediation of their husbands.[70] Their positionality was very different from white women who began to research Native American cultures in the late nineteenth century. White women's research extended, in part, from the philanthropic and reformist activities of white urban women's organizations,

[66] Ananías (2021).
[67] Derrida (1995: 2–3).
[68] See Giraudo (2022) on the role of three women in the Inter-American Indian Institute, including Henrietta Yurchenco, a key figure in Chapter 2 of this book.
[69] Kheshti (2015: 140).
[70] Bruchac (2018).

and in part, from efforts to claim forms of academic and scientific authority from which they were otherwise excluded.[71] Their politics and cross-cultural commitments varied widely and shifted over time, with white suffragists often abandoning Black and Indigenous allies as they came closer to voting rights. As Aaron Fox has argued in his analysis of the Laura Boulton collection of sound recordings, the reconstruction of particular histories of collections is important to interrogate the complicity of individual and institutional processes of exploitation.[72]

The analytical challenge is to move beyond a discourse of individual heroics or failures, to recover specific roles and relations within larger structures, as well as the continuing trajectories of reclaiming Indigenous culture. Though I focus in this book on institutions between the 1930s and the 1970s, this is not the end of anyone's story. The work of Robin Gray on the repatriation of Laura Boulton's recordings to Ts'msyen communities in British Columbia, Canada, makes clear the future stakes of collections. She writes, "Repatriation refers to a process of returning home, and decolonization refers to a process aimed at changing the larger social structure and therefore the actions of institutions and individuals."[73] This is the broader context and significance of analyzing power and networks in historical institutions.

Constellations of History

In this book, my analysis dwells at points of intersection, especially the geopolitical crossroads between North and South in the middle decades of the twentieth century. The narrativity of particular time/space relations shapes other sets of relations. In addition to examining intimate histories at close range, we need to telescope out to see and hear them in relation to other moments in time/space.[74] In 1940, Walter Benjamin wrote:

Historicism contents itself with establishing a causal connection between various moments in history. But no fact that is a cause is for that very reason

[71] Rhea (2016).
[72] Fox (2017).
[73] Gray (2015: 199).
[74] Narratives, both fictional and nonfictional, are embedded in and produce particular time/space relations, as Mikhail Bakhtin theorized in his notion of the chronotope (Bakhtin 1981). See Barr (2017: 205) on the importance of viewing Native American histories in the longue durée.

historical. It became historical posthumously, as it were, through events that may be separated from it by thousands of years. A historian who takes this as his point of departure stops telling the sequence of events like the beads of a rosary. Instead, he grasps the constellation which his own era has formed with a definite earlier one. Thus he establishes a conception of the present as the "time of the now" which is shot through with chips of Messianic time.[75]

As a German Jewish intellectual witnessing the disaster of Nazism, Benjamin was writing against a developmentalist history that assumed the teleology of modern progress. He considered history to encompass possibilities of rupture, combinations of temporality, and pathways toward different futures. Benjamin's work has been a productive resource for theorizing Latin American Indigenous movements. In a critique of linear historicism, Javier Sanjinés has proposed a sociocultural temporality that involves "'embers of the past,' which, buried and smoldering, are still capable of lighting new conflagrations."[76] Sanjinés draws out resonances between the alternative logics of Indigenous movements and the peripheral thinking of Benjamin. Alejandro Madrid also draws on Benjamin to conceptualize "dialectical soundings" in the context of Black Indigenous and transnational borderlands. In Madrid's words, "Music as dialectical sounding could work as a medium that makes visible the invisible." This is a matter of renarrating the relations among the past, present, and future in a way that lays claim to repressed histories and identities.[77]

In the following chapters I analyze the relations between actors and institutions, and the key moments when something changed and a new set of relations emerged. I begin and end the book in the United States not because that is the center, but because it is the location from which I tell these stories, and because I want to challenge dominant conceptions of "American" history and heritage by highlighting relations between the United States and Latin America in the context of deeper colonial histories.

---

[75] Benjamin ([1935] 1968: 263).

[76] Sanjinés ([2009] 2013: 25). Alejandro Vera (2014) has also shown how official music histories have often conformed to the myths of the development of civilization and the nation.

[77] Madrid (2011b: 186). This theorization comes from Madrid's work with the Black Seminole (Mascogo) community of Nacimiento in northern Coahuila, Mexico, with close ties to Bracketville, Texas.

The conditions of possibility for the narratives I trace are rooted in the following historic shifts:

The Caribbean, 1492: Spanish ships arrived in the Caribbean, which became the epicenter of trans-Atlantic contact and colonization. Conceptualizing this moment has become the stuff of kindergarten classes, parades, protests. The metanarrative splinters out into so many micronarratives, and yet still recalls the impacts of Spanish imperialism, often overshadowed by metanarratives of British imperialism. Representatives of the Spanish monarchy were also the first to claim territory to the north—Florida—in 1513, almost one hundred years before the English founded their first settlement in Jamestown. Europeans' violent destruction of the majority of Indigenous peoples in the Caribbean led to the mass enslavement and forced relocation of Africans to the Caribbean as a labor source for new networks of global capitalism. In one of the great absurdities of world history, First Peoples across the hemisphere were labelled "Indians," while Afro-Caribbeans were labeled "West Indians." The Indies were not so much a fixed place as a shifting target of European desire for domination over people and wealth, for ordering bodies and things across multiple horizons. African and Indigenous peoples and their descendants in the Americas remembered their pasts, remembered the ruptures, and envisioned other orders beyond the colonial order. Again in that Caribbean epicenter, the independent nation-state of Haiti was founded by Black people who rose up against slavery in 1791. The enslavement of Black people in the United States, the "land of liberty," continued another seventy-four years (three decades after the British abolished slavery in their Caribbean colonies).

Texas, 1821: Indigenous peoples dominated this territory that was claimed by Spain and then by Mexico, and then by Anglo settlers from the fledgling United States. In the seventeenth century, Spanish colonists had interacted with Caddo, Wichita, Comanche, and other peoples in the area. The Spanish used the name Tejas to refer to the Hasinai Caddo and their vast settlements, which struggling Spanish missions bordered.[78] In the 1820s, a newly independent Mexico encouraged immigration from the United States to Mexican territories in the north (Texas and Coahuila)

[78] Barr (2009).

in order to push out or extinguish Plains Tribes. Comanche, Apache, and Kiowa peoples had become agile warriors riding horses brought to the Southwest by the Spanish; they led raiding parties deep into Mexico. Although the Mexican government abolished slavery in 1829, Anglo settlers were allowed to keep enslaved Black people in Mexican territory and received tax exemptions to promote settlement. In the 1830s the Mexican government tried to centralize control over Anglo immigrant populations who had sworn allegiance to Mexico. Anglo settlers initially aimed to establish an autonomous Texan state within the Mexican nation, and then declared independence in 1836. For the United States, Texas was more than a potential slave state. It was a gateway to expansion into vast territories first colonized by Spain, and a means to gain control over lands where Indigenous peoples were still an obstacle to Anglo settlement. The US annexation of Texas in 1845 was part of this expansionist project, followed by the invasion of Mexico and the annexation of Mexican territory which became seven additional US states under the 1848 Treaty of Guadalupe Hidalgo. Due to its massive size and history of rebellious nationalism, Texas continued to play an outsized role in American narratives of taming the wild frontier, but also kept in play colonial tensions between Hispanic and Anglo heritage claims.

Cuba, 1898: The Spanish American War was the final blow against Spanish empire, decades after other colonies had gained independence. It was also a key moment in the rise of US empire through its seizure of Cuba, Puerto Rico, the Philippines, and Guam. US President Theodore Roosevelt built a career on his military service in Cuba during the Spanish American War. His "Rough Riders" took their name from Buffalo Bill's Wild West Show, forging an explicit link between westward and southward expansion. During his presidency (1901–1909), Roosevelt was a supporter of folklore as well as natural heritage in the west. He wrote an introduction for *Cowboy Songs and Other Frontier Ballads*, published in 1910 by the Texan folklorist John Lomax. In his handwritten introduction, Roosevelt expressed concern for preserving so-called native ballads of the Southwest, a term that christened Anglo cowboy lore as national heritage and erased Native American cultures and communities. The Spanish American War, along with the Mexican American War (1846–1848), sparked new collecting initiatives in US libraries and museums. US institutions expanded their acquisitions of Latin American materials, which were increasingly viewed as sources for developing US scientific and economic interests in the region.[79]

New York City and Washington, DC, 1928: The Pan American Association of Composers was founded in New York by modernist composers from the United States, Europe, and Latin America, with the objective of promoting new art music of the Americas. The same year, the Archive of American Folk Song was founded at the Library of Congress in Washington, DC; it initially focused on recordings of white and Black southern music, but later included Native American and Mexican American music, among many other collections. The Pan American Union also established its Division of Intellectual Cooperation in 1928. All three organizations fostered networks for inter-American cultural exchange. In the US political realm, the 1928 Meriam Report was a crushing indictment of assimilationist policies toward Native Americans and the beginning of a shift toward the reconstruction of Tribal governments. White Americans were increasingly fascinated by both Native American and Latin American cultures (sometimes conflating the two). The western regions of the United States and the countries across the southern border were overlapping objects of Anglo-American desire and incorporation. For example, a US journalist wrote in 1935 that "so many books on Mexico had been published in the past few years . . . that Americans [meaning Anglo Americans] were finding it difficult to escape their 'Mexican heritage.'"[80] Heritage was a malleable space, tied together with appropriation as much as ancestry, but it was also a space for imagining new relations of identity and difference.

These episodes and time/space relations set the stage for the interconnected case studies that I explore in the following chapters. The 1930s were a pivotal time for the development of national and international collecting projects in the Americas. Palomino writes that the 1930s were also a key period for the "invention of Latin American music" as a category in transnational discourses.[81] In 1933, the United States shifted its Latin American foreign policy away from direct military intervention and toward cultural diplomacy—an approach that President Franklin Delano Roosevelt called

[79] Salvatore (2005, 2014).
[80] Quoted in Delpar (1992: x).
[81] Palomino (2020).

the "Good Neighbor" policy. In 1935, the US government launched the Works Progress Administration (WPA), an assortment of cultural and infrastructure projects that put Americans back to work during the Depression and created new collections as well as heritage sites. The WPA arts programs were influenced by the cultural policies of revolutionary Mexico, following efforts at Indigenous arts revival across borders in the 1920s.[82]

Chapter 1 examines a lesser-known program of the WPA, a collection of "Indian and Pioneer" oral histories in Oklahoma, formerly Indian Territory, which I use as a lens for exploring Southwest borderlands history. I pay special attention to the representation of music, language, and dance in this oral history collection, and consider the cross-cultural construction of orality and the traces that may (or may not) reveal particular voices from the past. The constructedness of oral histories, their production through historical and cultural processes, should not invalidate them as sources. Rather, like all historical sources, oral histories are the product of multiple voices and political forces, some visible and audible, and others obscured in the archive. We need to listen and read beyond the referential function of this genre to place it in its own social-historical context and consider what it may reveal.

The 1930s and 1940s are pivotal throughout the book because this period represents a turning point in the relations between Europe and the Americas. Prior to this time, Latin American intellectuals often used cultural ties with Europe as a strategy for resisting US hegemony. But with the Spanish Civil War resulting in the dictatorship of Francisco Franco, and with the rise of the Second World War, "the European horizon no longer provided a support or a space of confluence . . . for Latin American intellectuals," as Fernández Bravo has written.[83] Spanish editors settled in Buenos Aires and Mexico City, establishing centers for publication that articulated new conceptions of Latinoamericanismo.[84] Other refugees fleeing Franco's regime scattered throughout Latin America. Among music specialists, Vicente Salas Viu settled in Chile and became involved in networks of the Pan American

---

[82] This influence moved through a variety of channels. Mexican mural painting with social and political themes was directly transferred to US contexts in the 1930s (sometimes hiring the same Mexican artists to paint the murals). In the 1920s, efforts at reviving and collecting Indigenous art and artisanry unfolded first in Mexico and then was modeled in the United States, with some of the same actors, such as Rene d'Harnoncourt, involved in similar projects across borders (López 2010; Meyn 2001).

[83] Fernández Bravo (2009: 120).

[84] Fernández Bravo (2009: 127) and Palomino (2020: 11) both identify the Fondo de Cultura Económica de México as a key site for the articulation of new concepts of Latinoamericanismo in the 1940s.

Union, while Otto Mayer-Serra settled in Mexico City and became involved in the Inter-American Indian Institute. Mayer-Serra was an especially interesting figure, a German Jewish and socialist refugee who first fled to Spain in 1933, where he acquired a Catalan identity and the surname Serra, and then joined the flow of Spanish refugees to Mexico City in 1939.[85]

Chapter 2 focuses on the emergence of the Inter-American Indian Institute in 1940, growing out of interaction between Mexican and US intellectuals, as well as earlier precedents in Latin America. In 1941, the US-based ethnomusicologist Henrietta Yurchenco followed WPA networks from New York to Mexico City and became deeply involved in the collection and broadcasting of Indigenous music under the auspices of the Inter-American Indian Institute. These projects resulted from multiple agendas and collaborations among institutions and individuals. My analysis shows how documentary recordings moved notions of authenticity from Indigenous communities to institutional archival collections. Yurchenco's activities had a variety of impacts. On the one hand, her work contributed to the hegemony of mechanical recording which displaced other modes of inscription, such as aural transcription, in fieldwork. On the other hand, Yurchenco made explicit the role of listening and active mediation to create a sense of liveness in field recording. She also reconfigured the instrumentality of institutional discourses to engage in dynamic social relations, which opened up new channels for the audibility of diverse repertoires across cultural and national borders.

Countries that joined the Inter-American Indian Institute created affiliated national institutes. Nicaragua was one of those sites, following the country's close cultural and political ties to Mexico and the United States. In Chapter 3, I analyze folkloric discourse in the writings of Nicaraguan *letrados*—the term commonly used in Latin American scholarship for "lettered" intellectuals who were also engaged in political projects of nation-building. While Indigenous peoples in western Nicaragua were considered sources for national heritage, Indigenous peoples in eastern Nicaragua were excluded from national heritage. The eastern, Caribbean coast of Nicaragua had initially been colonized by England prior to annexation by Nicaragua (with US support) in the late nineteenth century. The region included many English speakers with a range of racial/ethnic identities; those with some African ancestry were especially subject to exclusion from national belonging in folkloric writings. This Nicaraguan case study brings out the

---

[85] Alonso (2019).

contestation of who counts as Indigenous, tracing the different positioning of Indigenous peoples in western and eastern Nicaragua, as well as the exclusionary ideologies around African ancestry. There is also a tension in this chapter between political repression and psychological repression, which are linked in Derrida's conceptualization of the archive.

In Chapter 4, I examine networks and collections related to Indigenous Mapuche music and vanguardist art music in Chile. In the early 1940s, cultural diplomacy sparked a close relationship between two composers who were also administrators, Charles Seeger in the United States and Domingo Santa Cruz in Chile. Through their collaboration, the Pan American Union sent new recording and copying equipment to Chile. This transnational project shaped other projects of institutionalization already in progress at the Universidad de Chile, where Santa Cruz directed a national structure for the arts. Chile always had a marginal role in discourses of indigenismo, but several Chileans were involved in the Inter-American Indian Institute, and Chilean collection projects of the 1940s and 1950s increasingly turned to Indigenous music and folklore. I discuss the very different examples of Indigenous collections undertaken by the Chilean composer-anthropologist-artist Carlos Isamitt, the Argentine composer-ethnomusicologist Isabel Aretz, and the Chilean composer-artist Violeta Parra. This analysis leads to a reflection on different kinds of relations among archival collections, individuals, and communities and the processes of loss and recovery that they often entail.

In the epilogue to the book, I return to the Southwest United States as a key site for examining the representation of Indigenous culture at the intersection of North and South. My discussion of the historical work of Francis Joseph Attocknie (Comanche) challenges rigid divisions between orality and inscription. I argue that Indigenous communities and institutional archives should not be approached as dichotomous spheres. The idea of the "colonial archive" is often overgeneralized, obscuring the lively interaction and multiple affiliations of people who have created heritage institutions.[86]

Still, there is much work at hand to reactivate the cross-cultural and intracultural relationalities embedded in archives. I tend to use the terms recovery and recuperation to describe the work of reconnecting collections to communities, in part because both are associated with notions of returning to spiritual and physical health. Indigenous movements in Latin America often use the term *recuperación* to talk about the recovery of cultural memory

---

[86] Bruchac (2018) and Geismar (2013) also provide evidence of this co-construction.

as well as cultural property that has been detached, displaced, and quite often misplaced (lost and abandoned) in dominant institutions. Some of these institutions are within the same nation-state boundaries as the Indigenous heritage communities, but often they are located in the United States and Europe. The slowly emerging legal structures within the United States for the reclamation of Indigenous cultural property usually apply only to US federally recognized Tribes; they do not apply to Indigenous peoples from other countries whose cultural items are located in US collections.[87] The inter-American institutions, networks, and discourses that I examine in this book fed directly into the UN system at the end of World War II, though international legal frameworks were slow to protect Indigenous intellectual and cultural property. In 2007 the UN Declaration on the Rights of Indigenous Peoples provided a resource for pressuring states to recognize Indigenous rights to intellectual and cultural property within and across national boundaries. Yet even with the best of intentions, institutions can be slow to respond to changing legal and ethical mandates regarding Indigenous intellectual and cultural property. By locating my historical narratives within institutions while drawing out their contemporary significance, I hope to instigate more critique and dialogue that will contribute to opening up institutional collections to heritage communities of our day.

As Gabriella Giannachi writes, "the archive is not only an ordering system that facilitates the live transmission of knowledge, it is an ordering system that has a 'live force,' that is *(a)live*."[88] Part of the liveness of archives, I argue, comes from the traces left behind from human lives, traces which become audible when we listen, read, and think beyond the referentiality of the written text. Liveness also comes from the flux of the archive, always in a process of reconfiguration—adding new collections, transferring items to new formats, and building new architectures for safeguarding or access.[89] The four case studies that follow will explore the notions of aurality, authenticity, repression, and recuperation through intimate stories of Indigenous collections, and the traces of lives and voices that run through them.

---

[87] Legal scholars suggest that the right to international cooperation may be applied to relationships between Indigenous peoples and foreign institutions that hold their cultural materials (al Attar, Aylwin, and Coombe 2009: 333).

[88] Giannachi (2016: 8).

[89] Hamilton et al. (2002: 7).

1

Between the Ear and the Letter

Oral History and US Borderlands

In April of 1938, a twenty-eight-year-old Comanche man named William Karty met with a white fieldworker named Lillian Gassaway in Anadarko, Oklahoma, to participate in an oral history interview under the auspices of the Works Progress Administration (WPA). Karty was the head of a recreational and vocational program for the Kiowa Tribal jurisdiction of the Civilian Conservation Corps-Indian (CCC-I) Division, also tied to the Works Progress Administration. He oversaw programs related to agriculture, carpentry, blacksmithing, and typing, with Native boarding schools serving as a base for community education.[1] The interviewer, Lillian Gassaway, was the daughter of Reverend John Jasper Methvin, the first Christian missionary who worked on the Kiowa and Comanche reservation in US Indian Territory, which later became the state of Oklahoma. During the interview, Gassaway took notes with pencil and paper; mechanical recording equipment was not used during the project. The notes were later edited and typed for submission to the WPA Indian Pioneer history project.

The following narrative was an approximation of William Karty's own words, part of his biography which became an oral history text in archival collections:

> I am the reservation manager for the CCC-I at Anadarko. My father's name was Buffalo; he died in 1931. My mother, Tarsarer, was born about 1880 and is still living. My grandmother, To-see, was born in Mexico, in 1809; died in 1924. I was born on West Cache Creek in September, 1909. I am of Spanish and Comanche blood. My grandmother on my mother's side was a Spanish captive. She was captured in Mexico when she was only eight years old.
>
> My father was a Comanche and a member of the Indian Police force at Fort Sill before the opening of the country [to white settlement]. As you

[1] Hanneman (2000: 440).

Indigenous Audibilities. Amanda Minks, Oxford University Press. © Oxford University Press 2024. DOI: 10.1093/oso/9780197532485.003.0002

see, my name is not like the name of my family. They used never to have surnames. I will tell you how I got mine. One time when I was a very small boy, Buffalo Bill (Bill Cody) came to the Fort to make a motion picture and I was in that picture with him. When he left he gave me his name but in going through the government offices it became Karty instead.[2]

This brief story encodes deep histories of mobile Indigenous communities and of cross-border captives who became kin. It also encodes intertwined histories of US governmentality and mediated representations, which created new structures for Indigenous life in the early twentieth century, even in that most personal element of an individual name.

Beginning in the 1880s, Buffalo Bill's Wild West show—initially live performance and later film portrayals—was one of the popular spectacles that began to represent Indigenous culture for a mass audience. This practice was rife with paradoxes. Government agents and missionaries prohibited traditional Native music and dance when they were part of Native community activities. When performed for white audiences, however, Native music and dance could be tolerated or even encouraged. In a particularly egregious example, the federal government granted permission to Buffalo Bill Cody to incorporate Lakota prisoners into his performance troupe, bound for a European tour, just a few months after they had survived the US military's massacre of some three hundred men, women, and children at Wounded Knee in 1890.[3]

As media scholar Dustin Tahmahkera (Comanche) has emphasized, Native performers also claimed active roles in shaping the representation of their cultural practices. Comanches have been especially prolific actors and agents in cinematic representation. In Tahmahkera's words, "Within a Comanche history of migrations and movements off-screen and on, cinematic Comanches are a performative people in motion (and motion pictures) in the media borderlands."[4] Tahmahkera argues that the omnipresence of Comanches in the media borderlands is an extension of their historical power in the geopolitical borderlands. The dominant portrayals

---

[2] Birth years are often approximated in these histories, although it is possible that his grandmother lived to be well over a hundred years old. The parenthetical insertion "Bill Cody" was probably added by Lillian Gassaway or a typist. Interview with William Karty, April 29, 1938. Indian Pioneer Papers digital collection, WHC, https://digital.libraries.ou.edu/cdm/ref/collection/indianpp/id/4777.

[3] Carter (2000: 359–360).

[4] Tahmahkera (2022: 4).

of Comanche defeat fail to recognize Comanche continuance in life and in media, off-screen and on-screen.

In the oral history quoted above, William Karty locates his own biography in both the geopolitical borderlands and the media borderlands. What is the nature of this oral history? Since time immemorial, Indigenous communities have created their own practices and genres of recounting the past, but the narrative of William Karty came out of an intercultural space. In this chapter I focus on archived oral histories that emerged from encounters between Indigenous people and a particular institutional project of inscription. This kind of oral history is not a transparent conduit for information. I take the position that institutional oral history collections should be read and heard through the cultural processes of creating and compiling narratives. As Elinor Ochs has written, everyday conversation in many cultural contexts often involves embedded narratives, with multiple speakers and listeners co-constructing stories and probing their meaning.[5] Most archived oral history texts began with an interaction in which the interviewer and inter- viewee brought their own conversational practices to the encounter. Charles Briggs's early work showed how the social scientific interview tends to priv- ilege an abstract, decontextualized approach to knowledge, which can lead to miscommunications and misinterpretations in the interview encounter.[6] The voice of the interviewer, though often edited out of oral histories, is a powerful force in mediating, reframing, and representing the voice of the interviewee.

Briggs's work was part of a broader interdisciplinary analysis of discourse as performance, which moved away from the reification of texts (as music or speech) and toward the *emergence* of texts.[7] In this view, certain stretches of discourse (for example, a prayer or a song) are "lifted out" of their inter- actional setting, then recited in another oral setting, or captured in a me- chanical recording, or written down to become a tangible text. A memorable phrase, a recording, or a written text then moves into new contexts, accruing new meanings while also carrying "elements of its history of use within it."[8] Following these ideas, I approach oral histories as entextualized narratives that carry some traces of particular voices. These narratives must also be

[5] Ochs (2004).
[6] Briggs (1986).
[7] Bauman and Briggs (1990); Bauman (1977); Herndon and McLeod (1980); Feld (1984).
[8] Bauman and Briggs (1990: 73).

interpreted through attention to the mediating practices which led to their emergence as texts.

In this chapter I recover the history of an archival collection, now known as the Indian Pioneer Papers, which has been widely used by scholars as well as family researchers for the historical and cultural information it contains.[9] It is one of many collections in US institutions (museums, libraries, and archives) that emerged from the 1930s government-funded Works Progress Administration. In thinking about oral history "between the ear and the letter," I draw attention to the relations among voicing, listening, and writing that are recombined in heterogeneous, co-constructed narratives. Decentering "music" as an object in this case study enables a broader view of the mediated relations between orality and writing, which are also a key part of discourses focusing on Indigenous music. Within the bureaucratic instructions for the Indian Pioneer project was a pedagogy of listening, crucial to documentary transcription and collection. There are other layers of listening here, as well. We gain access to this past moment of time by listening to the archive, where oral histories encode mediating forms, interactive voices, and sociopolitical forces.

I begin with a broad context for considering this case study as part of Southwest US borderlands histories, which bring together layers of colonial and Indigenous interactions. Then I unravel the tangle of circumstances that led to the 1930s creation of the Indian Pioneer Papers, also referred to as the Indian Pioneer history project. This collection was made up of inscriptions of oral narratives about Indian Territory, which became the state of Oklahoma in 1907. Tribes from across the United States were forcibly removed to Indian Territory from the 1830s onward. I put special emphasis on the Southern Plains Tribes that played a crucial role in borderlands relations, but I also consider narratives from other groups represented in the Indian Pioneer Papers, which often problematized fixed racial categories. At the end of the chapter, I draw out connections between the Indian Pioneer project and other projects of Indigenous history, memory, and heritage.

---

[9] Copies of the Indian Pioneer Papers bound volumes are held by the University of Oklahoma Western History Collections (WHC) and the Oklahoma Historical Society (OHS). The WHC digital collection is currently located at https://digital.libraries.ou.edu/whc/pioneer/. Some of the interviews quoted in this chapter come from archived reports in the WHC and OHS rather than the bound volumes or digital collection, as specified in the footnotes. Selections from the Indian Pioneer Papers have been published in La Vere (1998).

Deep Histories of Southwest Interactions

The stories in this book spin up from undercurrents of interaction between the Americas, North and South. My focal points in twentieth-century institutional networks extended from metropolitan centers of government control, like Washington, DC, and Mexico City. Discussing a micro-history of collection in the Southwest borderlands requires consideration of deeper histories and broader intercultural dynamics that were distant and detached from metropolitan centers (colonial or national). In this sense, the borderlands region of the Southwest United States might be viewed as a vortex of North/South interaction that de-centers the dominant axes of contact.

Interaction among Indigenous peoples of the Americas goes back millennia, prior to European arrival, leaving evidence of mutual influence in the agricultural, architectural, and ceremonial practices of broad contact zones. These relations always included conflict as well as exchange, but European colonialism marked a significant shift, the beginning of a new system of global hegemony that involved interlocking ideologies of race, development, culture, and capital.[10] The Spanish were the first Europeans to attempt to colonize what is now the Southwest United States, establishing a long-term settlement in New Mexico at the end of the sixteenth century. The region is significant not only in its legacy of Spanish colonization but also in its legacy of Indigenous resistance. The Pueblo Revolt of 1680 vanquished the Spanish for over a decade. In the early 1700s, groups of Indigenous peoples migrated to the region from further north, gained mastery of the Spanish horse, and developed a mobile livelihood following buffalo herds across the Southern Plains. Among Southern Plains tribes, Kiowas, Apaches, and especially Comanches gained a dominant position in the region through mounted hunting and warfare.

In the eighteenth and nineteenth centuries, the pressures of colonial encroachment and the dispossession of Indigenous land and resources led to increased raiding for livestock, goods, and human captives. Spanish and Mexican settlements usually incorporated Indigenous captives into a life of servitude. Southern Plains and Southwest Tribes also incorporated

---

[10] My interpretation here contrasts with the notion of "reversed colonialism," which Pekka Hamalainen (2008) uses to talk about the rise of Comanche power in the Southwest borderlands in the eighteenth and nineteenth centuries. Without denying the broad range of intergroup power dynamics in American histories, I consider European conquest to be a new order of global power that constituted modern racial hierarchies.

captives into their communities—sometimes as subordinates and other times as adopted kin with full rights as Tribal members. As the US government exerted increasing control in the region in the late nineteenth century, Southern Plains groups of Comanche, Kiowa, and Apache were forced onto reservation lands in southwest Indian Territory, near the Texas border. Other Indigenous peoples, such as subgroups of Kickapoo and Seminole, fled further south to Mexico as a strategy for maintaining more independence outside of reservation confinement in the United States. In the latter half of the nineteenth century, new borders backed by military force regulated the movement of Indigenous peoples—between Mexico and the United States, and around the reservations in Indian Territory and the broader Southwest.

Still, the dense cultural heterogeneity and lively circuits of exchange continued in the region, with a particularly impactful development in the ceremonial use of the peyote cactus, whose natural habitat runs from south Texas to San Luis Potosí in northern Mexico. In the late nineteenth and early twentieth century, members of Southern Plains Tribes in Oklahoma developed a new peyote ceremonial complex that spread, with variations, throughout the United States and Canada. Comanche and Kiowa were leaders in this process, after two Lipan Apache brothers married into their reservation community and shared peyote practices with them in the 1870s. Carrizo, Tonkawa, and other borderlands tribes may have been earlier conduits of peyote, with multiple circuits of influence facilitating new ceremonial practices.[11]

Although recent histories of the Southwest have highlighted the ingenious strategies through which Southern Plains Tribes became dominant in the 1700s, some works tend to reinforce a teleology of Indigenous defeat which is divorced from Indigenous "survivance"—an active sense of presence, creative resistance, and continuity.[12] Most academic historians recognize the biases built into archives, but they still often emphasize accumulating masses of archival documentation more than interrogating concepts of race and power bound up with colonial knowledge structures. There is also a recurring slippage between popular concepts of indigeneity and scholarly analyses in anthropology and history. As Alcida Ramos has written, scholars often unwittingly bring popular stereotypes into their research, which takes on the guise of objectivity in its reception.[13] When preconceptions and stereotypes

---

[11] Swan (1990, 1999). On early nineteenth-century peyote use by borderlands Tribes, see also LaBarre (1975: 121); McAllester (1949); and Stewart (1987: 46–51).
[12] Vizenor (2008).
[13] Ramos (1998).

slip between popular and academic discourse, they become even more powerful and mobile, endorsing certain kinds of essentialist characterizations, historical teleologies, and "just so" stories.[14]

As Christopher Aplin has pointed out in relation to Apache histories, many popular and scholarly histories of the Southwest have focused on violent encounters. This begs the question of what kinds of stories get told, from whose perspectives, and what stories are overlooked or elided.[15] Many of the oral histories in the Indian Pioneer collection are mundane, focusing on daily life and local knowledge of people and places. These texts often reveal ideological divisions between white settler and Indigenous perspectives, but there is also diversity within each category. Generalizations run the risk of construing an authentic voice in oral history. These narratives represent textual constructions created by multiple actors in a particular cultural and historical context. We need to step back and try to understand how oral history, or at least these oral histories, came to be made—to try to hear the voices that formed them.

Indian Pioneer History

The Indian Pioneer history project was a research enterprise based in the state of Oklahoma with the dual intention of preserving historical memory and creating jobs during the Depression. It was funded by the federal Works Progress Administration and jointly sponsored by the University of Oklahoma and the Oklahoma Historical Society. The primary work of the project was carried out from December 1936 to April 1938, a period of seventeen months. This short-term project resulted in an astonishing quantity of oral history manuscripts—over 11,000—that represented the "reminiscences" of elderly white, Black, and Native American residents of Oklahoma. Like the oral history collections of the contemporaneous Federal Writers Project, the Indian Pioneer history project did not use

---

[14] An especially problematic example is Gwynne's 2010 book *Empire of the Summer Moon*, which I discuss in the epilogue.

[15] See Christopher Aplin's theorization of the relations between "overlook" and "amnesic elision" (Aplin 2010: 35–40, 71). This observation on the preoccupations of history does not imply that violence should not be analyzed, as it constitutes the core of colonial histories and often runs across relations between colonized peoples, as well (Brooks 2001; Blackhawk 2006; Jacoby 2008; Delay 2008). Crandall (2019) discusses the continuities of Indigenous governance in times of conflict as well as peace.

mechanical recording equipment. Rather, nonspecialists who were on the "relief rolls" (certified as unemployed) received guidance to conduct oral history interviews and create manuscripts based on notes written by hand, during or soon after the interview.

Documentation for the Indian Pioneer history project is uneven, but key actors included the Native intellectual Don Whistler (Sac and Fox) and the white historians Morris Wardell and Grant Foreman. Whistler had a wide range of experience in family business, Tribal politics, and cultural heritage collections; he would later become a long-serving elected leader of his Tribe, as well as the founder and host of a pioneering Native radio program.[16] Wardell was a professor of history specializing in Cherokee political history; he moved into administration as the "dean of men," and then assistant to the president at the University of Oklahoma.[17] Grant Foreman wrote the introduction to the bound volumes which were archived in the Oklahoma Historical Society and the University of Oklahoma. In that introduction, he neglected most others' contributions to the collection and oddly ignored the Indian histories contained therein. His intellectual and institutional authority was hegemonic in 1930s Oklahoma, and his own biography is significant for understanding the collections work he was involved in.

A lawyer by training, Grant Foreman came to Oklahoma in 1899 as a fieldworker for the Dawes Commission, the government entity that broke up Tribal landholdings and allotted smaller parcels to Native Americans in order to open land to white settlement. After four years working with the Dawes Commission, Foreman resigned to join a law practice in Muskogee, Oklahoma, a town that took its name from Indigenous Muscogee (Creek) people originally from the southeastern woodlands of the United States. His professional trajectory brings to mind the Latin American role of the *letrado* which I will discuss in later chapters. These "lettered" men of the nineteenth and early twentieth centuries used law as a springboard for research in history and folklore. Law and letters were interrelated projects that were both epistemic and pragmatic, aimed at regimenting diverse populations within new governmental structures. The new structures of land and law under Oklahoma statehood benefited Foreman. His land and oil holdings enabled him to retire from his legal practice in the early 1920s so that he could devote himself entirely to historical research and writing.[18] During this time he

---

[16] Garrett-Davis (2018, forthcoming); Ortega (2019).
[17] Levy (2015). See also description in the finding aid, Morris L. Wardell Collection, WHC.
[18] Clark (1953).

also became the director of the Oklahoma Historical Society, which enabled him to solicit and oversee collections activities as he researched and wrote his books and articles. These activities of soliciting and organizing collections went into overdrive with the support of the Works Progress Administration.

Beginning in 1935, the Works Progress Administration (WPA) supported a frenzy of historical and cultural collections work in Oklahoma, as in other states. Archaeologists loosely supervised excavation teams to unearth ancient (and not so ancient) artifacts and human remains to be sent to academic and museum collections.[19] In Oklahoma, the WPA Historical Records project and a related Historical Archives Survey prompted the solicitation of written records, manuscripts, and photographs from local, state, and national institutions—especially related to Indian Territory—as well as the private collections people held in closets and attics in their homes.[20]

Sometime in the summer of 1935, an idea was launched—probably by Grant Foreman—to propose an Indian history project that could garner WPA support. The initial proposal submitted to Washington was titled "Ethnological Survey of Indians," and it was a collaboration among Foreman, several faculty from the University of Oklahoma, and a Bureau of Indian Affairs employee based in Oklahoma City. WPA officials determined that the project was not feasible after consulting with Washington-based anthropologists, who doubted that nonspecialist employees taken from the relief rolls could conduct ethnological research with Native Americans. These anthropologists were defending their own expertise as they positioned themselves as Indian experts; they expressed concern that Indians would be even more reluctant to participate in professional research if they had been "antagonized" by WPA workers. The notion of "interviews" was itself subject to a statistical paradigm of social science and its arbiters in the governmental infrastructure.[21]

A major bureaucratic problem was that the majority of WPA-supported employees had to be drawn from the "relief rolls"—individuals who had been certified as unemployed due to the Depression and who met a number of other shifting criteria, such as being heads of their households. Most elderly Native Americans would not be eligible to be paid through the WPA, and many younger Native Americans were also excluded because they

---

[19] Regnier, Livingood, and Hammerstedt (2013).
[20] M1234 WPA Historic Sites and Federal Writers' Project, Box 56, File 6, WHC.
[21] University Archives RG 40/10, College of Arts and Sciences/History Dept. Morris L. Wardell Box 4, File 4, WHC. Grant Foreman Collection, Box 45, Files 13–15, OHS.

had already been pulled into Emergency Conservation Work through the Department of Indian Affairs and could not be transferred to WPA work.[22] The group organizing the Indian history project considered reworking the proposal into an ethno-botanical project, but decided even that would be hindered by the limited capacity to hire Native Americans through the WPA.

The group seemed to be at a dead end, but by June 1936 they were moving forward with another version of the project. In the coming months, they began to include non-Indian "pioneers" (early settlers) as sources of historical information, and they emphasized that the interviews undertaken would focus on the collection of narratives rather than social scientific methodology. They drew parallels with the work being carried out by the Federal Writers Project, the Federal Music Project, and the Federal Theater Project, which had successfully solicited stories from "old timers" in many parts of the country.[23] At that time, the project continued to be framed with a focus on Indian history, but the potential sources for this history opened up to include non-Indian settlers as well as physical collections and cemetery inscriptions. As the project unfolded, it included many white settlers' interpretations of Native American culture as they remembered encountering it in their youth, a context that tended to reproduce stereotypes and superficial judgments. In this way, the concerns of Washington anthropologists about sending WPA workers to Indigenous communities led to an often warped portrayal of Indigenous culture through the eyes and ears of white settlers. White settlers also contributed the largest amount of material reflecting on their experiences as pioneers and the formation of white communities in Oklahoma prior to statehood. These bureaucratic procedures split the temporality of competing claims to prior occupancy under settler colonialism, with Native peoples oriented toward the past and non-Native settlers oriented toward the future.[24]

When the official proposal was submitted to Washington on November 28, 1936, the project was focused on "Indian and pioneer histories," but still emphasized Native American knowledge that was assumed to be slipping away. The project description listed the general aims as follows:

[22] Letter from Homer Heck and WS Key to Oklahoma Historical Society, January 23, 1936, Foreman Collection Box 45, File 14, OHS.

[23] Moe Clauber to William Leonard, WPA, September 19, 1936, Foreman Collection, Box 45, File 9, OHS.

[24] See Povinelli (2011: 35–37) on the "governance of the prior."

The collecting of biographical information on both living and dead Indians and pioneers whose lives have been in some manner important in the history of the State from its earliest historical beginnings. The collecting of information on family customs, tribal histories, social organization, including folk lore and legends so far as not to duplicate work already being done. The collecting of unrecorded facts now known only to those living, such as stories of removal, the Civil War, life in the schools, and the transition from tribal life to statehood. The locating of family and other Burial grounds, copying the inscriptions and collecting information on those known to be buried in these areas (emphasizing the period prior to 1900). The collecting of information from those living who know of old trails, forts, posts, camps, trading centers, villages, etc., so far as not to duplicate work already being done. This material will be collected and written by field workers who will send it to headquarters for supplemental information. Here it will be classified, edited and put in the proper form for typing. Final copies will be deposited with the Oklahoma Historical Society and the University of Oklahoma.[25]

This framing emphasized the activities of collecting, compiling, copying, and typing rather than composing new analytical works of anthropology or history. The caveat of avoiding duplication was a nod to the biographical and folkloric research undertaken by the Federal Writers' Project and the Federal Music Project, as well as the collecting and classification work undertaken by the Historical Records and Historical Archives projects. The total funding requested was $41,915.50, with most of that allocated to the salaries of project personnel, including the director, supervisors, editors, interviewers, secretaries, readers, timekeepers, and typists.[26]

The Indian Pioneer history project shared common ground with the Federal Writers' Project in valuing the historical memory of people who did not have extensive written records of their lives, as elites usually did. The following passage from the proposal conveyed this understanding along with the need for transcription and preservation of oral history and memory:

[25] This initial project description was most likely written by Grant Foreman, judging from the annotation of an identical text in the OU Western History Collections. M1234, WPA Historic Sites Box 56, File 6, "Indian Pioneer History Project S-149. Character and Purpose," and WPA Project Proposal S-149, November 28, 1936, Wardell Box 4, File 4, WHC.

[26] The percentages of the salary categories were listed as follows: intermediate (typists), 5.1%; skilled (secretaries, readers, timekeepers), 36.1%; professional and technical (interviewers and others), 37.2%; superintendences (1 director, 1 clerical supervisor, 2 editors, 6 superintendents), 19.7%.

Much of the history of this country and of the people who have made it lies in the minds of living people. It consists of information that has come to them either through their own experience and observation or from accounts and traditions handed down to them by their ancestors. The people who have this information are usually advanced in years and they are daily being carried away by death. Every death of such person is a distinct loss of historical material that might have been preserved. The object of this project is to see these people while they are yet living and able to impart the information that they possess, to secure and transcribe it and preserve it in such manner that it will be available for all time to come.[27]

The impending risk of losing cultural memory was most pronounced for Native American oral history, because the dominant ideology of the time was that Native Americans were undergoing a process of assimilation and extinction. The same proposal stated: "The aged Indians—and others for that matter—have valuable contributions to make to Indian history of the State of Oklahoma. This information is valuable and absolutely essential for the history of a race that is fast losing its original status as it is being absorbed into the white race." This formulation did not say that Indians were vanishing, as so many other publications had claimed, but rather suggested that they were being culturally assimilated through education and intermarriage. Most strikingly, Indians were expected to lose their "original status" as a result of this assumed "absorption" into whiteness. Dominant US ideologies of indigeneity equated racial purity with cultural survival, and racial mixing with cultural loss. Many Native participants in the project recognized the reality of cultural loss in the face of federal policies designed for extermination and assimilation, but many also attested to cultural survivance. This passage about "original status" went further than an acknowledgment of cultural loss and seemed a threat to revoke the heritage of Native Americans as originary inhabitants.

As news of the project spread in Oklahoma, prospective researchers wrote to the sponsoring institutions to express their interest in working on the project. Angie Debo was one of them. Debo had completed her PhD at the University of Oklahoma in 1933 under the sponsorship of Edward Elliott Dale, a close friend and colleague of Wardell. Dale was an Oklahoma ranch boy turned schoolteacher turned history professor, having earned his PhD

---

[27] WPA Project Proposal S-149, November 28, 1936, Wardell Box 4, File 4, WHC.

at Harvard under Frederick Jackson Turner. Dale embraced Turner's frontier thesis, which valorized the settlement of the American west by white settlers who were destined to take the place of Native peoples.[28] Amanda Cobb-Greetham (Chickasaw) has analyzed Debo's complicated relationship to the frontier thesis. Debo often appears as a critic of white settlement but, as Cobb-Greetham points out, even Debo's critiques failed to challenge a sense of the inevitable decline of Native peoples and cultures.[29] Debo's name did not come up in the planning discussions for the Indian Pioneer project, but her letter to Wardell managed to secure a position as an editor. Although the position was short-lived, Debo used Muscogee oral histories from the project for her ongoing research. She found a remarkable degree of continuity between the Muscogee oral histories and other documentary sources, suggesting that oral history could parallel written records (see Figure 1.1).[30]

The organizers anticipated a six-month project and were prepared to begin within two weeks of approval. On December 14, 1936, five powerful male decision makers came together to flesh out the implementation and personnel for the project, and a female secretary made a detailed transcription of the meeting. In addition to Foreman, they included an Indian Affairs officer based in Oklahoma City (John Woolery), a historian and university administrator (Morris Wardell), and two other state-level administrators (Lanson D. Mitchell from the Oklahoma WPA and James W. Moffitt from the Oklahoma Historical Society). Wardell suggested hiring superintendents who were "young men" so that they might "energetically carry on the program, thus relieving Dr. Foreman of as much of the detail as possible, permitting him to devote his time to writing etc."[31] Foreman was sixty-seven at the time, an age that accorded respect and consideration for his health. In addition, both Woolery and Wardell were focused on Native participation in the project, and they may have been strategizing to moderate Foreman's influence. While Oklahoma women took on leadership roles in the Federal Writers Project, they were rarely considered for leadership in the Indian Pioneer project. Later in the project, when Foreman recommended Winifred Clark (in his words, "a very capable woman") for a supervisory role during

---

[28] Loughlin (2005: 75); Cobb-Greetham (2022).

[29] Cobb-Greetham (2022).

[30] Leckie (2000: 79). The book that resulted from Debo's research at the time was *The Road to Disappearance: A History of the Creek Indians* (1941). This book title, among others, illustrates Cobb-Greetham's argument that Debo portrayed Tribes in a teleology of defeat and decline.

[31] December 14, 1936 report, University Archives RG40/10, College of Arts and Sciences/History Dept. Morris L. Wardell Box 4, File 4, WHC.

Figure 1.1 Angie Debo, scholar of Oklahoma Native American histories, who worked on the Indian Pioneer history project and the Federal Writers' Project. 1935. Angie Debo Collection, Oklahoma State University Library.

one of his extended absences, he instructed the administrator to pay her less than the usual rate.[32] Labor practices repeatedly put women in a subordinate position in institutions, tied here to a veritable "patriarchive."[33]

---

[32] Foreman to Key, June 17, 1936, Grant Foreman Collection, Box 45, File 13, OHS.
[33] Derrida (1995).

Woolery, the Indian Affairs officer, continually suggested strategies for drawing more Native American personnel into the project, but the other decision-makers found them unfeasible based on the budget and WPA protocols. Two of the names that came up for consideration as superintendents, and who did enter into those roles, were Chauncey Moore and Don Whistler. In his application letter, Chauncey Moore said he was part Indian and had served as president of the Oklahoma Folk Festival. His work as a regional superintendent for the Indian Pioneer history project involved extensive Native networks in northeastern Oklahoma, though his own cultural identifications were unclear in the project documentation. Don Whistler identified strongly as Sac and Fox, his father's Tribe, while his mother was of European descent. Whistler was especially well prepared for the dual investigation of Indian and pioneer histories, as he had close relations with families and communities in both areas. None of the preliminary discussions mentioned Oklahomans who were not white or Indian. However, some fieldworkers later interviewed Black and Black Indigenous Oklahomans who provided rich narratives that challenged racial dichotomies as well as sentimental nostalgia for old times.

The project was implemented rapidly, with limited foresight in matching state goals to the budgets and policies of the federal government. Native Americans with the deepest traditional knowledge often lived furthest from urban centers, and they spoke most comfortably in their Native languages, but there was no allocation for travel or translation. The prominent white men developing the structure of the project lamented that few Native Americans in the western part of the state would qualify for employment as relief staff. Southern Plains Tribes, among others, were located in the western part of Oklahoma; they tended to be traditionalist and did not have the same kind of access to formal education and employment opportunities as those in the eastern part of the state. Eastern Oklahoma was the domain of the Five Tribes from the Southeast United States who had long been labeled "civilized" because their economic and governmental practices were viewed as compatible with white ways.[34] Members of the Five Tribes tended to have greater access to formal education at an earlier date than many other Tribes; some had their own Tribally run schools. People of white and Native mixed descent, especially from the eastern regions of the state and from the Five

---

[34] This group historically includes Cherokee, Chickasaw, Choctaw, Muscogee (Creek), and Seminole Tribes.

Tribes, were more likely to work on the project than other Native Americans in Oklahoma.

Woolery still hoped that Native personnel from southwest Oklahoma could be brought into the project as non–relief workers. He recommended Robert Coffey (Comanche), George Hunt and James Daugomah (Kiowa), Howard Soontay (Apache), John Downing (Caddo), and John Haddon (Wichita).[35] Wardell was a strong supporter of Don Whistler (Sac and Fox), who was hired as a superintendent soon after the December meeting. Wardell attested to Whistler's preparation of the manual for fieldworkers in January and February of 1937, writing to Foreman, "I should like to report to you that Mr. Whistler is doing a nice piece of work" (see Figure 1.2).[36]

Whistler's family and professional background are important for understanding his role in the Indian Pioneer project. He was the son of a poor white mother and a Sauk father from a prominent Native family who ran a general store at the Sac and Fox reservation. Whistler spent his childhood immersed in Native culture while also maintaining close relations with his white relatives. His parents divorced when he was an adolescent, and his mother eventually moved the family to Norman so that her children could attend the University of Oklahoma. Don Whistler and his siblings helped to shape Native student culture, and the Whistler family built several successful businesses at the edge of campus.[37]

Whistler was an ideal person to develop the Indian Pioneer project, not only because of his intercultural knowledge and networks, but also because he was well educated and had experience working with collections. He became an OU student around 1916, a time when many Native students advocated for cultural collections reflecting their communities, and he contributed to Native collections at the university at various points in his life. In the 1920s he worked as an assistant curator and lecturer at the University of Pennsylvania Museum, an opportunity facilitated by his aunt on his mother's side of the family, Bee Mayes Barry.[38] Bee Barry built a career in the northeast as an "Indianist" performer, a popular dramatic approach at the time which involved selectively (and often imaginatively) combining tropes of Native

---

[35] Native Americans recommended for employment in other parts of the state included Thomas Alford (Shawnee), Alice Young Jones (Potawatomi), Solomon Kent (Iowa), Ernest Murdock (Kickapoo), Alford Wilson (Cheyenne), and Jesse Rowlodge (Arapaho). December 31, 1936, Wardell Collection Box 4, File 4, WHC.

[36] Wardell to Foreman, Jan 9, 1937; February 10, 1937; Wardell Collection Box 4, File 4, WHC.

[37] Ortega (2019).

[38] Garrett-Davis (2018, 2020, forthcoming).

Figure 1.2 Don Whistler (Sac and Fox), who worked on the Indian Pioneer history project and was founding host of the Indians for Indians radio show. Accession No: 237.B, Oklahoma Historical Society.

culture.[39] Barry was of Euro-American descent, but presented herself as Chippewa in performances in the northeast. She drew on knowledge gleaned from her sister's Sauk in-laws and from other intertribal social networks (she had attended Haskell Indian School and worked for many years in the Indian school service). Barry also worked for the WPA Music Project in the 1930s,

---

[39] Troutman (2009).

with the charge of making recordings of Tribal music across Oklahoma.[40] Some WPA reports mention the existence of this collection, but the collection appears to have been lost, if it ever existed at all.

Methodologies for Interviewing

WPA projects were large, unwieldy operations that resulted from negotiated agendas across institutions at the local, state, and national levels.[41] The Indian Pioneer history project was distinct from several other WPA cultural heritage projects because the methodology of the project was developed in Oklahoma rather than in Washington, DC.[42] The manual included Foreman's description of the character and purpose of the project, along with an elaboration of the duties for supervisors and workers that he had drafted in an earlier document. In addition to expanding the section on personnel duties, Whistler apparently wrote the specific instructions for the "Field Workers Guide for Interviews" below:

A. Always, without exception, know the name of the person to be interviewed before you meet him. Some of the ways in which you will secure these names are: from your superintendent, from Indian tribal rolls, from 89ers or Old Settlers organizations, from Old county maps showing original land owners, from other interviewees. . . .

B. DO NOT produce a notebook and pencil at the beginning of the interview. In fact it is better to avoid a note book entirely. Small cards which can be used, one at a time, are much better.

C. The field worker will find in most instances that a simple friendly chat will produce the best results. Take as few notes as possible in the presence of the person interviewed. This will be particularly true of full blood Indians, old people, and the less educated.

---

[40] Barry was still planning to publish her research in 1942, as the remaining WPA projects were shifting focus to war efforts. "Report of the Community Service Programs of the WPA Sponsored by OU," University of Oklahoma Archives RG 3, Office of Pres. Joseph A. Brandt, Box 15, WPA file, WHC. Barry's letters to her mother and sister are archived in the Snow Collection, WHC.

[41] See, e.g., Hirsch (2003); Gough (2015).

[42] The manuals for the Survey of Historical Records and the Survey of Federal Archives, which involved some of the same institutional actors in Oklahoma, were written and distributed from Washington in January and February 1936. Foreman Collection, Box 45, File 11, OHS.

D. (If necessary) Explain very briefly your purpose in gathering material, for what it is to be used, and how taken care of.

E. Let the person interviewed do most of the talking. If he or she wants to tell about his hogs or her favorite pickle recipe, let them do it.

F. Do not ask too many direct questions. Do not interrupt a story for minor details—ask about them later.

H. A good procedure in starting the interview is to ask a question about some local event, or place. For example:

"Do you remember Scott's trading post down on North Fork?"

"Were they still using that old cattle trail when you came here?"

I. Be extremely careful to get the name of the person absolutely correct.... This instruction about names, is purposely put toward the end because that is where it properly belongs in your procedure.

J. As soon as possible after your interview, write the whole story out. Do not abbreviate and do not condense. Write out everything that you have learned, whether it seems important or not.

K. Absolutely—Do Not begin another interview until you have written a first manuscript on the previous one.

The above are not absolute rules. They are a condensation of suggestions made by people who have had experience in this line of work. If you find a situation where they are not practical, do not hesitate to use some other approach. Remember the purpose of this project and get the information.[43]

Whistler's guidelines provided an explicit pedagogy of elicitation, listening, and inscription. This approach to interviewing prioritized the communicative norms of the interviewee, rather than the objectifying, segmented approach of social scientific interviewing.[44] Close listening and remembering cultural knowledge were important skills in Native communities and families. Avoiding direct questions and interruptions was also in keeping with many Native communicative norms. Minimizing the appearance of note-taking helped to keep the interaction in the realm of sociality and avoided the power dynamics of bureaucratic inscription. Fieldworkers were expected to have some bits of local knowledge to use as

---

[43] WPA Manual of the Indian-Pioneer History Project for Oklahoma, p. 6–7, M1234 WPA Historic Sites Box 56, File 6, and Dale Collection Box 208, File 2, WHC.

[44] See Briggs (1986).

a spark for memory and storytelling. They were also expected to remember and reproduce in writing "the whole story" after the interview. Many Native Americans had two names, one in their Tribal language and a conventional English language name. In the manual and forms for collecting information, Whistler instructed fieldworkers to ask about and write down both names for each individual. Despite the admonition to get names spelled correctly, there are many variable spellings in the collection.

Whistler advocated for a kind of history that reflected the texture of daily lives, without objectifying them as detached historical or anthropological objects. "History should not be just a series of dates," he wrote in the manual. "We can better understand a people if we know something of their every day mode of life."[45] He provided different lists of topics to be explored when interviewing Indians and pioneers, and he positioned the Indian list first. His instructions to avoid note-taking in the presence of "fullblood" Indians, elderly people, and the less educated suggest complicated relations among literacy, ethnicity, generation, and social class. These relations could not be corralled in neat categories in Oklahoma; many Native Americans such as Whistler had more formal education and more skill with the written word than poor whites.[46]

As the project unfolded, Whistler sent out bulletins that provided supplementary instructions for fieldworkers, based on his assessment of the reports and questions that came to his office. In the first bulletin, Whistler recognized the variety of temporalities in oral storytelling, but he encouraged interviewers to reorganize events into the linear temporality that dominated written works.[47] He wrote:

> Within the above limitations, the life story of the person interviewed should be a simple narrative, carried out in the chronological order. (Did you ever read Robinson Crusoe or Treasure Island?) You will find that in

[45] WPA Manual of the Indian-Pioneer History Project for Oklahoma, p. 10, M1234 WPA Historic Sites Box 56, File 6, and Dale Collection Box 208, File 2, WHC.

[46] Cobb (2000) notes that the Chickasaw academies, among other Tribally run schools, provided a stronger education than any schools available to whites in Oklahoma. Indian schools run by the US government and/or missionaries were a mixed bag. They generally focused on manual labor, but they sometimes provided stepping-stones for students to continue higher education. Whistler's aunt, Bee Barry, attended Haskell Indian School as a non-Native American student because it was her only opportunity to attain an education, coming from a poor family in a rural area. Snow Collection, Box 1, File 2, WHC.

[47]. Temporal variability is a common feature of conversational narrative, and can also be shaped by different speech genres and cosmologies across cultural contexts (Ochs 2004; Bacigalupo 2013).

most instances the person interviewed will not stick to the time order in telling his story. Do not let that bother you—too much. But when you write the Biography put the facts into their regular time order. In other words— Write the things first that happened first. Your completed biography should read like a story. It should not be a jumble of facts.

Do the best you can.[48]

Whistler's final note of encouragement seems to recognize the challenges of the task, as well as the novice status of his fieldworkers. In all his bulletins, Whistler demonstrated a voice of authority and clearly directed fieldworkers, the majority of whom were white. This is also the voice of the manual, but his coauthorship and leadership went unacknowledged in public presentations of the project.[49] Whistler left the project after a few months, apparently due to budget cuts from the national WPA office, but he had already made his mark. He co-created an institutional design for putting the heterogeneity of voice in some kind of legible order, without subsuming it entirely by the dominant order. Listening was a key methodology, but neither administrators nor fieldworkers could completely control the workings of the voice, ear, or transcribing hand. This is aurality in a broader sense—the capacity of sounds and voices to "seep into and restructure the paradigms that appear to contain or exclude them."[50]

Native Stories from the Indian Pioneer Collection

The stories inscribed in the Indian Pioneer collection are co-constructed texts involving not only the interviewer and interviewee, but also editors and typists.[51] Though they are written as monologues, we can guess about many of the questions asked (based on topics listed in the manual) and about moments when information was withheld. Most of the written narratives are brief, which may suggest a reticence on the part of interviewees, or editorial work that condensed longer narratives. Whistler's interest in everyday life

---

[48] Dale Collection, Box 208, File 2, WHC.

[49] In the WHC files, some copies of the manual had Whistler's name on the title page and others did not. The one copy I found in the OHS files did not have Whistler's name.

[50] Minks and Ochoa (2021: 25); Ochoa (2014).

[51] The notion of co-construction entails interaction that jointly produces discourse in speech, writing, or some other medium such as musical performance. Co-construction often involves contestation as well as collaboration (Jacoby and Ochos 1995).

comes through in many texts about daily activities in the old days, such as children's games and food preparation.

Some interviewees resisted the project objective of artifact collection. One report noted that Mr. D. A. Homer (Choctaw) "has collected a few Indian relics, but does not care to exhibit them to the public." Mr. Homer worked in the adjoining office of the interviewer as an Indian field clerk for the federal government, and his father had owned an Indian newspaper. This was not someone who would be perceived by project directors as a traditionalist living in a rural location, yet he maintained cultural boundaries and cultural privacy in an interethnic professional context.[52] He was highly literate but not culturally assimilated, challenging dominant perceptions of the Five Tribes.

Other oral histories challenged dominant narratives of white settlement. The narrative of Mrs. Cora Smith, also called Wa-wa-tha (Sac and Fox) described the strange disruptions of land runs, when white settlers arrived to claim plots of land:

> When this territory was opened to the whites, I was still living at the Kansas Sauc village [in Indian Territory]. We did not know the land was being opened, but about the middle of the morning we began to see an unusual amount of wild animals all seeming to be headed in one direction. Later groups of white men with their families in wagons or men on horseback or in surrey commenced coming from the same direction. Some of them acted as if they were crazy, running around as if they were looking for some thing. Then all of a sudden they would stick a pole into the ground and hang some thing on it. Many set fire to the grass after they had done this. Within a half an hour the smoke was thick. Two or three days after that we went to Chandler, and the streets were crowded. We had a hard time getting about.[53]

Paul Gokey, also called We-to-tha-qua (Sac and Fox), noted how White settlers burned the prairie to find the markers for Indian land, so that they

---

[52] Indian-Pioneer History Project report, January 27, 1937, Dale Collection, Box 205, File 1, WHC. The narrative in the Indian Pioneer Papers is at https://digital.libraries.ou.edu/cdm/ref/collection/indianpp/id/44.

[53] Dale Collection, Box 207, File 8, WHC. This narrative was apparently not included in the edited volumes of the Indian Pioneer Papers. Cora Smith (Sac and Fox) lived in Avery, Oklahoma. The narrative of another Cora Smith in Henrietta, Oklahoma, who was not Native American, appears in the bound volumes.

could claim unmarked land. The leveling of the landscape and the violence between rival claimants laid bare the immense destructiveness of the enterprise:

> I must have been fourteen or fifteen. We had been in Oklahoma just a few years, having come from Kansas. My folks and I went to a Drum Dance at the old dance ground four miles east of Adelotte across the road from Pattequah's place. Towards noon we saw a whole lot of people coming from the south but we didn't know what they were there for. We knew that the government had given the government surveyors the right to enter the territory, but this couldn't be they, because there were women and children besides the men. They kept coming all day, and they seemed to be very excited. There was a lot of shooting and fighting going on, and I saw several men killed. They burnt the prairies and there sure was lots of smoke. I found out afterwards that the land had been opened to the whites and that they were burning the prairie to find the eighty-acre markers. The Indian land was already marked, and they had to find land that didn't belong to the Indians. After all the excitement was over, we continued our dance.[54]

The Drum Dance was a ceremonial event, and the completion of the ceremony was not optional; it had to be carried out, even in conditions of world-changing rupture.[55]

Narratives often grappled with the experiences of boarding schools, part of the institutional apparatus intended to eliminate Native culture. The text of Ella Wer-que-wa (Comanche) pointed out the coercive aspects of this system, and the importance of language as a site of attempted control:

> In the early days here when rations [food supplies] were issued, after schools were established, the Government wouldn't issue any rations if the Indians didn't send their children to school, and they were punished if heard speaking the Indian language. This was to bring them closer to civilization, causing them to forget their Indian ways.[56]

---

[54] Dale Collection, WPA Materials, Box 205, File 6, WHC, https://digital.libraries.ou.edu/cdm/ref/collection/indianpp/id/4306.

[55] I thank Lina Ortega (Sac and Fox), the Associate Curator of the OU Western History Collections, for helping to contextualize this story which involves some of her relatives, and for correcting the spelling of names.

[56] Indian Pioneer Papers, WHC, https://digital.libraries.ou.edu/cdm/ref/collection/indianpp/id/5739.

An interview with a "full blood Choctaw," Mr. Jesse Henry, conveys the sense of the interviewer pulling out information (with effort) about schools, a key site for exposure to English speech and writing:

> The first day I went to school, when I was six years old, my father took me. It was a little country school, with only one large room and the name of it was Brazil. It was located several miles from Shady Point. A white man was my teacher. I don't remember his name. I could not speak English then, I could only understand Choctaw language. I just went to the second grade, but I learned all the letters of the alphabet and all the numbers and how to read and write and spell . . . I don't know anything to tell, except that times were hard then just like they are now.[57]

Alphabetic letters were an introduction to a different episteme and system of control, but literacy also provided mobility within that system. At the end, Henry seems to resist the interviewer's prodding questions and disrupts a linear narrative of progress: "I don't know anything to tell, except that times were hard then just like they are now."

Different Indigenous groups had different kinds of relations with Southwest borders. Many Kickapoos from the upper Midwest fled south to Mexico, rather than settle on their reservation land in Oklahoma, because they could maintain more independence in Mexico. The following narrative of Rachel Franklin, also called Ma-ka-the-da (Sac and Fox), attested to these cross-border movements (which continue today):

> I have a faint recollection of a group of Kickapoos coming from Mexico who stopped for a short while on the Sac and Fox reservation. While they were here, the Sac and Foxes entertained them royally with feasts. They were here only a short time, and then went on to their own reservation near Shawnee.[58]

Like the Sac and Fox, the Kickapoo were a Great Lakes Tribe, displaced by US colonialism. This passage suggests the maintenance of long-term cultural relations despite the ruptures of displacement. The story also points to the

[57] Indian Pioneer Papers, WHC, https://digital.libraries.ou.edu/cdm/ref/collection/indianpp/id/2507.

[58] Indian Pioneer Papers, WHC, https://digital.libraries.ou.edu/cdm/ref/collection/indianpp/id/4114.

multiple trajectories of border crossings, where Tribal Nations never fully conformed to the geopolitics of the US or Mexican nation-state.

The Indian Pioneer oral histories referred to multiple systems of slavery that shaped border crossings in the nineteenth century. Mexico had abolished slavery in 1829 (thirty-six years before US abolition) and was a common destination for Black Americans fleeing enslavement on US plantations.[59] Many Indigenous and Black people also created interracial families. Regardless of ancestry or legal status, people perceived as Black were always vulnerable to the slave system in the southern United States. This motivated many mixed families to settle in Mexico.[60] In the United States, some members of the Five Tribes held Black slaves, following the white plantation system which dominated in their southeastern homelands. After the Civil War, these formerly enslaved people became known as freedmen. They often had mixed Black and Indigenous ancestry, though the dominant racial ideologies in the United States rarely recognized these mixtures.[61]

The Southwest system of enslavement had emerged from Spanish colonizers' interaction with Indigenous peoples of the Southwest and Southern Plains, and also drew on Old World notions. The ambivalent category of *genízaro* (adapted from the Ottoman term Janissary) encompassed Indigenous people who had been captives but came to serve important intermediary and military functions for Spanish settlements.[62] Spanish and later Mexican communities in the region often employed euphemistic terms of kinship and service for incorporating captives; they paid "ransom" to Southern Plains Tribes for captives from a range of cultural backgrounds, thereby obscuring the status of enslavement. Southern Plains Tribes provided more possibilities for the full inclusion and social mobility of captives in their communities. Sometimes captive histories carried stigma in Tribal communities, but many prominent Tribal leaders passed down the memory of captive ancestors in their family histories.[63]

---

[59] Jacoby (2016); Baumgartner (2020).

[60] See Madrid (2011b) as an example.

[61] Sturm (2002); Yarbrough (2008); Miles (2005); Roberts (2021); Gayle (2022).

[62] Brooks (2001) relates that Spanish colonial records documented the specific Tribal origins of many genízaro communities and individuals, but later Mexican and US records erased their particular histories and Tribal affiliations. This erasure prevented genízaro recognition and rights under US Federal Indian law as it developed in the nineteenth and twentieth centuries. This is one of many examples of the relations between archival records and governmentality. See also *Nación Genízara* (Gonzalez and Lamadrid 2019), the first book from the perspective of Genízaro communities.

[63] See, e.g., Roy (2007).

Some narratives convey the dense weight of colonial histories in only a few lines. John Johnson of Atoka, Oklahoma, was apparently interviewed twice, first by Etta D. Mason on April 27, 1937, and then by Joe Southern on November 23, 1937. The first interview is labeled with the index card topic: "Comanches-Texas Raids," making clear the interpretive frame of "wild Indians" raiding ranching or farming communities. In that first interview, Johnson was identified as a Choctaw freedman; in the second interview, he was identified as a "mixed-breed Indian of Cherokee-Comanche blood." Both narratives tell the story of the capture of his mother, Mary Johnson, by Comanche raiders; he was born while she was living in captivity. Both narratives identify his father as Brit Johnson. The first narrative says that Brit Johnson lived at Belknap, Texas, but was away from home most of the time, as he was owned by the rancher Allen Johnson. Both narratives say that following the raid, his father searched for over a year before finding his wife's location. The second narrative says he did so with the help of "a Mexican boy, an interpreter and guide." According to the second narrative, his father negotiated to ransom his family: "My mother has related to me that in this trade, I was not included as Father was unaware of my presence in this world." Johnson was raised by a Comanche widow until he was eight years old, when he went to live with his mother and father. In adulthood, Johnson outlived his first wife and their three children, and later married a "Choctaw freedman," Julie Fields. The terse narration ends: "She is living with me now. She is something about my age."[64] Both probably born into slavery, these elders of the 1930s had witnessed and survived the shocks of colonial relations, a time when violence ruled the borderlands. Yet the differences between the two accounts remind us that these oral histories are inscriptions and interpretations, rather than the unmediated voice of the interviewee.[65]

Published narratives of former captives were especially powerful in the public imagination, and they are still sometimes reproduced as historical evidence without considering the processes of inscription, editing, and editorializing that created the text. The historian James Brooks, for example, considers the narrative of the Mexican captive Andele Martínez as eyewitness testimony in his republished edition of 1996. At the same time,

---

[64] The term freedman was often used in historical discourse for both men and women. Indian Pioneer Papers, WHC, https://digital.libraries.ou.edu/cdm/ref/collection/indianpp/id/3373.

[65] Indian Pioneer Papers, WHC. The first narrative is at https://digital.libraries.ou.edu/cdm/ref/collection/indianpp/id/3606, and the second narrative is at https://digital.libraries.ou.edu/cdm/ref/collection/indianpp/id/3373.

Brooks recognizes the moralizing tone of the missionary, Reverend John Jasper Methvin, who initially wrote Andele's life history and published it in 1899 with the Pentecostal Herald Press. The text includes close description of scenes and events that Andele could not have witnessed first-hand, which underscores the literary and moralizing imagination through which Reverend Methvin co-created the text. This example is especially relevant when we consider that Methvin's daughter, Lillian Gassaway, became a fieldworker for the Indian Pioneer project, as noted at the beginning of this chapter. Some narratives undoubtedly had blurry boundaries as they moved across modalities of communication, including stories told and retold aloud from memory, the inscription of oral history, and the popular dissemination of captive tales along with many other thrilling and terrifying depictions of the Wild West.

Some texts in the collection reinforced the dominant perceptions of Southern Plains Tribes as wild and violent. A few specific acts of violence were repeatedly described in similar language across different narratives of the Indian Pioneer collection as well as popular published narratives of the early twentieth century. This recurrence suggests that they took on the role of metacultural narratives, in the sense of mobile frameworks for interpreting peoples and cultures which propagated ideologies of morality and value. Still other stories challenged those dominant metacultural narratives. S. W. Ryan (labeled a "mixed blood Choctaw") was interviewed at the age of eighty-one near the border of Texas in Ryan, Oklahoma, a town named for his family. His narrative states:

We came to this country from Arkansas in 1876 near Tishomingo. I am a Choctaw and I married a Chickasaw, and drifted out here. When I first came I cut herds, that is, I kept our range cattle from getting mixed up with the trail cattle, that were always being driven through here in large herds. That was in the time when the gun was law. If a man did not know how to shoot a gun to protect himself he might as well stay away from this country, for there was no law to protect him.

I held all the land around here. I didn't have to pay a permit, lease or buy. The Indians gave it to me. I had a ranch and I am just now tearing down my barns. I really hate to see them go, but I don't need them any more.

The Kiowa and Comanche Indians came through here often but they never bothered me. I had to give them a beef once in a while, but occasionally I would give them one on my own.

I had more trouble with the Texas Cattlemen. They would come through my land on drives and worry my stock. I brought people in here and placed them up and down the river. Helped them to build their fences, then these Texas Cattlemen would come up, cut the fences and drive through. They even tried to drive me out, but they are gone now and I am still here.[66]

Ryan's narrative rejects the expectation that Kiowas and Comanches would bother him and his business. (We can imagine the question he was responding to.) The text includes the logic of exchange, but the logic of the gift plays a stronger role. Ryan developed his cattle enterprise by building local relationships and material infrastructure. The Texas cattlemen disregarded both in a single-minded quest to move livestock to distant markets. But Ryan claimed the last word: "They are gone now and I am still here."

Contestations of Value and Voice

Already by April 22, 1937, the project had collected 600 oral history manuscripts and 1,300 responses to questionnaires eliciting historical information and interviews. There were 78 relief workers at the time. Twenty-five of them were stenographers, clerks, and typists working under Foreman's direction, while the other 53 were fieldworkers collecting interviews and other historical data around the state. As the WPA followed the rollercoaster of federal funding and politics, the non–relief employees were reduced. Whistler's position was cut from the project, but he showed no signs of hard feelings as he facilitated the transfer of work in progress. Government-sponsored cultural work was notoriously unpredictable. A Native artist in southwest Oklahoma preferred to undertake physical labor in the Civilian Conservation Corps, which guaranteed a long-term salary.[67] Foreman tended to denigrate the output of the fieldworkers and most of the supervisors; he attributed more value to the few who had professional historical training. Nevertheless, in evaluating the interviewees, he confessed, "With some exceptions, the best stories did not come from educated people" (see Figure 1.3).[68]

[66] Indian Pioneer Papers, WHC, https://digital.libraries.ou.edu/cdm/ref/collection/indianpp/id/1788.

[67] Hanneman (2000: 43).

[68] Foreman report on Indian Pioneer History project, April 22, 1937, Foreman Collection, Box 111, OHS.

Figure 1.3 Grant Foreman reviewing the first bound volumes of the Indian Pioneer oral histories. 1938. Photograph by Alphia Hart. Oklahoma Historical Society.

Though Washington anthropologists had assumed that Native Americans would be reluctant to share information about their cultural histories, Foreman found that many were eager to attain employment to conduct this work in their own communities. Rather than acknowledge the bureaucratic problems that hindered Native employment, Foreman was defensive in this early report:

There is being evinced a feeling that the Indians have been discriminated against in the employment of persons on this project. This feeling is not well founded for the fact is that a large percentage of the people employed on the project possess Indian blood. I am not able to say just how many, but of the five supervisors originally employed, four were of Indian blood.[69]

The most prominent Native figure to shape the project was undoubtedly Don Whistler, who would serve as principal chief of the Sac and Fox Tribe from 1938 until his death in 1951.[70] Foreman was probably counting Chauncey Moore in the group of supervisors with "Indian blood," though in his later collection of Southwest folk songs, Moore did not identify with or include any discussion of Native heritage (his own, or anyone else's).[71] Foreman thought of using prizes to solicit Native stories as a means to overcome the financial restrictions of the project. The Cherokee Nation donated some money for prizes, with the request that the funds be distributed in Cherokee communities and in Indian schools.[72]

The official framing of the balance between "Indians" and "Pioneers" in the project shifted at different moments. The project was initially envisioned as an Indian history project. Even after it was expanded to include white settlers, the popular perception of the project was still focused on Native American history and culture. But in one of his first summary reports, Foreman included twelve pages of excerpts of white settler stories, and only 1.5 pages of Indian stories. Black and Black Indigenous people were not included in the vision or summary reports for the project, and yet narratives were incorporated into the collection from some of those families and communities, probably through the initiative of individual fieldworkers. On the local level, the Oklahoma "old timers" who were central objects of inquiry turned out to be a heterogeneous group, and many of their stories problematized the fixed categories assumed by racial ideologies.

The decreasing emphasis on Native American narratives in the project may have been shaped by the powerful politics of white Anglo-Protestant nationalism. Foreman was undoubtedly familiar with the Oklahoma establishment's unease with Benjamin Botkin, a professor of Jewish

[69] Foreman report on Indian Pioneer History project, April 22, 1937, Foreman Collection, Box 111, OHS.
[70] Garrett-Davis (2020: 286).
[71] Moore and Moore (1966).
[72] Foreman report on Indian Pioneer History project, April 22, 1937, Foreman Collection, Box 111, OHS.

immigrant heritage at the University of Oklahoma who worked on the Federal Writers' Project in Oklahoma and became its national folklore editor. While Botkin did not engage extensively with Native American histories, he did work with Black American histories and narratives. He promoted a pluralist view of American culture and considered folklore as part of a process of critical reflection and social reform. His left-leaning presentation at the American Writers Congress in the summer of 1937 led to direct interventions by Oklahoma powerholders, and Botkin was forced to resign from the university in 1938. In Washington, the House Committee on Un-American Activities, led by Texas politician Martin Dies, targeted Botkin and other WPA figures for their alleged association with Communist figures or organizations. The rhetoric of the Dies committee explicitly promoted white Anglo-Protestant nationalism, attacking efforts at racial inclusion as much as vague associations with Communism. Following these political attacks, some WPA cultural projects were revised and others terminated. The institutional frameworks for connecting cultural documentation to democratic pluralism and cross-ethnic inclusion were largely dismantled.[73]

The Historical Records projects of the WPA, which Foreman had directed or facilitated in Oklahoma, were considered more conservative and less controversial than other WPA cultural programs.[74] Foreman was by no means a leftist, but the Dies Committee hearings must have had a chilling effect on intellectual production across the political spectrum. The attacks on Botkin and other cultural workers may have led Foreman to focus almost exclusively on white settler history in his official summaries of the project.

Indigenous voices in Oklahoma had already been marginalized by the bureaucracy and expert authority of WPA networks in Washington. Cultural work with Native Americans tended to be assigned to programs run through the Department of the Interior and the Smithsonian Institution's Bureau of American Ethnology. After the federal government created the Civilian Conservation Corps as an emergency relief measure in 1933, Oklahoma officials had to exert pressure to get Native Americans included. This involved setting up a separate Indian Division, the same entity that William Karty (Comanche) worked for in southwest Oklahoma, as

[73] Hirsch (2003, 2013); Davis (2010). Hirsch (2013) makes the point that the dissolution of the WPA programs also led to a kind of institutional historical amnesia for later generations of oral historians.
[74] McDonald (1969: 768).

noted at the beginning of this chapter. Without this institutional apparatus, officials made clear, all the jobs would go to whites, either because of bias or because of legal restrictions for enrolled Tribal members and their land allotments.[75]

Although Franz Boas's cultural relativism informed WPA approaches at the national level, older assumptions of evolutionary anthropology were deeply embedded in institutional and popular discourses, promoting a view that Native American culture was part of the past, rather than the present and future.[76] Nevertheless, the long-term impacts of historical discourses can be surprising. Recall that the Indian Pioneer project served as a source for Angie Debo's research on Muscogee histories. At the same time, she was trying to find a publisher for her earlier book manuscript, *And Still the Waters Run: The Betrayal of the Five Civilized Tribes*. That book was too controversial for Oklahoma gatekeepers (including Wardell) because Debo named still living, powerful individuals as grafters in the exploitation of Indigenous land, people, and resources.[77] In 1939, *And Still the Waters Run* finally moved toward publication at Princeton University Press, where the Oklahoma editor Joseph A. Brandt had relocated. Brandt wouldn't take the risk of libel charges at Princeton, either; he excised names that could be cause for litigation. Many decades later, Amanda Cobb-Greetham's analysis makes clear that despite its ideological shortcomings, Debo's rigorously documented historical work provided resources for later legal defenses of the Five Tribes.[78] Debo's book revealed the violations of the US federal government in their legal and treaty obligations to the Tribes. While Grant Foreman moved in his career from law to history, the impact of Debo's book moved from history to law. In this case, the research and writing of history facilitated the strengthening of legal mechanisms for Indigenous sovereignty.

[75] Cultural and infrastructural programs sometimes overlapped. At least one CCC-ID program in Oklahoma included training in Native arts and crafts (Hanneman 2000: 440).

[76] Hirsch (2003: 24, 38).

[77] Leckie (2000: 76–77) notes that Wardell played a key role in evaluating the book's legal risks on behalf of the University of Oklahoma leadership. Another instance of power machinations behind the scenes of institutions was the WPA-sponsored guidebook, *Oklahoma: A Guide to the Sooner State*. Debo directed this Oklahoma-based project under the Federal Writer's Project. Just before publication in 1941, Debo's historical essay in the guidebook was mysteriously replaced by an anonymous essay riddled with errors (Morgan 1986: x).

[78] Cobb-Greetham (2022).

From Oral Histories to Historical Auralities

At different moments and in different institutions, varying frameworks for oral history have attempted to codify the recording, transcription, and preservation of narrative voices. This chapter has provided a case study of the mediating practices and interactive co-construction that produce archival texts and collections. Orality and inscription are not discrete spheres, but rather modes of communication that are often intertwined in projects of documentation, collection, and interpretation. Early discourses of nationalism and heritage tied orality to notions of tradition, rurality, and indigeneity. More recently, an interdisciplinary turn toward aurality has brought practices of listening into sharper focus, with a broader range of actors and forces taken into consideration. Whereas discourses of orality have tended to corral voices under particular regimes of classification, discourses of aurality recognize how subaltern voices often overflow the categories they are assigned.[79] If we shift our attention from oral histories to historical auralities, we might better hear the multiplicity of voices within collections, fueling both history and heritage, often bridging speech and song as well as other realms of creative activity.[80]

The Indigenous voices encoded as oral history in 1930s Oklahoma were connected to bodies, lives, relationships, and networks that extend beyond the collected texts. In these oral histories (and in keeping with discourses on orality), accounts of ritual, kinship, food, music, and dance often filled the culture category with ethnographic intelligibility. Yet the heterogeneity of cultural practices, the violent impacts of colonialism, and the diverse genealogies of many Oklahoma Tribal members destabilized categories of race and civilization. The dual accounts of the life of John Johnson, described as a "Choctaw Freedman" and as a "mixed-breed Indian of Cherokee-Comanche blood," stretch the limits of intelligibility in oral history and stake the claims of aurality—the seeping of discordant voices into the institutional structures that were supposed to order voices and histories. The sprawling, decentralized nature of the project, and its implementation by nonprofessional researchers, may have intensified the forces of aurality. The outcome was the accumulation of a multivocal, mediated archive, rather than a tightly

---

[79] Ochoa (2014); Minks and Ochoa (2021).

[80] See Aplin's (2010: 22) discussion of the "shadows," including silences and ambiguities which are "omnipresent in public and ceremonial observances, in official written histories, *in aurally transmitted oral histories*, in the visual arts, and most importantly in song" (italics added).

controlled ethnographic analysis by an anthropologist of the time, like the "Indian experts" in Washington who opposed the project to begin with.

The massive collection of oral history manuscripts by Oklahoma fieldworkers in 1937 and 1938 became the Indian Pioneer Papers, now accessible via a digital repository at the University of Oklahoma Libraries.[81] These oral histories should be interpreted through the cultural mediations of their day, as well as the mediations of our day. The collection contains traces and representations of voices, rather than the voices themselves. Multiple actors and agendas came together in constructing this collection. Foreman continually claimed the most prominent role in his accounts of developing and directing the project, and he minimized or omitted the contributions of others. The Oklahoma Historical Society was his domain, and its board of directors intended the Indian Pioneer collection to be called the Grant Foreman Papers.[82] That the collection was not ultimately tied to his name in the annals of library classification demonstrates the limits to his claims of authority and authorship.

The Indigenous narratives that WPA workers elicited, heard, inscribed, edited, and typed in the Indian Pioneer history project were larger than the project itself. Long before European colonization and continuing to the present day, Indigenous peoples have maintained and encoded their histories in many different forms, including voices in speech and song; instrumental music; inscriptions on stone, clay, cloth, animal skins, and parchment; and graphic designs on bodies and items such as pottery. There have also been blurry lines, at times, between Indigenous histories emerging from Indigenous communities and those which have been co-constructed with non-Indigenous researchers. To be clear, many anthropologists, ethnomusicologists, and other kinds of cultural collectors exploited the communities where they worked, violated cultural protocols, and appropriated the intellectual contributions of their Native collaborators. Many institutional collections were created by the extraction of material, artistic, and spiritual items from Native communities, often without their consent. The rapaciousness of collecting even extended to Native bodies that had been extinguished through military violence and the spread of European disease. This is a central part of the coloniality of knowledge which continued to be institutionalized after US independence and is still with us today.

---

[81] The search interface is at https://digital.libraries.ou.edu/whc/pioneer/.
[82] Grant Foreman Collection, Box 111, OHS.

While continuing to critique that history of exploitation, we can recognize the active participation of Native Americans who willingly brought their stories into institutional projects. The prominent Kiowa intellectual Guy Quoetone (1884–1975) participated in oral history interviews and collection activities for the Indian Pioneer project, building on his earlier work as a mediator among government agents, researchers, and Kiowa communities (see Figure 1.4). In the 1960s he participated in more extensive interviews through the Doris Duke American Indian Oral History Project, which involved seven

Figure 1.4 Guy Quoetone (Kiowa) as a young man. Division of Manuscripts Southwest Oklahoma Collection #137, Western History Collections, University of Oklahoma Libraries.

universities across the United States and produced tape recordings as well as transcriptions of interviews.[83] In one of the Duke interviews recorded in 1967, Quoetone talked about the research visits of James Mooney as he was conducting research on Kiowa calendars—an Indigenous genre of history— and other topics for the Bureau of American Ethnology. For a while, Mooney was living in a government building at Mount Scott, and he would ask Kiowa elders to come tell him stories. Quoetone recalled:

> And those old men, Adalpepte, Haitseke, Anko, and, oh, there's about ten of them. They gather every day and talk to him just like we's talking. I'd go sometimes and just sit in and listen. I'm not asked to take part, but I was just a young man. Just listen in, because it's interesting stories. I didn't care for the story, but I interested just to listen to them all. And I got a lot of those stories. I didn't write them down, but I heard them. I just heard these stories. . . . And he paid them well. He paid them all every day, paid them by the hour. It's a government project and he paid them lots of money. . . . They always come to him. They like it. They're out every day, every day. And they camped for weeks and weeks. He don't run them down. They're old men, you know, but they kind of like it, because they like to talk and tell stories anyway. And they all—maybe one of them overlook a story and then they call him down, "You forgot this." And then they'd go back. "Oh, yeah," and then they'd—and that way Mr. Mooney, he got all of it. Near as they could.[84]

Quoetone repeatedly emphasized his acts of intensive listening to Kiowa elders' stories. His account also portrays the co-construction of narrative in the Kiowa elders' interaction ("You forgot this . . . Oh yeah").

Mooney's visit provided a stimulus for these narrative events, but, as Aplin notes, "the intellectuals of southwest Oklahoma are consummate scholars well seasoned by a relished intellectual sparring that, like their land tenure, long preceded the arrival of James Mooney."[85] In discussing oral histories of

[83] Repp (2005). The overarching project is currently called the Archive of Native American Recorded History. See https://www.nativeoralhistory.org/.

[84] Oral history interview with Guy Quoetone, conducted by Julia Jordan, June 14, 1967, p. 10–11, WHC. Quoetone recalled that Mooney was conducting research and writing about "Indian stories and history of the ten-calendar-history, and peyote worship and all that" (p. 9). Quoetone may have been remembering multiple periods of Mooney's research, including his extended residence from 1894 to 1896, when he was studying the Kiowa calendars, as well as a shorter period in the summer of 1918, when he drew the ire of government officials for supporting peyote practices in the Native American Church. See Moses (2002). Quoetone's 1967 interview is at https://digital.libraries.ou.edu/cdm/ref/collection/dorisduke/id/6690.

[85] Aplin (2010: 124).

Fort Sill Apache in southwestern Oklahoma, Aplin points out that framing devices such as "my father told me" serve to "demarcate the scope and limits of knowledge" and constitute a form of citation. This epistemic framing, he notes, is also apparent in Anthony Webster's study of evidentials in Chiracahua Apache oral histories.[86] Cultural protocols and epistemic stances that are encoded in Indigenous languages often move to a second language, even when that acquired language becomes the first language of subsequent generations. These framing devices are also Indigenous forms of documentation, creating oral/aural traces to sources from the past.

Quoetone's oral history seems to portray the interaction between Mooney and the elders as a mutually productive, reciprocal exchange. Quoetone's comment about the elders being paid well for their stories brings to mind Jenny Tone-Pah-Hote's theorization of "culturally relevant forms of labor."[87] Tone-Pah-Hote's study of Kiowa arts in the early twentieth century demonstrates how and why Kiowa people engaged in ethnological work and artistic production for academic researchers and for popular collectors. They adapted many of the artistic practices of their ancestors to the interests and markets of the time as a strategy for maintaining their cultural knowledge and identities while earning supplementary income.

Like Guy Quoetone, Don Whistler's intertribal work with Native cultural heritage transcended his involvement with the Indian Pioneer project. In April 1941, four years after leaving the Indian Pioneer project, Whistler launched the Indians for Indians radio show at the University of Oklahoma, often with live studio guests who sang, told stories, and shared news of upcoming cultural events. With an audience of 75,000, the weekly broadcast became a lively intertribal forum for social and cultural connections, as well as political advocacy for the rights of Native Americans. Members of Southern Plains Tribes, especially Comanche and Kiowa, played a prominent role as live radio guests. As Josh Garrett-Davis and Lina Ortega have noted, the promotion of social events in the powwow circuit contributed to the frequency of guests from western Oklahoma.[88] These song and dance events expanded during the war years as they celebrated the return of Native veterans, who served (and continue to serve) in the US armed forces at exceptionally high rates.

---

[86] Aplin (2010: 124); Webster (1999).
[87] Tone-Pah-Hote (2019: 29).
[88] Garrett-Davis (2018); Ortega (2019).

Garrett-Davis also notes Whistler's archival tendencies in the show.[89] Whistler made preservation recordings of broadcasts as much as he could, and assigned a number to each program which was shared on air and inscribed in his written records. In 1943 and 1944, Benjamin Botkin, at that time directing the Archive of American Folk Song at the Library of Congress, arranged to have some blank discs sent to record the Indians for Indians show.[90] The heritage work of Whistler and his radio guests represented a sharp contrast to collectors who assumed that Native American music was dying out. The Indians for Indians radio show supported the energetic vitality of Native music as it continued to be passed from one generation to the next, with adaptations and innovations.

A few months after Whistler launched the Indians for Indians show, Grant Foreman and his wife, the historian Carolyn Thomas Foreman, found themselves traveling in Mexico amidst the hordes of American tourists who seemed to be overwhelming local culture. In addition to escaping the late summer heat of Oklahoma, Grant Foreman was gathering material for his biography of an attorney for Sinclair Oil Company, involved in a "settlement with the Mexican government for the oil lands expropriated."[91] Foreman may not have been aware of the new institutional framework taking shape with the Inter-American Indian Institute, which involved some representation from Native Oklahoma, and some reciprocal influence with US New Deal programs. I begin the next chapter with a description of the founding congress of the Inter-American Indian Institute, narrated by another Oklahoman who found himself in Mexico at that time.

[89] Garrett-Davis (2018, 2020: 286–287).
[90] Ortega (2019: 63).
[91] Correspondence, August 9 and September 3, 1941, Foreman Collection, Box 93, File 8, OHS.

2

Radio, Recording, and Inter-American
Indigenismo in Mexico

On April 18, 1940, John Joseph Mathews (Osage) was driving his roomy station wagon to Pátzcuaro, Mexico, the location of the founding congress of
the Inter-American Indian Institute. Well known as a mediator in Indian affairs, Mathews was sent to the Inter-American congress as part of the US delegation and the only representative from Oklahoma. He was a free-wheeling
intellectual and literary writer from Pawhuska, Oklahoma, with Native
Osage as well as European ancestry (his Osage father was part Welsh, and his
maternal grandparents were French immigrants). Growing up in a prominent family during the oil boom years, Mathews had studied at Oxford and
spoke fluent French. In 1940 he was in Mexico on a Guggenheim fellowship,
a means of renewing his writing vocation during a second term serving on
the Osage Tribal Council. He was apparently not counted as an Indigenous
delegate but was filling in for Elmer Thomas, a non-Indigenous US Senator
from Oklahoma.[1]

Mathews had an irreverent sense of humor; his diary entries demonstrated
various tussles with writers and artists he met in Mexico. Upon arrival in
Pátzcuaro (four days late), Mathews wrote in his diary:

> After dinner I went to the El Lago hotel, where I was assigned a room with
> [Vincenzo] Petrullo, who wrote the book called the "Diabolic Root," which
> the University of Pennsylvania Press published on Peyote [in 1934]. He is
> prematurely grey, has a glowing complexion, and is short and rather prom-
> inent buttocked. We talked from bed to bed about many things, and I told
> him that I thought his book on Peyote was rather misleading. He wasn't
> offended. My opinion of him is that he is not a great anthropologist by any
> interpretation.[2]

---

[1] Snyder (2017: 128–130).
[2] Diary entry, April 18, 1940, John Joseph Mathews Collection, Box 1, File 39, WHC.

Indigenous Audibilities. Amanda Minks, Oxford University Press. © Oxford University Press 2024.
DOI: 10.1093/oso/9780197532485.003.0003

Though Mathews was not intimately involved in Native spiritual practice in Oklahoma, he grew up in close proximity to Native traditionalists and had an understanding of their cultural context.[3] He did not have much familiarity with the Indigenous communities around Pátzcuaro, but he closely observed the interaction between the multinational delegates (the majority of whom were not Indigenous) and the Indigenous people living and working in the area. There were some friendly exchanges, but also signs of cultural and social distance.

On the last day of the congress, Mathews attended a presentation at a monument to Don Vasco de Quiroga, a Spanish magistrate who had governed the region during the colonial era and became a bishop in 1538. Mathews recounted the varied accomplishments of Don Vasco, then told the lively story of the presentation:

> But that which happened yesterday was the last chapter in the long history. Leading from the Pasada [Posada] Don Vasco is a road to the village. On the road in a small plaza is a very ugly memorial statue to Don Vasco. Hot and unlovely in the sun and dominating the dusty plaza (cross roads really). To this monument came the guardians of the present day Mexico to hold a ceremony in memory of Don Vasco, and to impress the visiting delegates to the Indian conference. The business of speechmaking was just begun, when a number of white garbed Tarascans [Indigenous P'urhépecha] came up and started a commotion. A Tarascan woman with tears rolling down her dirty face, clawed her way into the center of the crowd, and would not be calmed. Men in glaring white cotones came with machetas [machetes] and other weapons, and the ceremony was broken up. They were only able to continue when the Indians were satisfied that they did not intend to move the bones of the beloved Don Vasco, from the place where they now rest to this ugly pink monument.
>
> Sr. Martinez, in charge of the arrangements of the Conference, had his glasses torn off and broken, and when I last saw him he was squinting at his dominoes, and reaching for the wrong glass of beer.
>
> And again sayeth Mathews, who has been in the Republic of Mexico all of seven months, HE WHO WOULD RULE ALL MEXICO, MUST DO SO THROUGH RELIGION.[4]

---

[3] See Swan (1990) for discussion of Mathews's and Petrullo's work on Peyote.
[4] Diary entry, April 25, 1940, John Joseph Mathews Collection, Box 1, File 39, WHC.

Although Mathews made his own judgments about the Indigenous cultures of the area, he seemed to recognize the limits to his understanding as he poked fun at himself and at the other delegates. We can only imagine the consternation of the Mexican officials who were trying to demonstrate their expert knowledge and progressive management of Indigenous affairs, only to have their commemorative event disrupted by local Indigenous people.

Mathews's story illustrates the distance between Indigenous communities and the officials who developed policies to manage them. By the 1940s these officials were often known as *indigenistas*, and they continued to develop multiple fields of *indigenismo*, discourses about Indigenous peoples as well as programs for them. Some indigenista movements focused on artistic and literary representation of Indigenous histories and cultures, and other movements focused on government policies, especially issues of education, modernization, and economic development. Leftist variants of indigenismo developed in Peru and Mexico through efforts to work through the relations between class and racial subordination. Indigenista movements often involved transnational influences, but the founding of the Inter-American Indian Institute represented a new kind of centralization and institutional networking across governments. This transnational inter-American organization developed its own discourses and fields of action, which coexisted and intersected with national indigenista discourses in variable ways.[5]

At the Pátzcuaro congress in 1940, the Inter-American Indian Institute was founded through the collaboration of nineteen countries of the Americas— all but Canada and Paraguay—in a heterogeneous ideological field. Some actors were aiming for social and political transformation in order to integrate Indigenous peoples into nation-states, giving them citizenship rights as well as specific collective rights. Official Indigenous delegations from Mexico, the United States, and Panama attended the founding congress; other participants who identified as Indigenous formed part of their countries' delegations. A range of Indigenous protagonists corresponded with the Inter-American Indian Institute in the interests of advancing their political demands.[6] Over time, the programs of the Inter-American Indian Institute were not radically transformative in the realm of governance. Still, they influenced international organizations and national governments in their

[5] Giraudo (2012); Giraudo and Martín-Sánchez (2012). As an example, Rios (2020: 48) notes the influence of the Inter-American Indian Institute on the creation of state-run folklore departments in Bolivia.

[6] Giraudo (2006); Giraudo and Martín-Sánchez (2016).

approaches to Indigenous peoples in the second half of the twentieth century. The sociohistorical reality of this field was dynamic, with diverse actors and ideologies moving across loosely regulated spaces.

In this chapter I consider activities of the Inter-American Indian Institute (III) as part of the prehistory for discourses about intangible cultural heritage.[7] From the beginning, the III used "culture as a resource" for a range of social, political, and economic objectives.[8] The III aimed to promote Indigenous music, dance, and theater; to protect Indigenous arts and artisans; and to organize inter-American festivals of Indigenous arts.[9] These activities would serve as resources for developing national cultures as well as local and regional economies, for example, through marketing crafts to tourists. The first congress of the III recommended education in Indigenous languages and the publication of Indigenous literature, in addition to facilitating proficiency in national languages as a means to participate in the full rights of citizenship.[10]

In the early 1940s, the III directed a range of projects related to Indigenous music and media, especially field recording, archiving, radio broadcasting, and musical arrangements and composition. These projects revealed the ideological slippage between reproduction and representation of Indigenous music. Officials did not always distinguish between documentary field recording and transcription, on the one hand, and art music compositions which incorporated Indigenous motives, on the other. The media projects were, however, a key site for distinctions between field recording and field transcription—which I refer to as "aural transcription." This is not a new term in ethnomusicology, but I use it specifically as a translation of the Spanish term *audiotranscripción*, as I heard it in the discourse of the archivists at the Fonoteca Nacional, the National Sound Archive of Mexico. Aural transcription is the practice of transcribing music by ear and by hand. Beginning in the 1920s, Mexican cultural institutions used aural transcription in documentary music projects which focused more on the development of national heritage

[7] For studies on late twentieth and early twenty-first-century paradigms of intangible cultural heritage, see Kirshenblatt-Gimblett (2004), Smith and Akagawa (2009), Seeger (2009), Bigenho, Stobart, and Mújica Angulo (2018), and Stefano and Davis (2017).

[8] For analysis of "culture as a resource" in more recent times, see Yúdice (2003) and Luker (2016). For historical studies of the arts in inter-American indigenismo, see Giraudo and Gallardo-Saborido (2022) and the articles within their coedited special issue.

[9] "Editorial," *América Indígena* (1941: 6).

[10] Tercero (1940). An irony, here, is that Spanish literacy programs often obscured systems of Indigenous writing which preceded and continued into the colonial era (Faudree 2013: 52).

than on attempts at universalizing scientific theories. They relied on the sharp listening skills and symbolic systems of classically trained musicians, who listened to repeated performances while inscribing Indigenous and folk music in the field. This practice changed in the early 1940s as the direct result of the introduction of sound recording by the Inter-American Indian Institute.

Field recording entailed ideologies of temporality which created an interface between the past and the future. The sound recorder was used to conjure and preserve the past. Intellectuals, officials, and composers would then use elements of this past to combine with other cultural sources in order to promote the development and progress of unique American civilizations, an orientation toward the future. These projects helped to create new ideologies of authenticity which relocated what was perceived as authentic Indigenous culture from living Indigenous communities to distant archives. Close analysis of institutional discourses reveals how practices of listening contributed to the creation of new publics, moved by the visceral encounter with Indigenous field recordings.[11]

Discourses of technology, then as now, often encoded power-laden ideologies of race, gender, and sexuality. For example, recording blanks—blank discs to be used for field recording or broadcast recording—were called *discos vírgenes* (virgin discs) in Spanish.[12] The Inter-American Indian Institute, like the Pan American Union and most other international organizations of the time, was dominated by upper-class men from white or *mestizo* (mixed) backgrounds. However, some of the first people to make field recordings of Indigenous and other musics from around the world were women. One of these was Henrietta Yurchenco, a charismatic US expatriate with radio experience who was residing in Mexico in the early 1940s. Yurchenco came to play a central role in music projects of the Inter-American Indian Institute and forged new terrain in field recording techniques. She did not carry out these projects alone, but rather entered into an institutional field in collaboration with other actors.

[11] See Gray (2020).

[12] January 2, 1946, File "Propaganda por Radio, México, 1945–1947," AHIII. Here and elsewhere, AHIII documents were consulted in Espinosa Velasco and Cruz González (2002).

Hemispheric Indigenismo and the Arts

Because the III was headquartered in Mexico City, it was inevitably shaped by Mexican cultural projects already in process. After the Mexican Revolution (1910–1917), a diverse group of intellectuals, artists, and officials began to describe and document Indigenous cultures of Mexico, not only the ancient Mayas and Aztecs (a focus of nineteenth-century historians) but also living Indigenous cultures.[13] Already in 1916, the anthropologist Manuel Gamio rejected the idea that Indigenous culture was undergoing a process of extinction; he considered the obligation of a country like Mexico to integrate and modernize its extensive Indigenous population.[14]

The postrevolutionary institution that directed the majority of cultural projects was the Secretariat of Public Education (SEP), founded in 1921 by José Vasconcelos. The SEP supported the documentation of Indigenous music through the Department of Fine Arts (Section of Music, Subsection of Folklore) beginning in 1926.[15] Rural teachers participated in the collection and teaching of Indigenous music.[16] The purpose of music-centered projects at the SEP was to preserve the diversity of regional music and to use it to create new canons of Mexican music, generally drawing on folkloric motives as a basis for art music compositions, which would be taught in schools throughout the country. On the one hand, an accumulative process aimed to store and preserve musical objects (musical notation and sometimes instruments) in the new national archives. On the other hand, according to Jessica Gottfried Hesketh, "the compiled materials were viewed as original samples that could be taken from their context and converted into national emblematic symbols, giving the nation authentic elements with which to identify."[17]

Though Latin American intellectuals and officials had long discussed an international organization oriented toward indigenismo, its realization in Mexico in 1940 came about through the intervention of John Collier, a US social reformer and then Commissioner of the Bureau of Indian Affairs (BIA). Collier had a special interest in Indian expressive culture; he had been inspired to become a reformer of Indian policy in 1920 after witnessing ritual

[13] López (2010).
[14] Gamio (1916); López (2010: 8).
[15] Gottfried (2017).
[16] Alonso (2008); Vaughan (1997).
[17] Gottfried (2017: 8).

performances of song and dance at Taos Pueblo, New Mexico, which was becoming a magnet for artists, writers, and cultural critics.[18] Collier viewed Indian culture as one of the few surviving remnants of communal society, an idealized vision he had unsuccessfully tried to construct as a social reformer among immigrants in New York.

In 1931, two years before Collier was named BIA Commissioner, he had traveled to Mexico to meet with the country's "anthropological and 'Indianist' leaderships," which had gradually emerged from the nation-building projects of the Mexican Revolution.[19] Subsequent meetings developed concrete plans for an inter-American institute that would assist governments across the Americas in solving problems associated with their Indigenous populations, such as poverty and political marginalization. The immediate call for such an institute was made in 1938 at the VIII Pan-American Congress held in Lima, Peru. The congress founding the Inter-American Indian Institute was originally planned in Bolivia but ultimately realized in Mexico based on the invitation of Mexican President Lázaro Cárdenas, who had made Indigenous land reform a key part of his administration. Collier, who had attended the 1938 congress in Lima, took advantage of US diplomatic agendas during the rise of World War II to secure funding for the founding of the III. US funding came from Nelson Rockefeller's Office of Inter-American Affairs, a wartime federal agency which aimed to combat German Nazi and other Axis influences in Latin America.[20] President Cárdenas also contributed significant funds for the III staff and established the III headquarters in Mexico City.[21]

In the early 1940s, officials and intellectuals in the United States and in Mexico shared concerns about Indians' poverty, health standards, and marginalization from national affairs. However, these policy makers were influenced by different political projects emerging from different national histories. US federal Indian policy had undergone a radical shift after decades of government programs aimed at forced assimilation and disintegration of Native American Tribes.[22] Music and dance played a central role in assimilationist policies and Native resistance to those policies beginning around

---

[18] Kelly (1983: 119).

[19] Collier (1963: 356); Rosemblatt (2018: 106). See also Dawson (2004).

[20] On the Office of Inter-American Affairs, see Cramer and Prutsch (2006, 2012).

[21] The III continued to operate in Mexico City for several decades after US funding ceased, suggesting that it was not entirely a puppet of the United States. In 1948 the III became part of the Organization of American States.

[22] Philp (1977).

the 1870s.[23] The US government prohibited traditional music and dance, and used boarding schools to teach bourgeois parlor music and brass band music to Native youth. Government efforts at culturally assimilating Native Americans were linked to the breakup of Tribal lands and political organizations, purportedly paving the way to national integration and citizenship, as well as increased economic opportunities for non-Indians on former Indian land. The official reversal of these policies came in 1934 in the guise of the Indian Reorganization Act, directed by Collier. The Indian Reorganization Act ended allotment (the breakup of Tribal land) and established the means for Tribal self-government, land consolidation, and Tribal businesses. As BIA Commissioner, Collier incorporated traditional music and dance into the curriculum of Indian schools as a means of preserving Native culture.

Mexico was in a process of post-revolutionary nation-building that responded to US imperialism as well as European colonization. An important outcome of this nation-building project was the idea of *mestizaje* as a source of unique identity rather than a disadvantage in the global hierarchies of sociocultural evolution. Boasian anthropology helped to push back against assumptions of European superiority, but this emerging discipline was subject to adaptation and innovation in Mexico. Guillermo de la Peña has traced the close, complicated relationship between Franz Boas, the founder of American anthropology, and his Mexican protégé Manuel Gamio, who earned a doctorate from Columbia University while riding the waves of the revolutionary decade of 1910 to 1920. De la Peña uses the term "intellectual intermediary" to conceptualize the role of national intellectuals like Gamio in mediating and transforming the paradigms of anthropology in the Mexican context.[24]

As de la Peña demonstrates, Boas showed some resistance to revolutionary transformations because of the disruptions to the institution he was trying to develop in Mexico City with international support, the International School of American Archaeology and Ethnology. American anthropology was bound up in the political structures of US institutions, both academic and commercial—structures supported by the dictatorship of Porfirio Díaz. In 1913, Boas wrote a letter to the Mexican university official Ezequiel A. Chávez in which he critiqued US intervention but also justified the dictatorship, arguing that "under a state of disorder such as prevails at present,

---

[23] Troutman (2009).
[24] De la Peña (1996: 44).

only a strong hand can bring relief—a Cromwell, or a Napoleon, or a Díaz."[25] Gamio made his own way by forging a nationalist agenda for anthropology which sought a path to development that would take into account cultural difference, while also aiming for cultural unification. Gamio's anthropology was committed to preservation of the Indigenous past and transformation of the Indigenous present, in order to achieve a common national culture in the future.

More possibilities for cultural pluralism were articulated in the 1930s, but the Cárdenas government tended to limit Indigenous mobilization according to "the definition of politics within revolutionary populism."[26] The III congress took place in the final months of Cárdenas's six-year term as president of Mexico. The succeeding government was more conservative, and Gamio also moderated his indigenista politics to a more conservative stance. This shift followed the imperatives of Mexican politics as well as US academic notions of detached social science (no less political in the context of conservative US backlash against 1930s cultural pluralism).[27] The vision of the III under Gamio focused on detached scientific research without explicit political agendas. A pivotal force was the alliance of Collier and Gamio in advocating the state institutionalization of applied anthropology. Music and media were also key elements of their toolkit.

Performance in the Pátzcuaro Congress

Radio broadcasting and musical performance were part of the III from its inception. Radio spots promoting the III Congress were broadcast on the Mexican radio program "La Hora Nacional" (The National Hour) from the Secretariat of Government. The opening session of the Congress was also broadcast on national radio. In one of the promotional radio spots, the III Congress was presented as an opportunity to bring Indigenous

[25] Quoted in De la Peña (1996: 55). Boas to Ezequiel A. Chávez, November 21, 1913, Franz Boas Papers, American Philosophical Society.

[26] Dawson (1998: 300). See also Rosemblatt (2018: 136–137).

[27] The shift in focus may also have been related to the change in the III leadership from Moisés Sáenz to Manuel Gamio in 1941. Sáenz was a student of John Dewey who became an influential education policy official in Mexico in the 1930s. Sáenz carried out the early planning of the III, including the music and media project, but he contracted pneumonia and died in Peru in 1941. Giraudo (2012) suggests that Sáenz was pushing research and policy of the III toward a more transformative politics for Indigenous peoples' rights, in comparison to the conservative turn under Gamio's and Collier's leadership.

representatives together to speak freely about their problems, within the international order and in dialogue with the "wise, the specialist, and the scholar" (*del sabio, del técnico, y del estudioso*). Yet the broadcast took a strong position of condescension toward Indigenous peoples, as in the following excerpt:

Identifying themselves with the social spirit of the Mexican Revolution, the delegation of Mexico before the VII International American Conference proposed the Indigenous assembly in the terms noted, which seeks the recognition, by the governments of our continent, of the necessity of installing a more just modality in the treatment and solution of the problems of the Indian groups. The rectification of that state of social disequilibrium will have a great significance, because surely upon modifying the biological and cultural necessities of those inferior masses of the American population toward a greater satisfaction, they will be able to establish the bases for fulfilling a closer future, the foresight of the most advanced mentalities of the present, that augur the flourishing of a great culture specific to the New World, as one of the highest expressions of man.[28]

Here, the "problem of the Indian" is associated with a "state of social disequilibrium." Rather than mandating governmental changes, the broadcast assumes the need to modify the "biological and cultural necessities" of Indigenous peoples. This need for change was oriented toward the future, in the selective combination of cultural characteristics that would bring about an advanced stage of civilization—in some ways breaking out of the paradigm of European superiority, but without questioning the hierarchical stages of progress.

The congress in Pátzcuaro that founded the III was accompanied by two nights of musical performance in honor of the delegates. The first night,

---

[28] "Spots para la Hora Nacional que la Dirección General de Información, de la Secretaría de Gobernación, radiará por su estación X.E.D.P., el día 7 de abril de 1940, de las 22 a las 23 hs." File "Propaganda por Radio, México, 1940–1943," AHIII. "Identificándose con el espíritu social de la Revolución Mexicana, la delegación de México ante la VII Conferencia Internacional Americana propuso la asamblea indígena en los términos apuntados, que busca el reconocimiento por los Gobiernos de nuestro Continente, de la necesidad de instaurar una modalidad más justa en el trato y solución de los problemas de los grupos indios. La rectificación de ese estado de desequilibrio social tendrá una gran trascendencia, pues de seguro que al modificarse hacia una mejor satisfacción de las necesidades biológicas y culturales de esas capas inferiores de la población americana, podrán sentarse las bases para que se cumpla en un futuro más próximo, el vaticinio de las mentalidades más avanzadas del presente, que auguran el florecimiento de una gran cultura peculiar al Nuevo Mundo, como una de las más altas expresiones del hombre."

April 15, 1940, was conceived as a "festival of regional popular music" which primarily featured musicians and singers from nearby Indigenous communities.[29] Indigenous music was portrayed as a key component of a patchwork of cultures comprising Mexican national identity. The second night of performances on April 21 was promoted as a "cultural festival" that began with *"danzas aborígenes y bailes regionales"* (aboriginal and regional dances) from Michoacán. In the program, different terms to denote "dance" (danza, baile, ballet) distinctively categorized Indigenous, folkloric, and art traditions.[30] The featured event of the evening was a "Prehispanic Ballet" called "Xochiquetzalli" (the name of an Aztec goddess). The music for the ballet was composed and directed by Francisco Domínguez, a Mexican musicologist and composer who had been among the first to conduct research on Indigenous music in Mexico and to advocate for recognizing its status as Mexican heritage.[31] The ballet was performed by young women of the Society of Pátzcuaro and students of the school "Hijos del Ejército" (Sons of the Army)—performers who portrayed an Indigenous past as a shared national heritage. According to the program description, the ballet depicts the Aztec goddess of flowers, Xochiquetzalli, attended by slaves, maidens, and priests, with other dancers representing birds and butterflies. When priests begin to hunt the birds and butterflies, the goddess intervenes and forces all except the priests into poses of submission, some resembling flowers and leaves. In this ballet, performers from a higher sector of society took on Indigenous identities from the distant past, intertwined with images from nature. The temporal effect is one of preceding the contemporary Indigenous communities, thus making the indigenista performers closer to the origins of the nation. This displacement of Indigenous authenticity was characteristic of indigenista discourses to come.

[29] The performers included a musical group from the Island of Jarácuaro directed by Nicolas B. Juarez; songs by José´S. Ortizánchez, who directed a trio performance; a regional "Tarascan" (Indigenous P'urhépecha) band with songs by Ortizánchez; a musical group directed by Jacobo Cruz; and a "Canto a la India" (Song to the Indian Woman) by Ortizánchez with voices accompanied by the Band of the State.

[30] Program, "Primer Congreso Indigenista Interamericano," File "Propaganda por Radio, México, 1940–1943," AHIII.

[31] Alejandro Madrid discusses Francisco Domínguez's role in debates of the 1920s, in which Domínguez advocated for field research directly engaging with Indigenous music and communities, to serve as a true autochthonous basis for Mexican art music and national heritage (Madrid 2009: 123–125).

Mediating Culture

Music and media continued to be a central means of promoting activities of the III after its founding. The III Convention (Article V.4), the founding document ratified by member states, included a proposal to use phonograph records for publicity to promote the work of the Institute. Proposals were made to broadcast promotional spots for the III in the United States and throughout Latin America, with some success. The National Broadcasting company of New York, the Crosley Corporation of Cincinnati, Ohio, and X. E. W. of Mexico offered free radio time to the III on a weekly basis.[32]

A central part of the early work of the III was a project bringing together field recordings and art music composers' representations of Indigenous music, which Gamio took over in 1942. Collier helped to arrange for funding through the Office of Inter-American Affairs, which channeled money for the project through the Pan American Union in Washington to the III office in Mexico City.[33] The initial plans were to acquire copies of existing field recordings, compile them in an Indigenous music archive in the III headquarters, and commission composers to write Indigenous-themed music based on the recordings, to be used in radio broadcasts. The III would be responsible for distributing the recordings for radio broadcast throughout the Americas.[34]

In December 1941, the musicologist Otto Mayer-Serra submitted a proposal for the "Creation of the Department of Research on Indo-American Art," which would be sponsored by the Universidad Nacional Autónoma de México, but housed within the III. In his proposal, Mayer-Serra wrote that what little research existed on Latin American Indigenous music had been carried out by "composers and maestros" and was rarely published. He advocated for the disciplinary framework of comparative musicology (which he called "the latest branch of musical historiography") and the methodology of field recording to advance studies in this area. He also advocated an anthropological approach when he wrote that "it is necessary to study the melodies of primitive peoples from their own aesthetic categories, keeping in mind the peculiar mode of their intonation, their scales (many times based

[32] "Propaganda por Radio del Instituto Indigenista Interamericano," File "Propaganda por Radio, México, 1940–1943," AHIII.

[33] John Collier to Carlos Girón Cerna, May 23, 1941. Description of correspondence in file "John Collier," and file "Propaganda por Radio, México, 1940–1943," AHIII.

[34] Carlos Girón Serna to Charles Seeger, June 27, 1941, File "Dr. Charles Seeger, 1941–1942," AHIII.

on extra-musical concepts and completely different from our modern musical experience), their ritual (magical) function, their ethnological, phonetic and cultural factors in general, and their degree and possibilities of evolution."[35]

Mayer-Serra had a transnational personal and intellectual history which facilitated connecting anthropology, musicology, and media. The musicologist Diego Alonso has recently brought to light key aspects of Mayer-Serra's biography which had been obscured by political necessity during his lifetime.[36] Of German Jewish ancestry, Otto Mayer studied musicology in Berlin; one of his professors was Curt Sachs, a founder of comparative musicology. In 1933, Mayer's socialist affiliations forced him into exile in Barcelona, where he learned Spanish and Catalan, built a musicological career, and continued to pursue a critical theory of music based on Marxist principles. He was legally adopted by a Catalan socialist politician, Manuel Serra, in order to avoid extradition to Nazi Germany. Mayer-Serra had a special interest in radio and recordings dating back to his studies in Berlin, where he associated with musical intellectuals who were exploring the potential of media for proletarian art and social revolution. With the defeat of the Popular Front in the Spanish Civil War, he was exiled again in 1939 and settled in Mexico City, along with many other refugees escaping Franco's dictatorship.[37]

Mayer-Serra conceived of the proposed III archive as a means "to centralize the remains [*restos*] of the marvelous aboriginal cultures in the American continent, conserve them for the knowledge of future generations and permit researchers of the entire world to study them, interpret them and corroborate the results of our investigations." This was in keeping with other researchers' preoccupations with salvage ethnography and the preservation of cultures presumed to be disappearing. Mayer-Serra wrote that recordings would be collected, organized, and studied scientifically. Resulting studies would be disseminated "through lectures, inter-American radio programs, expositions, film exhibitions, etc. to provide knowledge about the most valuable samples of indigenous art, to inspire interest of the youth toward these

[35] "Proyecto de Creación del Departamento de Investigación de Arte Indoamericano," Otto Mayer-Serra, December 1941, File "Propaganda por Radio, México, 1940–1943." AHIII.

[36] Alonso (2019).

[37] Palomino (2020: 163–166) discusses Mayer-Serra's correspondence with Francisco Curt Lange, who had left Germany for Uruguay for economic reasons almost two decades earlier. They began their correspondence writing letters in German in 1935, when Mayer-Serra was still living in Barcelona. Beginning in 1940, after Mayer-Serra had moved to Mexico City, they wrote each other in Spanish, perhaps a sign of their embrace of Spanish American discourses.

autochthonous monuments of ancient American cultures, and to create a source of inspiration for the American authors in their nationalistic production."[38] Here, Indigenous music recordings were viewed as resources for science, history, and the nation.

The III interest in radio programs followed the systematic use of radio for educational purposes in postrevolutionary Mexico. Since the 1920s, the Secretariat of Education had produced radio programs of educational courses as well as music—programs which were intended to bring rural populations into ideal forms of citizenship. While many of these broadcasts had nationalist overtones, explicitly with the "Hora Nacional" program founded in 1937, the programming also included transnational content.[39] With some of the same cultural policy officials involved, the III brought international perspectives on Indigenous peoples and cultures into a national broadcasting space.

Nevertheless, producing radio programs based on Indigenous music and indigenista compositions proved to be a challenge. It was difficult for III staff to acquire Indigenous music either in the form of written notation or recordings.[40] There was evidence of tension between the initial III proposal and the directives of the Pan American Union (PAU) and John Collier. The project approved by the PAU was for each program to include "a piece of indigenous music with a commentary and an example of how that theme had been used in contemporary music." Collier suggested that the III first acquire the contemporary music compositions, and then the Indigenous music upon which they were based. But for the III staff, "the difficulty is that we wouldn't know how to locate the primitive themes corresponding to the modern music that we acquired."[41] Creating a one-to-one linkage between a contemporary composition and an Indigenous source music was problematic because of the modernist idiom in which many Latin American composers worked, and the multitude of influences that shaped their compositions. Even if project staff were able to identify or develop notation for a particular Indigenous motive

[38] "Proyecto de Creación del Departamento de Investigación de Arte Indoamericano," Otto Mayer-Serra, December 1941, File "Propaganda por Radio, México, 1940–1943." AHIII.

[39] Joy Elizabeth Hayes (2000) discusses the ambivalent coexistence of US commercial radio technology with national content in Mexico. The Mexican government used radio to instill national consciousness and a particular political hegemony which was not open to debate.

[40] Curt Lange, Harold Spivacke, and Laura Boulton were singled out as some of the first to come to their aid by offering to send recordings. Frances Densmore sent recordings, as did Gilbert Chase on behalf of the Library of Congress. File "Propaganda por Radio, México, 1940–1943," assorted documents, including Chase to Gamio, October 12, 1942, AHIII.

[41] Archived summary notes in File "Propaganda por Radio, México, 1940–1943," AHIII.

used in a composition, Latin American composers and musicologists in correspondence with the III expressed concern that having a motive performed by musicians outside the Indigenous community in which it originated would result in an entirely different sound that would misrepresent the source music. An alternative proposal would use Indigenous music only as background for broadcasts about other themes (health, education, etc.), but the III remained committed to keeping music in the foreground of the radio broadcasts. They ultimately settled on a plan to commission composers of the Americas to write short pieces based on Indigenous motives captured in field recordings, which would be loaned to the composers for that purpose.

The radio programs would include an original piece of Indigenous music, ideally played on Indigenous instruments, followed by an indigenista composer's interpretation of that music. Gamio wrote to the Brazilian composer Heitor Villa-Lobos, "Playing in succession the Indigenous musical motive and the orchestral adaptation based on it will better make evident the importance and aesthetic value of Indigenous music."[42] This estimation was from the perspective of erudite listeners. Elsewhere, Gamio wrote that "when those discs are played before an Indigenous audience, they will appreciate more, much more, the first part of the program than the second, while the audience with European cultural criteria will prefer the second part."[43] His comments suggest the desire to bring together a cross-cultural national audience while recognizing the different ways of listening that divided them. This was also a racial compartmentalization that did not reflect the cultural fluidity of people with multiple or hybrid aesthetic frameworks.

Yurchenco in Mexico

It must have seemed fortuitous when, around the time of these negotiations, Henrietta Yurchenco appeared on the scene in 1942. A US citizen, Henrietta Yurchenco had been residing in Mexico for almost a year with her husband, the Argentine American painter Basil Yurchenco. Henrietta Yurchenco had grown up studying classical piano in Connecticut, but she found her calling in New York as a pioneering broadcaster of folk and world musics

---

[42] Gamio to Villa-Lobos, October 8, 1942, File "Propaganda por Radio, México, 1940–1943," AHIII.

[43] Gamio (1942: 22). "Cuando esos discos sean tocados ante un auditorio indígena, este apreciará más, mucho más, la primera parte del programa que la segunda, en tanto que los auditorios de criterio cultural europeo preferirán la segunda parte."

on the radio station WNYC. This path followed an interest sparked when she was a teenager and heard George Herzog give a lecture on African music at Yale.[44] US-based networks of the Works Progress Administration (WPA) facilitated Henrietta's move into public cultural production and policy. The WPA employed Basil Yurchenco in a mural project, one of many inspired by Mexican mural painting, and he facilitated an introduction for Henrietta to interview at WNYC.[45] Henrietta Yurchenco's programs on WNYC included "Adventures in Music," on folk music from around the world; "Folksongs of America," which debuted singers such as Leadbelly, Woody Guthrie, and Pete Seeger; "Songs of the Seven Million," representing the cultural diversity of New York at the 1941 World's Fair; "Calypso," on popular music from Trinidad; and "American Music Festivals," which featured art, folk, and jazz music of the United States. Before moving to Mexico, Yurchenco had also made field recordings of Portuguese fishermen in Cape Cod.[46]

The Yurchencos caught the "Mexican vogue" in the 1930s in New York City, a key destination for Latin American artists and musicians breaking away from European aesthetic hegemony. Henrietta and Basil initially traveled to Mexico City in 1941 on the invitation of the Mexican painter Rufino Tamayo, who had recently returned to Mexico after living in New York since 1926, when he shared an apartment with the Mexican composer Carlos Chávez.[47] The Yurchencos settled into a bohemian international milieu in Mexico City and made extended trips to explore the arts and cultures of Guanajuato, Guerrero, and Oaxaca (see Figure 2.1).

In the spring of 1942, John H. Green, a New York friend and recording engineer, came to visit the Yurchencos with the intention of making recordings of Mexican music. Henrietta Yurchenco successfully solicited support from the Palace of Fine Arts, as well as the Universidad de San Nicolás de Hidalgo and the governor of Michoacán. They planned an expedition to Michoacán accompanied by Roberto Téllez Girón, who had carried out music research in the area as the official music documentarist for the Mexican government's Department of Fine Arts (see Figure 2.2).[48]

---

[44] Yurchenco (2002: 36). Here and elsewhere, I am citing from the 2002 English version of Yurchenco's memoirs. Bitrán Goren (2018) and Giraudo (2022) discuss the 2003 Spanish version which included more information and documentation.

[45] Yurchenco (2002: 30).

[46] Curriculum of Henrietta Yurchenco, File "Propaganda por Radio, México, 1940–1943," AHIII.

[47] López Hernández (2022: 6) notes that Rufino Tamayo was among the Mexican artists involved in museum-based projects to adapt Indigenous pieces to "modern life."

[48] Francisco Domínguez had also carried out field research in Michoacán as early as 1923, supported by the Mexican Secretariat of Public Education (Madrid 2009).

Figure 2.1 Henrietta Yurchenco in Oaxaca, Mexico, 1942. Photo by Basil Yurchenco. Used with permission of Peter Yurchenco. Henrietta Yurchenco Collection, Centro Nacional de las Artes, Mexico City.

Téllez Girón was almost exactly the same age as Yurchenco and also a pianist, though he had studied and performed piano more extensively than she had. His Spanish father had been a successful businessman but died unexpectedly without a will and left the family impoverished. Téllez Girón learned quickly in piano lessons from a neighborhood teacher and began playing professionally as a child accompanying silent films in the movie

Figure 2.2   Roberto Téllez Girón, classical pianist and Indigenous and folk music specialist in the Secretaría de Educación Pública, Mexico. Used with permission of Roberto and Ricardo Téllez-Girón López. Henrietta Yurchenco Collection, Centro Nacional de las Artes, Mexico City.

theater, proudly helping to support his family. He received excellent training at the National Conservatory, and it was his musical skill that won him the position as a folk music collector, because he had an acute ability to hear and transcribe musical sound with great detail. He conducted field research with singers and musicians who patiently repeated their performances as he adapted the system of Western art music notation to represent folkloric genres.[49]

Undoubtedly, Henrietta Yurchenco's charisma, intelligence, and drive helped rally support for her plans. Perhaps more importantly, recording equipment was hard to come by in Mexico, and her friendship with John Green provided Mexican institutions, at least temporarily, with access to a professional Fairchild machine that recorded on acetate disks. Yurchenco, Green, and Téllez Girón spent three weeks traveling through the state of Michoacán, recording 135 songs in a wide range of musical styles, primarily in the Indigenous language now referred to as P'urhépecha (the term "Tarascan" used in earlier publications is considered derogatory). We can only imagine the relationship between Yurchenco and Téllez Girón during that first expedition. Yurchenco was outgoing; Téllez Girón was more serious and reserved, but amiable and respectful. He would soon marry a telephone operator in one of the towns where he conducted research, and he maintained a great love of media and cinema throughout his life.

In this and other recording expeditions, Yurchenco took a broad approach to recording the musical creativity of the people she encountered. The communities she described in her reports were in the process of rapid change, and she viewed herself as an agent of preservation as well as dissemination of regional musics, whether or not they were purely "aboriginal." She recognized that even "traditional" Indigenous genres also involved creativity and innovation, as in the *pirekua*, the P'urhépecha song form that is associated with particular composers who are esteemed for their new compositions.[50]

The mediation of Yurchenco's project was embedded in many other layers of mediation—technologies, disciplines, scholarly voices, languages, and nation-states. Yurchenco was critical of the blunders of the American Embassy in Mexico City as it attempted to implement the Good Neighbor policy through cultural exchanges without demonstrating much cross-cultural knowledge or sensitivity.[51] Yet it must have been difficult to avoid falling into this structure of international relations. When Yurchenco and Téllez Girón returned from the expedition, they gave a presentation to the Mexican Society of Anthropology. The event took place at the Benjamin

---

[49] Gottfried Hesketh and Téllez Girón López (2010).
[50] For more on the pirekua, see Chamorro Escalante (1991).
[51] Yurchenco (2002: 90–91).

Franklin Library of the American Embassy, which had been established that year to promote friendship and exchange between Mexico and the United States.

Yurchenco had not yet mastered Spanish, and so she wrote the lecture in English, then Téllez Girón translated the text and delivered it at the American Embassy. The presentation foregrounded the revolutionary effects of "the recording machine in field work," which enabled a new kind of collecting with "greater honesty and significance."[52] Yurchenco's ideology of authenticity and objectivity in sound recording can be traced back to Jesse Walter Fewkes's and Benjamin Ives Gilman's publications around the turn of the twentieth century.[53] They perceived the phonograph as a means of transcending the cultural bias of the researcher, and they considered transcriptions made from recordings to be more objective than transcriptions made in fieldwork because the recording enabled repeated listenings in a controlled space without distractions.

Yurchenco's presentation emphasized the revolutionary results of applying recording technology in fieldwork, in contrast to the aural transcriptions of previous researchers, which she considered "insufficient and sometimes incorrect."[54] One wonders if Roberto Téllez Girón, who had carried out research using aural transcription, felt uncomfortable when he presented Yurchenco's words about the authenticity of recordings in fieldwork. Jessica Gottfried Hesketh has suggested that Téllez Girón's transcriptions in other regions effectively encoded the music he studied, to the extent that performances based on his notation were recognizable to heritage communities decades later.[55] Western staff notation can never serve as an exact reproduction of musical sound, even for European-based music, and much less for other musical systems. Nevertheless, the methodology of on-site aural transcription required more interaction and communication with the singers and musicians than the methodology of field recording alone. Some of the field recordings made on the expedition were barely audible, and hardly a transparent conduit to the musical performance.

Yurchenco wrote a report describing her first field expedition and sent it to Charles Seeger (representing the PAU), Alan Lomax, and Charles Stevens

---

[52] Yurchenco, manuscript of lecture delivered in translation in the Benjamin Franklin Library in Mexico City (1942), Fondo Henrietta Yurchenco, CENART.

[53] Brady (1999: 80–82); Hochman (2014: 77).

[54] Yurchenco, manuscript of lecture delivered in translation in the Benjamin Franklin Library in Mexico City (1942), Fondo Henrietta Yurchenco, CENART.

[55] Gottfried Hesketh (2010).

(the latter two representing the Library of Congress). Lomax and Seeger are both prominent figures in the development of documentary music recording and the discipline of ethnomusicology in the United States, along with their family members who participated in the work of recording, archiving, and disseminating vernacular musics. Alan Lomax was from Texas. He and his father, John Lomax, made a few recordings of Spanish language music in south Texas. In early adulthood Alan spent time in Mexico, but apparently could not learn enough Spanish to launch a recording project at the time.[56] Yurchenco's report on her first expedition shows that she was part of the Lomaxes' and Seegers' networks at least from 1942. In this report, Yurchenco also noted plans for constructing a recording archive housed in the Palace of Fine Arts and built by the Ministry of Public Education.[57]

Yurchenco's early work at WNYC proved to be good preparation for her work in Mexico. Following that first expedition, Manuel Gamio asked her to prepare a series of radio programs jointly sponsored by the Inter-American Indian Institute and the Music Division of the Pan-American Union.[58] Her WNYC program "Adventures in Music" became "Adventures in Music of the Americas" in Mexico. With the project in full swing, Gamio wrote letters to art music composers from the United States and across Latin America, often following Seeger's recommendations. Seeger's suggestions included Colin McPhee (Canada), Aaron Copland (United States), Alberto Ginastera (Argentina), and Camargo Guarnieri (Brasil). Gamio would send the composers recordings of Indigenous music as the basis for culling Indigenous motives that would be incorporated into the compositions. Gamio solicited 5–7 minute pieces, usually in exchange for a $100 honorarium.[59] Interestingly, the III offered Aaron Copland less than they offered the Latin American composers ($75 as opposed to $100 per composition). Copland may have declined due to other commitments, but the payment is

---

[56] Szwed (2010: 54, 92). Considering that the Lomax family was from south Texas, it is striking that Spanish language music received much less attention than white and Black southern music in their field recordings. Their choices may have been shaped by personal aesthetic preferences, and by the fact that they could not wield as much power in Spanish speaking contexts in Texas. Rodriguez and Torres (2016) are diplomatic in their assessment of the recordings that Alan's father John Lomax made in South Texas in 1939, focusing on their value as a heritage source for contemporary Tejanos.

[57] Undated memorandum, "Re: Results of expedition to record the folkmusic (sic) of the state of Michoacán, Mexico," Fondo Henrietta Yurchenco, CENART.

[58] Yurchenco (2002: 98).

[59] Seeger had developed close relations with Ginastera and Guarnieri through his work at the PAU. See Seeger to Gamio, December 16, 1942, File "Dr. Charles Seeger, 1941–1942" and Sady to Copland, January 14, 1943, File "Propaganda por Radio, México, 1940–1943," AHIII.

an important point since it showed the III paid Latin American composers competitive rates and did not privilege US composers in their budget.[60]

The challenge was to locate appropriate recordings, obtain copies, and establish agreements with composers. For making the radio transcriptions they also needed acetate discs, which were scarce in Mexico during the war years, but Seeger helped Gamio acquire them from the United States.[61] Older cylinder recordings of Mexican music were scattered in places such as the Smithsonian Institution, Columbia University (Herzog's collection which had moved there with him from Yale), the Museum of Natural History of New York (an early collection recorded by Carl Lumholtz in 1898), and the Southwest Museum of Los Angeles (including cylinders of Mexican and Indian music recorded by Charles Lummis in California in 1901–1905).[62] The technology for copying cylinders was still evolving; the National Archives said it would take two years to make copies of selected recordings, following the installation of new equipment. Seeger offered to serve as a behind-the-scenes mediator to facilitate an arrangement through which the Library of Congress would copy the Columbia cylinders of interest to Gamio and send copies to both Gamio and Herzog.[63] The III also contacted a number of US Indianist composers in the hopes they would have recordings, transcriptions, or their own compositions to share. Indianist composition had fallen out of favor in the United States by that time, and it was difficult to identify the current publishers of their pieces, but the III seemed to be casting a broad net without making clear distinctions between Indigenous music and composers' representations of it.[64]

There was some debate about whether commercial recordings could also be a source of authentic Indigenous culture. In his work at the PAU, Seeger had emphasized the value of commercial recordings of Latin American music, as Alan Lomax had done for US folk music at the Library of Congress. Writing from Peru, Andrés Sas cautioned Gamio that commercial recordings

---

[60] Gamio to Copland, January 14, 1943, File "Propaganda por Radio, México, 1940–1943," AHIII. See Hess (2013b) on Copland's cultural diplomacy in Latin America.

[61] Gamio to Seeger, November 12, 1942, File "Dr. Charles Seeger, 1941–1942," AHIII.

[62] Seeger to Gamio, July 31, 1942, File "Dr. Charles Seeger, 1941–1942," AHIII.

[63] Seeger to Gamio, October 15, 1942, File "Dr. Charles Seeger, 1941–1942," AHIII.

[64] The US composers who were targeted for Indigenous music materials included Arthur Farwell, Charles Wakefield Cadman, Homer Grunn, Thurlow Lieurance, Harvey Worthinton Loomis, Frederick Jacobi, and Charles Sanford Skilton (via his daughter, as he had recently passed away). Most of these solicitations did not come to fruition. See Browner (1997, 1995) and Troutman (2009) for discussion of some of these US Indianist composers.

should not be taken to represent Indigenous music. Gamio had inquired about the existence of "discs already made of Indigenous music . . . recorded by musicologists, ethnologists and other competent experts."[65] Sas responded: "Understanding that you refer to recordings of folkloric music that is not 'arranged,' made without commercial ends but with illustrative intentions, I have to tell you that unfortunately no Peruvian disc exists of this kind. There are versions of Indian folkloric or popular airs arranged and recorded by RCA Victor, with commercial ends. Some of these arrangements are well done, although none can claim the rank of art music [*música culta*]."[66] Here, Sas makes a distinction between folkloric music and commercial music, and between commercial music and art music. The elusive target of the search for recordings was caught between ideologies of Indigenous authenticity and the transformative mediation of arrangements, whether commercially or artistically motivated.[67]

In the end, it appears that the III contracted Andrés Sas (Peru), Carlos Chávez (Mexico), Carlos Isamitt (Chile), Luis Sandi (Mexico), Candelario Huízar (Mexico), Jesús Castillo (Guatemala), Earl Robinson (United States), and Colin McPhee (Canada) to contribute compositions for the radio broadcasts. Scripts were prepared for broadcasts including the compositions by Sandi, Castillo, Isamitt, and Huízar, focusing on Indigenous music of Mexico, Guatemala, Chile, and Colombia.[68] In the broadcasts focused on Mexican music, they used the documentary recordings that Yurchenco had helped to realize together with John Green and Raúl Guerrero. Other documentary recordings planned for use in the broadcasts were made by Gabriel Ospina in Colombia and Seamus Doyle in Peru.[69] It appears that at least one script (involving music by Huízar) was broadcast on November 22, 1943, on short-wave radio by the International Broadcasting Company of New York,

---

[65] Gamio to Sas, October 8, 1942, File "Propaganda por Radio, México, 1940–1943," AHIII.

[66] Sas to Gamio, October 24, 1942, File "Propaganda por Radio, México, 1940–1943," AHIII. Tucker (2013: 55–56) notes that foreign record companies made 78 rpm recordings of indigenista music in 1927 and 1928, but it was only in the mid-1940s that Peruvian record companies emerged and began to record Andean music.

[67] The French-Belgian composer Andrés Sas was contracted by the Peruvian government in 1924 to develop national music institutions and spent most of his career in Peru. A Chilean tribute at the time of his death in 1967 also described him as an "investigator of indigenous musical folklore" (Comité Editorial, *Revista Musical Chilena* 1967). Romero (2017: 99) suggests that Sas was not antagonistic to indigenista music in Peru (at least not as much as his colleague Rudolph Holzmann).

[68] Huízar was contracted for compositions using Indigenous music from Colombia as well as Mexico, and Sandi was contracted for compositions using Indigenous music from Peru as well as Mexico.

[69] See Pernet (2007: 148–149) for a discussion of Seamus Doyle's 1941 recording activities in Latin America while on tour with the American Ballet Caravan.

audible on WNBI (11870 Kc-25 metros) in Mexico.[70] In that case, the broad-cast recording made in New York was apparently sent to other cities in Latin America for broadcast in those countries.

The mediation of the Inter-American Indian Institute made this work a project of cultural diplomacy and scientific collection, goals that were distinct from the commercial objectives of recording companies. The mediation of the recording itself brought together senses of immediacy and distance. Recordings enabled people to hear, in their immediate en-vironment, voices and instruments from another time and place, but those recordings also created a sense of distance from an authentically Indigenous object.

Collaborations

With the entrance of Henrietta Yurchenco on the scene, the pieces came to-gether for the launching of systematic field recording expeditions. In 1943, a formal partnership for sponsoring recording expeditions was established among the Inter-American Indian Institute, the Mexican Secretariat of Public Education (SEP), and the US Library of Congress, with additional support from Seeger at the Pan American Union. The Bureau of Indian Affairs staff member Emil Sady worked with both the Pan American Union and the III, and he was also a key actor facilitating the purchase and transfer of equipment (see Figure 2.3). The partnership was sparked by letters the III had sent to Washington since 1941 seeking recordings of Indigenous music, combined with the increased interest of the Library of Congress in acquiring music recordings from Latin America.[71]

In April 1943, Gilbert Chase, the assistant for Latin American Music in the Library of Congress Music Division, suggested to Gamio that cooperation between their organizations would be mutually beneficial, and that the III could prepare a proposal to be sent through diplomatic channels.[72] Chase outlined what the Library could offer:

---

[70] Gamio to Huízar, October 19, 1943, File "Propaganda por Radio, México, 1940–1943," AHIII.

[71] Bartis (1982); Salvatore (2005).

[72] Gilbert Chase was a key figure in inter-American musical diplomacy, and his biography emerged directly from US imperialist networks. Born in Cuba in 1906, Chase's father was an American naval officer and veteran of the Spanish American War; his mother was Danish, a daughter of the Danish Consul in Havana (Biondi 2004: iv).

Figure 2.3 US Bureau of Indian Affairs official Emil Sady with two Native American delegates from the United States at the Inter-American Indian Institute founding congress in Pátzcuaro, Mexico, 1940. NAA INV 00853200, National Anthropological Archives, Smithsonian Institution.

We are able to provide the recording machine and the blank discs for recording and for making copies. The usual procedure is for one copy of each record to be deposited in the Library of Congress, and one copy in the local institution with which we are collaborating, which in this case, of course, would be the Instituto Indigenista. We provide funds for shipping this material to and from Mexico, and we can also dispose of a certain sum for field expenses.[73]

Gamio then secured the support of the Mexican Secretariat of Public Education, which had more resources than the III. In a proposal to the US Ambassador in Mexico, Gamio wrote that the Secretariat of Education would not only contribute to the travel expenses of recording expeditions, but would also provide the personnel for carrying out the project, including Roberto Téllez Girón, the composer Luis Sandi (chief of the Music Section of the SEP), and Henrietta Yurchenco (whom Gamio listed as an employee of the SEP rather than part of the international cooperation). The III would serve as "coordinator and organizer" of the project. In this proposal to the US Embassy, Gamio described the object of the field recording not as "indigenous music" (a term he had been using to discuss the radio project) but rather "folkmusic [sic] of Mexico."[74] This may have been an attempt to develop the broadest possible interest among funders, or an attempt to cast the recording net widely·as an official government-sponsored project. In early 1944, the project was extended to Guatemala through support of the Guatemalan government in collaboration with the III. As was common at the time, indigenista and artistic networks overlapped with diplomatic roles. Carlos Girón Cerna, who had initiated the radio project as Provisional Interim Director of the III in 1941, was then the Consul of Guatemala in Mexico. The Library of Congress offered to give copies of recordings to the government of Guatemala.[75]

Yurchenco's accounts of the recording expeditions echo many other explorers and ethnologists who emphasized the physical challenges of traveling long distances through wilderness or rough terrain to reach the Holy Grail of authentic, remote Indigenous communities. Many of her representations of the people and communities she encountered reflected the biases of her time and her outsider perspective. However, she did not create purist representations of Indigenous music, but rather observed with equal curiosity the interchange between autochthonous and imported musical styles. Even viewing her writings with a critical eye toward the politics

[73] Chase to Gamio, April 26, 1943, File "Propaganda por Radio" México, 1940–1943," AHIII.

[74] Gamio to US Ambassador Messersmith, July 5, 1943, File "Propaganda por Radio, México, 1940–1943," AHIII.

[75] Gamio to Don José Castañeda (Secretaría de Relaciones Exteriores de Guatemala), December 28, 1943, File "Propaganda por Radio, México, 1940–1943," AHIII.

of cross-cultural representations, we can acknowledge the endurance and drive to transport heavy equipment across long distances, often traveling by foot and horseback. Getting strangers to sing and play music from their own cultural repertoires must have required special communication skills as well as the effective wielding of economic and social power. We can begin to grasp the project results by turning our ears to an archived radio script and to Yurchenco's contemporaneous analysis of her recording methods.

Methodologies for Sound and Listening

The radio programs and the documentary recordings that Yurchenco helped to produce created specific positionalities through listening. As an example, we can imagine a radio listener in Mexico tuning in to a broadcast of a prerecorded spot based on the following script:

> This is a program of the Inter-American Indian Institute with headquarters in Mexico City. You are listening to our musical theme, performed by the indigenista orchestra of the Institute. If you are an indigenista—if you are an educator, intellectual, musician, architect, archaeologist, linguist, sociologist, ethnologist—collaborate with us. Write to us and we will send you our publications. Send us your works. And, if you are not an indigenista, BECOME AN INDIGENISTA! Remember that the problem of the Indian is one of the most important of our America.

After a pause, the listener would hear through soft radio static the sharp sound of a reed flute creating an angular melody with punctuating percussion. The announcer continues:

> You just heard an indigenous theme of the Quiché Indians of Guatemala, played on their traditional instruments, the chirimía—a kind of vernacular oboe, ritual drums, and turtle shells. The Maestro Gerardo Castillo, of Guatemala, is now going to perform for you all, with the indigenista orchestra of the Institute, a symphonic arrangement of the Indigenous theme that you just heard.

The name Gerardo Castillo in the script was probably supposed to be Jesús Castillo, a well known Guatemalan composer and researcher to whom the project directors had written. The symphony orchestra was probably that of the Universidad Nacional Autónoma de México, a sixty-piece ensemble whose sound was mediated by the recording and radio transmission of the time. The announcer goes on:

> And now let us recollect the sacred voice of the Popol Vuh, that marvelous book of Quiché myth, which inspired Maestro Castillo's beautiful composition that we just heard: Quiché myth says that the first men were made of corn masa, and they stayed with that presence, similar to people. They knew their intelligence upon realizing that they saw, they looked, ultimately knowing everything there is below the sky, on the ground. From the clouds, they saw everything without needing to walk first . . . Great was the wisdom that they possessed, which they used to penetrate in their beings the trees, the rocks, the lakes, the sea, the mountains and the coasts. But the gods Ajtzak and Ajbit were afraid of that wisdom of the first men. So they clouded the eyes by mandate of the Heart of the sky, covering them like the breath covers the surface of a reflection; thus their eyes remained clouded, and they could only see what was near.

We may surmise from the script that Maestro Castillo's inspiration came from at least two sources at two different points of history: an inscription of an Indigenous melody that was probably current in his day, and an older inscription of Mayan cosmology—the colonial-era text known as the Popol Vuh. Both sources of inspiration were mediated by documentary practices of different times. It is unclear if the Indigenous melody came from Castillo's own research or from Yurchenco's recordings in Guatemala. The Popol Vuh was a Spanish friar's translation in 1701–1702 of an earlier text which used Latin script to represent the K'iche' language.[76] The radio script aligns the "sacred voice," the "marvelous book," and the "beautiful composition" in a way that blurs the boundaries between orality and writing.

At the end of the script, the radio announcer concludes:

> And to finish we will tell all of you the indigenista phrase of today: "America will be saved by the Indian," José Martí. Thus, distinguished radio listeners, we bring to an end our listening of today, reminding you that this has been

---

[76] Quiroa (2017).

a program of the Inter-American Indian Institute, with headquarters in Mexico City.[77]

This III radio broadcast script mediated among Indigenous music, art music, and "radio listeners." In planning the programs, the organizers considered that Indigenous people would be among the listeners, but here the targeted listeners appeared to be intellectuals, academic specialists, teachers, and musicians who might be persuaded to "become an indigenista!"

Other techniques of mediation become apparent in Yurchenco's descriptions of her recording processes. In 1946 Yurchenco published a how-to article on field recording methods in *América Indígena*.[78] Part of this is practical advice, for example, to use long-lasting sapphire needles to record in the field, and to bring a gas motor to power the recording machine, thereby avoiding an even larger combined weight of batteries, converter, and carrier. Yurchenco also provides a view of the changing nature of music research, noting that musicology, like ethnology, had undergone rapid progress in the twentieth century, but that musicology was slower to incorporate recording technology and cultural analyses into its methodology. She writes that ethnologists had collected many recordings without attending to specialized musical knowledge and structures, but they were still quicker to cross disciplinary boundaries than the musicologists were. What is needed, in her interpretation, are "ethnologist-musicologists" or "musicologist-ethnologists." She mentions several music researchers—George Herzog, Frances Densmore, and Helen Roberts—who had succeeded in garnering respect from ethnologists as well as musicologists.

Yurchenco's recording expeditions fall somewhere in between the long-term anthropological fieldwork model and the brief collecting trips of comparative musicologists. In places where "pre-Hispanic rites" were carried out in secret, she says, recording music would require longer periods of time and more extensive efforts to build trust. In other cases, field recordings could be made during brief visits if the communities had good relations with local authorities and if the recordist had the official backing of those authorities (teachers, priests, government officials, etc.). By all accounts, Yurchenco had a special talent for building rapport with people from all walks of life, and she wrote sincerely of her respect for a broad range of musical styles. She

[77] File "Propaganda por Radio, México, 1940–1943," AHIII.
[78] Yurchenco (1946).

also noted the practical benefit of this approach by saying, "If the researcher can make the Indian feel that he admires his/her songs for their beauty and rhythm, then half the battle has been won."[79]

In writing about the recording process, Yurchenco de-essentialized the Indigenous music object and represented Indigenous music-making as constantly changing, adapting, and embedded in specific historical moments. Her discussion reveals that field recording was a creative project more than a mechanical reproduction or transmission. In her advice for field recordists, she privileges a notion of liveness, which is related to ideologies of authenticity, but she also shows how liveness is created through the craft of recording. Yurchenco outlines three possible approaches to recording ritual music: 1) recording during the ceremony or fiesta itself, which has the benefit of expressive intensity but does not always result in the best sound quality; 2) orchestrating a reproduction of the fiesta with the motivation of recording it; and 3) bringing only the musicians together exclusively to record the music normally performed during the fiesta. In discussing the second approach, she moves from the recordist's techniques for capturing liveness to the multiple audiences the recording should serve:

> The microphone should be used as a camera, in a very free manner among the distinct performers, giving emphasis to the rhythm of a drum, to the sound of the feet of the dancers, to the "chin chin," to the comments and shouts of the spectators. A disc made in this form is something more than the faithful reproduction of the music, and it is transformed into an oral document of the live scene. Researchers should never forget that a disc is not only the manner to easily transcribe music, but rather that it is an oral "record" [a word she uses in English in quotes], in the same way that film is a visual "record" that ought to have multiple uses: it can serve the composer for creative ends, it can be used by radio programs, as a musical source in documentary films, etc. In other words, it is a document that is going to be heard and listened to [oído y escuchado] by large human groups and it should not be enclosed in libraries and museums for the exclusive use of specialists and scientists.[80]

[79] Yurchenco (1940: 325).

[80] Yurchenco (1946: 326): "El micrófono se debe usar como una cámara, de manera muy libre entre los distintos ejecutantes, dando énfasis al ritmo de un tambor, al sonido de los pies de los danzantes, al 'chin chin', a los comentarios y gritos de los espectadores. Un disco hecho en esta forma es algo más que la reproducción fiel de la música, y se transforma en un documento oral de la escena viva. Los investigadores nunca deben olvidar que un disco no es sólo la manera de transcribir fácilmente la

Yurchenco uses terms denoting archival authenticity ("faithful reproduction," "oral document," "oral record") at the same time that she reveals her active role in creating a sense of liveness in the recording. In some ways, this text reaffirms Jonathan Sterne's assertion that "sound reproduction is 'always already' a kind of studio art."[81] Recording entails an active, strategic process of manipulating bodies and machines to create a semblance of fidelity and liveness. But Sterne tends to use studio recording more than field recording as a paradigm in analyzing the "cultural origins of sound reproduction."[82] As Sterne points out, the techniques of field recordists sometimes aimed to create studios in the field, but their motivations for doing so were entirely different from commercial studio recording. This is where Brian Hochman's intervention helps us to see and hear the impact of Indigenous orality and aurality in media histories. Field recordings of Indigenous music were "archives of the real" because they were the product of an arduous quest seeking cultural difference, and because they were taken to be objective, faithful conduits of race and culture.[83]

Yurchenco emphasized the "quest" aspect of her work, but she maintained a broad approach to documenting the musics that people actually performed and listened to, rather than limiting her recording to music that seemed entirely autochthonous. Her reflexive analysis of field recording points in the direction of later ethnographic work pioneered by Steven Feld that is sometimes called "anthropology in/as sound."[84] Yurchenco did not carry out long-term ethnographic research which would become central to "acoustemologies"—the union of acoustics and epistemologies, a concept developed by Feld dialogically through ethnography and sound recordings.[85] Still, Yurchenco's methodologies captured a kind of ethnographic recording of its time. In the article quoted above, Yurchenco was also pushing against the dominant paradigm of archives as enclosed spaces and sites of power. She wanted her recordings to be available to the Indigenous source communities,

---

música, sino que es un 'record' oral, del mismo modo que el film es un 'record' visual que debe tener múltiples utilizaciones: puede servir al compositor para fines creativos, para programas de radio, como fondo musical en films documentales, etc.; en otras palabras es un documento que va a ser oído y escuchado por grandes grupos humanos y no debe ser encerrado en bibliotecas y museos para el uso exclusivo de los técnicos y científicos."

[81] Sterne (2003: 223).
[82] This is the subtitle to Sterne's (2003) book.
[83] Hochman (2014: xxiii).
[84] Feld and Brenneis (2004); Feld (2015a).
[85] Feld (2015b).

and she wanted them to be available to broader audiences in Mexico and in the United States.

Even after Yurchenco returned to the United States in 1946, she continued to work on III affairs—above all, overseeing the copying of her field recordings at the Library of Congress and their transfer to Mexico. She continued to receive paychecks from Mexico for the work she had completed. Gamio wrote warmly to her in Connecticut, where she was visiting family: "Precisely now that you are far is when I am realizing more the efficient labor that you were undertaking for this Institute with the energy, seriousness and good results that you got us accustomed to and that unfortunately is not found with all collaborators. I trust that some time we will have you with us again."[86] For her part, Yurchenco wrote, "Mexico is my second home and I love it very dearly. Life in the States is hard and at times almost unkind."[87] Gamio signed his letters to her with abbreviated versions of the genteel, effusive diplomatic language of the time: "De usted Afmo. Atto. Amigo y S. S." was short for "from your affectionate and attentive friend and sure servant."[88]

Yurchenco was proud of her achievements and later wrote to Gamio from Washington: "Yesterday, while at the Library of Congress I tested the records out and found to my utter surprise that in spite of technical difficulties which I had on the expedition, the results are excellent. The engineers say they are the best yet."[89] She was not immune, however, to gaps in documentation. After she had returned to the United States, her Mexico City collaborators repeatedly asked her to send captions for the photos taken during an expedition.[90] When frustrated with the bureaucratic complications of the Mexican government in fulfilling her payment contract, Yurchenco suggested she would withhold information or services, thereby jeopardizing the project outcomes. During this time, she was also overwhelmed with the challenges of living in the United States with a shortage of housing and rapidly rising prices in the immediate aftermath of World War II.[91]

The project was concluded at the beginning of 1947, with copies of recordings and extra blanks finally in their proper destinations, along with

[86] Gamio to Yurchenco, December 17, 1946, "Propaganda de Radio, México, 1945–1947," AHIII.
[87] Yurchenco to Gamio, October 13, 1946, File "Propaganda de Radio, México, 1945–1947," AHIII.
[88] Gamio to Yurchenco, January 6, 1947. File "Propaganda de Radio, México, 1945–1947," AHIII.
[89] Yurchenco to Gamio, October 1, 1946, File "Propaganda de Radio, México, 1945–1947," AHIII.
[90] Gamio to Yurchenco, October 3, 1946, File "Propaganda de Radio, México, 1945–1947," AHIII.
[91] Yurchenco to Gamio, September 23, 1946, File "Propaganda de Radio, México, 1945–1947," AHIII.

recording equipment which was generally returned to the United States.[92] The order of international affairs had shifted considerably since the project had begun in 1941. The United Nations system began to take shape at the end of the war in 1945, including the establishment of UNESCO. Charles Seeger had expressed discontent at the displacement of international cultural policy development from the Americas to Europe, but he did his best to channel collaborators and professional allies into the new system.[93] Others moved through their own networks to UNESCO. In 1948, Torres Bodet, the Mexican Secretary of Public Education with whom Yurchenco had worked on the III project, moved to Paris to take over as Secretary General of UNESCO. Despite the geographical and ideological distance of distinct paradigms of heritage, these actors from the Americas recognized the cultural diversity of their societies and did not take Europe to be an ideal paradigm. On a global scale, the lines of influence were not continuous from the 1940s to the 1990s, but inter-American paradigms undoubtedly contributed to national cultural policies in the Americas, which came back into play with global heritage discourses in the 1990s.[94]

Legacies

In Mexico, Yurchenco is recognized as a pioneer and "precursor of field recordings of Indigenous music."[95] We must also recognize that Yurchenco entered into a national context of Indigenous music research in Mexico which was already in process from the 1920s.[96] Yurchenco moved fluidly across the class and racial hierarchies that created the conditions of possibility for her research. It is a tribute to her ethics and social graces that she treated people of all social statuses with warmth and respect. However, her approach impeded

---

[92] Some later projects overseen by Seeger at the Pan American Union enabled collaborating countries to keep the equipment. Yurchenco to Gamio, October 13, 1946, File "Propaganda de Radio, México, 1945–1947," AHIII.

[93] These included Gustavo Durán, Vannet Lawler, and Luiz Heitor Corrêa de Azevedo, all of whom had worked closely with Seeger in the PAU (Pernet 2007: 153). For more on Corrêa de Azevedo's documentary work in Brazil affiliated with the PAU and the US Library of Congress, see Barros (2013).

[94] Future scholarship may be able to track the influence of actors such as Torres Bodet, Gustavo Durán, and Luiz Heitor Corrêa de Azevedo in the early years of UNESCO.

[95] Castillo (2003).

[96] Key figures included Francisco Domínguez, Ignacio Fernández Esperón, and Concepción (Concha) Michel (CENIDIM 2016, Alonso 2008). One of the most frequent Mexican contributors to inter-American music publications was Vicente Mendoza, a composer, pianist and folklorist who had carried out research on Otomí music in the Mezquital Valley in 1936.

a structural critique of the positioning of her colleagues and benefactors in the United States and Mexico. As a mediator between the Mexican and US governments, Yurchenco had more opportunities to direct expeditions, sometimes relegating experienced Mexican researchers to the position of assistant.[97] Yurchenco's cross-cultural engagements were not as politically transformative as they could have been. Giraudo suggests that Anne Chapman, another US expatriate working for the III at the same time, made more political demands on behalf of Indigenous and peasant communities, leading to tensions with Gamio. Chapman's assigned mission was to study a parasitic illness in Chiapas. Gamio apparently thought Chapman was going too far in writing letters to regional authorities criticizing the exploitation and marginalization of impoverished communities and making concrete demands based on community meetings. These tensions contrast with the close and protective relationship between Gamio and Yurchenco.[98]

In the United States, Yurchenco is often considered a pioneer of "applied ethnomusicology," but her impact also needs to be viewed in relation to an earlier paradigm of "applied anthropology," which Collier and Gamio institutionalized in the 1930s and 1940s in the United States and Mexico. This applied anthropology (like state-sponsored indigenismo) was a bureaucratic system for managing marginalized populations within modernizing nation-states. Yurchenco broke apart its rigid categories, its dry functionalist analyses, and its hierarchies of value. Hers was a deeply engaged, bottom-up approach to human aesthetics informed by keen listening, eclectic creativity, and zest for life. Yurchenco departed from the objectives of academic folklorists and bureaucratic officials in her music recordings. She wanted to keep her recordings circulating in the popular sphere, and she released many of her field recordings from around the world on commercial labels. Over time, her work linked 1930s radio and recordings, which were beginning to articulate a notion of "world music," to the World Music industry of the late twentieth century. For example, Yurchenco's Nonesuch album *The Real Mexico in Music and Song*, originally released in 1966, was rereleased in 2003 in the Nonesuch "Explorer Series." The quest for authenticity in field recording was reframed for World Music listeners of the new millennium. But Yurchenco also kept in mind more local and regional listeners. She

---

[97] This was the case with Raúl Guerrero, who served as an assistant to Yurchenco in a 1942 expedition to the Valle Del Mezquital (Gottfried 2017: 11, Bitrán Goren 2018: 4, Yurchenco 1943).
[98] Giraudo (2022: 181,192).

continued to travel to Mexico periodically into her eighties, bringing copies of recordings to some of the communities she had known for sixty years.[99]

Yurchenco's interventions should not obscure the overall structure of the III music projects. One of the common threads in this history is the technological mediation of field recording which turned music into a new kind of object, authentically representing particular peoples and places, but also facilitating their detachment from those social contexts and their accumulation in archives. Archives were supposed to be resources for objective social science and for folklorization and nationalization of marginalized groups within the framework of state policy. As we have seen in this chapter, archives also became a resource through which non-Indigenous composers used Indigenous music for new compositions. There was often a slippage between representation and reproduction in these discourses, which put art music compositions on a higher realm of artistic creation.

The key legacy of these music projects was the establishment of field recording as a site of aural experimentation and archival production. The link between Indigenous authenticity and field recording had consequences for disciplinary paradigms. Gottfried Hesketh points out that after the introduction of the sound recorder, most Mexican researchers stopped making aural transcriptions in their fieldwork, even when they did not have equipment or supplies to make recordings. This new approach to research did not involve a total abandonment of transcription. Researchers in Mexico, as in the United States and Europe, continued to adapt staff notation to represent Indigenous music, but the site of transcription was often relocated from the Indigenous community to a laboratory or archive in a metropolitan location.[100] While aural transcription in fieldwork was the product of repeated interaction between the researcher and the music-maker, the new "scientific" transcriptions resulted from interaction between the researcher and the playback device. Indigenous music had to pass through the recording device to become an authentic and authorized source for the constitution of national heritage or scientific data.

Ideologies of authenticity—of the real and the original—acquire new forms in contemporary archives and in professional methodologies for preservation and listening. Yurchenco's recordings are considered testimonies

---

[99] Archived photographs of her visit to the P'urhépecha community of San Lorenzo in 2002 suggest the warm feelings between Henrietta, the composer Juan Victoriano (also in his eighties at the time), and his family (Fondo Henrietta Yurchenco, CENART).

[100] Gottfried Hesketh (2010: 37).

representing Indigenous cultures, as well as vestiges of technologies from the past.[101] Often, the technologies of that time period resulted in audio quality that sounds distorted compared to recordings of today. Considering the fragility of the discs and their technological limitations, it is surprising that many discs or at least copies of them survived. The protocol of the III-sponsored projects in Mexico was to send the original discs (some of which had a glass base) from Mexico to the US Library of Congress, which would return copies to the partner institutions in Mexico.

The Mexican institution that is the primary heir to Yurchenco's early music recordings is CENIDIM, which stands for the Carlos Chávez Center of Musical Research and Documentation. In 2013, CENIDIM launched a project to digitize the 1940s copies of Yurchenco's recordings, in conjunction with UNESCO intangible heritage recognition as "Memory of the World." This is a clear example of inter-American heritage discourse from the 1940s feeding into global heritage discourse of the twenty-first century. The proposal for this project refers to the discs using the marvelous term "sonorous documents." CENIDIM transferred these sonorous documents to the Fonoteca Nacional (the National Recording Archive), which had equipment and specialists who could restore and digitize the recordings. When I began communicating with the teams at the Fonoteca Nacional in the fall of 2020, I learned about the laborious work they had undertaken, in collaboration with CENIDIM, to catalog, restore, and digitize the recordings. They conducted research to determine the needles to use for playback, and the speed at which to digitize the recordings, based on information, for example, about the age and gender of the singer.

Curiously, the first recordings that Yurchenco made in Michoacán were not found in the collection at CENIDIM. The originals were still in the Library of Congress in Washington, but the challenges of communicating across languages and institutions led archivists in Mexico to believe the recordings had been lost. I connected them to staff at the American Folklife Center at the Library of Congress, who put the early Yurchenco recordings in queue for digitization. As the Mexico City archivists drew others into our email chains, Octavio Murillo Alvarez de la Cadena, an archivist at the National Institute of Indigenous Peoples, found DAT copies of the missing Michoacán recordings. The significance of this part of the story has to do

[101] Fonoteca Nacional, CENIDIM, PUIC (2015). See also the website devoted to the Yurchenco collection, "Micrositio—Henrietta Yurchenco, https://fonotecanacional.gob.mx/yurchenco (accessed June 4, 2023).

with the ongoing quandaries of technologies of reproduction, the continued migration of formats in archival preservation, the proliferation of copies on various media formats, and the challenges of keeping track of all these copies within and across institutions. It was a thrill to witness the reactivation of networks between the Library of Congress and the stewards of Yurchenco's collections in Mexico City, almost eighty years after the beginning of their collaboration.

In 1942, when Gamio was writing about the III radio programs, he thought that the non-Indigenous public would much prefer indigenista compositions rather than field recordings of Indigenous music. On the contrary, these projects increased public interest in recordings of Indigenous music. Today, these discs provoke desires for listening with ears of the past. The technology of mechanical reproduction, as Walter Benjamin wrote, sparks feelings of intimacy and proximity that appear to bridge temporal, cultural, and geographic distance.[102] Nevertheless, we should not forget the cultural processes that mediate between the moment of recording in the past and the moment in which we now listen to these recordings. Even more important is the recognition that there are still different ways of hearing, and that the descendants of those whose voices were recorded can have a very different relation to these sonorous documents.

Viewed broadly, inter-American indigenismo was a means to negotiate the form and status of cultural heterogeneity as a bridge between the past and the future. "Por el indio, se salvará la América" is a quote that the indigenistas attributed to José Martí in their radio broadcasts. It may be a paraphrase of Martí's essay "Nuestra América," which made ambiguous reference to "estos hijos de nuestra América, que ha de salvarse con sus indios" ("these children of our America, who must be saved along with her Indians").[103] Indigenista leaders recognized that their national futures were bound together with the futures of subordinated populations. In their revalorization of Indigenous cultures, they pushed back against European racial hierarchies and a unilinear notion of human progress. Much more than their counterparts in the

---

[102] See Benjamin's classic essay "The Work of Art in the Age of Mechanical Reproduction" ([1935] 1968).

[103] This is David Frye's translation of the phrase from José Martí's essay, as quoted in *Writing across Cultures* (Rama [1982] 2012: 89). The III apparently avoided reproducing the second half of Martí's sentence which excoriated the United States for its destructive policies toward Native Americans. In Esther Allen's translation, it reads: "These sons of our America, which must save herself through her Indians, and which is going from less to more, who desert her and take up arms in the armies of North America, which drowns its own Indians in blood and is going from more to less!" (Martí 2002: 289).

United States, Latin American indigenistas foregrounded mixture and coexistence rather than total assimilation or segregation. But indigenistas of the III, from North and South, assumed that it was their duty and right to direct the changes they deemed fit for Indigenous peoples—changes that would connect the past to the future in a trajectory of modernizing progress. Most did not listen well enough to discern the makings of future social movements in which Indigenous peoples would draw on their own histories to intervene more powerfully as political actors combining local, regional, national, and international networks in new ways, and forging alternative relations between the past and the future.

3

Folklore, Region, and Revolution in Nicaragua

The Nicaraguan government ratified the Pátzcuaro Convention creating the Inter-American Indian Institute (III) on December 27, 1941, following a brief period of pro-Indian legislation in Nicaragua in the 1930s.[1] The Nicaraguan National Indian Institute was created in 1943 by President Anastasio Somoza García's executive decree. Anastasio Somoza García was the first in a line of Somoza dictators who ruled Nicaragua from 1936 until the Revolution of 1979. The early directors and executive committee members of the National Indian Institute were generally close associates of the Somozas and members of prominent families from western Nicaragua. The majority had official positions in government ministries, while also maintaining careers in law, medicine, engineering, history, and literature. The institute published a journal, *Nicaragua Indígena*, periodically from 1946 until around 1970, which included essays on Indigenous history and culture, as well as reports and policy statements associated with the larger inter-American network.

In Nicaragua, indigenista networks of the 1940s built on an earlier cultural movement called the Vanguardia. Beginning in the late 1920s, Nicaraguan intellectuals loosely grouped as the Vanguardia explored how they saw and heard the nation in their writings, especially poetry and essays, which were published in newspapers, magazines, and books.[2] They grappled with the legacies of the two most famous Nicaraguans who came before them, Rubén Darío and Augusto C. Sandino—both revolutionaries in different ways, with transnational influences and impacts. Though most members of the Vanguardia were from elite backgrounds, the prominence of folk poetry in Nicaragua created dynamic relations between the literary and the popular.

[1] *La Gaceta Diario Oficial* (1942: 301). Thanks to Bernard Gordillo for locating the original source and correcting the date of ratification.
[2] Strictly speaking, the movement of the Nicaraguan Vanguardia took shape between 1927 and 1933, according to Arellano (1969). Though members of the Vanguardia went in different directions in the 1930s, I continue other authors' practice of using the term Vanguardia for their later writings, as well.

Indigenous Audibilities. Amanda Minks, Oxford University Press. © Oxford University Press 2024.
DOI: 10.1093/oso/9780197532485.003.0004

The figurative language of poetry also made it a powerful tool of political critique under authoritarian governance, enabling the collective imagining of other paths beyond the letter of the law. These poet-folklorists published collections of songs, stories, prayers, and other oral genres, but I focus more in this chapter on the literary essays they wrote about Indigenous folklore. Their essays included many descriptions of sound and music, presumably filtered through their own methods of aural transcription, less tied to musical training than in the last chapter. It was clear from the Vanguardia's discourse that they considered these literary writings as forms of collection—ways of taking stock of local and regional cultures as patrimonial resources. Their approach was captured in the term *acervo*, which can mean "cultural treasure" as well as "archival collection." As with all patrimonial discourses, close examination of this literature reveals tensions between what is included and what is excluded in the treasures of the nation.

The Mexican Revolution had repercussions throughout the Americas and specifically for Nicaragua, as a fertile ground for thinking about the role of Indigenous peoples and folk or popular culture in the construction of the nation. However, Jeffrey Gould draws out the contrast between ideologies of *mestizaje*—cultural/racial mixture—in Mexico and its variants in Central America:

> Although formally similar to the Mexican discourse in its praise of the historical contribution of Indians to the nation, the middle isthmus version of mestizaje effaced Indigenous communities from modern history with the violent bursts and silent fumes of ethnocide. In contrast to the Mexican case, by 1940 official and popular discourse in El Salvador, Honduras, and Nicaragua not only described their societies as mestizo, they posited that Indians had ceased to exist at some forgotten time in the deepest recesses of historical memory.[3]

At stake here is the placement of Indigenous peoples in national histories, and the consequences of this placement for political activity. Gould argues that in Central America, hegemonic discourses pushed Indigenous peoples further back into the distant past while erasing them from the recent past and present. As we saw in the last chapter, the inter-American structure of indigenismo also weakened the potential for Indigenous

[3] Gould (1998: 167).

communities to gain a strong voice in national affairs. This was even more extreme in Nicaragua than in Mexico, in line with Gould's argument. But in this chapter, I provide a more nuanced interpretation of the relationship between mestizaje and indigeneity, suggesting that the silencing of Indigenous voices was not complete.

From the beginnings of the modern nation-state in Europe, the construction of national culture and folklore was always a selective process.[4] Like many countries of Central America, the Nicaraguan nation-state encompassed territories with very different histories of Indigenous and Afro-descendant peoples, as well as different histories of colonial conquest. Both hegemonic and resistant movements of Nicaraguan nationalism constructed different representations of Indigenous culture in the western and eastern regions of the country, a division most often glossed in historical texts as the Pacific and the Atlantic. The Atlantic Coast was part of the Caribbean rim, and it was historically shaped by a British protectorate called the Mosquitia. In the 1940s, indigenistas identified the Atlantic Coast as the site of primitive indigeneity. They considered folklore to be absent or degenerate on the Atlantic Coast, while they embraced Indigenous folklore of the Pacific region as national heritage.

These different modes of positioning ironically opened up the possibility for those excluded from national belonging—communities of the eastern littoral—to maintain stronger claims to land and culture. Indigenous communities of both western and eastern Nicaragua became political protagonists through armed conflict in the 1970s and 1980s, but those in eastern Nicaragua were able to leverage conflicts into legal frameworks for autonomy—however incomplete and flawed they turned out to be. Discourses of Indigenous arts and heritage on both sides of the country were shaped by transnational networks. Examining aurality in this context shows that elite inscriptions of subaltern voices included characteristics that could not be completely controlled or repressed within their ideological frame. Thus, the possibility emerges for hearing traces of political subjectivities among the peoples who had been rejected and silenced in the initial construction of a national culture.

[4] Bauman and Briggs (2003); Bendix (1997).

Indigeneity and Revolutionary Roots

In the early 1920s, as the dust settled from the Mexican Revolution, Augusto C. Sandino left his native town in western Nicaragua to work in the oil fields of Tampico, on the eastern coast of Mexico. Sandino (1895–1934) was the son of an Indigenous woman and a Spanish-descendant man, and he would become well known throughout the hemisphere for fighting against the US Marine occupation of Nicaragua from 1927 to 1933.[5] As an illegitimate child of a powerful landholder, Sandino grew up partly with his mother, under-taking heavy labor in the coffee plantations, and partly on the margins of his father's family, where he was treated more as a servant than a son. Sandino's move to Mexico introduced him to the ideologies of the Mexican Revolution and its relevance to Nicaragua, as well as an eclectic mix of mystical spiritu-ality and political philosophy.[6]

In 1926, Sandino returned to Nicaragua to join a Liberal revolt against the US-supported Conservative government. The Liberal army received military aid from Mexico, aiming to spread the ideals of representative government, modernizing capitalism, and the separation of church and state, but Liberal party leaders ultimately backed down from a confrontation with the US Marines.[7] Sandino split from the Liberal command and became a renegade general leading a popular nationalist army against the US Marines. In doing so, he became a symbol of anti-imperialist struggle in Latin America, win-ning the support of leftists across the continent.[8] Sandino fought on behalf of the "Indo-Hispanic" race, with which he identified. Some Comunidades Indígenas took advantage of the political instability to advance their collec-tive demands, but this was not part of Sandino's struggle.[9] His nationalist project assumed the necessity of cultural assimilation.[10]

The US Marines withdrew from Nicaragua in 1933 following the mandate of Franklin D. Roosevelt's Good Neighbor Policy. Sandino halted his mil-itary operations and entered into negotiations with Nicaragua's President

[5] The US Marines occupied Nicaragua between 1912 and 1934, with a brief interruption in the 1920s.
[6] Hodges (1986: 5). For more recent biographies of Sandino, see Bendaña (2016) and Wunderlich (1995).
[7] Hodges (1986: 8).
[8] Hodges (1986: 95–97).
[9] Gould (1998: 155–157). Comunidad Indígena, "Indigenous Community," was a legal term that applied to specific people/places in the Pacific region with claims and sometimes titles to Indigenous land stretching back to the colonial period.
[10] Gould (1998: 159).

Juan Bautista Sacasa, including a demand for the dissolution of the National Guard because of its close ties to the US military. Leaving a meeting at the Presidential Palace in 1934, Sandino was assassinated on orders from the head of the National Guard, Anastasio Somoza García, an ambitious leader whose family would control Nicaragua for the next forty-five years.

The influence of the Mexican Revolution in Sandino's guerrilla movement was iconically audible in corridos sung by his soldiers that had new lyrics set to classic Mexican corrido melodies.[11] Sandino's military operations were strongest in the northern mountains of the Segovias, and these corridos were most widely heard and remembered in the northern regions. In his 1946 book *Romances y Corridos Nicaragüenses*, the Nicaraguan poet and folklorist Ernesto Mejía Sánchez wrote:

> The people of Mexico and Guatemala also sang corridos to general Sandino, and the melody of "La Adelita" gave life to many Sandinista "songs," which proves a common brotherhood and protest among the peoples of América, when one of them has been unjustly knocked down.[12]

Mejía Sánchez used the term *América* in the sense of Latin America, highlighting a perception of common bonds among Latin America countries. This passage also suggests some sympathy with Sandino's cause. But a few lines later, he writes,

> In general the political corridos are less sung [in Nicaragua today], since the people, who naïvely have believed in the "revolutions" and the parties that they represented, have forgotten them with contempt, because these "revolutions" and "parties" have systematically betrayed the people, they have exploited and debased them. The Nicaraguan political corrido has not yet been written. The people will produce political corridos and will keep them on their lips when the "revolution" that they sing about signifies their dignity and justice. The people of Nicaragua wait for that revolution.[13]

---

[11] The corrido is a narrative genre that became popular in Mexico in the revolutionary period, when it served as a popular form of journalism in providing news and commentary about current events. On the Sandinista corridos in Nicaragua, see Landau (1999: 127–134).

[12] "El pueblo de México y Guatemala también cantó corridos al general Sandino y la melodía de 'La Adelita' dió vida a muchas 'canciones' sandinistas, lo que prueba una común hermandad y protesta entre los pueblos de América, cuando alguno de ellos ha sido injustamente atropellado" (Mejía Sánchez 1946: 24).

[13] "En general los corridos políticos son los que menos se cantan, ya que el pueblo, que ingenuamente ha creído en las 'revoluciones' y partidos que ellas representaban, los ha olvidado con

Mejía Sánchez's text posits a rejection of the past and an anticipation of a new revolutionary future. This trajectory presumes the forgetting of political songs, and then the writing of new ones, kept "on the lips," ready for action and oral irruptions. Sandino was not, in fact, forgotten, and neither were the songs about him.[14]

Nicaragua Indígena and the Vanguardia

At the time of the founding of the National Indian Institute in 1943, President Anastasio Somoza García acknowledged the culture of the popular classes while generally privileging the interests of the elites.[15] A common focus on the distant past, or on quaint folkloric practices perceived to be in decline, enabled Somoza to nurture nationalist sentiment while flooding Nicaraguan media with US products.[16] Somoza's rise to power also depended on strategic support for the labor movement and its forms of popular culture from the late 1930s to the late 1940s, until it escaped his control and became subject to repression.[17] Somocista forces established some strategic alliances with western Comunidades Indígenas in an attempt to establish political hegemony and keep rival powers in check. The publication of *Nicaragua Indígena* spanned a period of government repression and censorship as well as increasing opposition, including such events as a coup attempt in 1954, the assassination of Anastasio Somoza García in 1956, military assaults on student protesters in 1959, and the government's ongoing assassinations of political dissidents. In 1961, a socialist guerrilla organization took the name of Sandino, the Frente Sandinista de Liberación Nacional (FSLN), with the objective of overthrowing the Somoza dictatorship and the rigid class structure

desprecio, porque estas 'revoluciones' y 'partidos' sistemáticamente han traicionado el pueblo, lo han explotado y envilecido. El corrido político nicaragüense está por escribirse. El pueblo producirá corridos políticos y los conservará en sus labios cuando la 'revolución' que ellos canten, signifique su dignidad y su justicia. El pueblo de Nicaragua espera esa revolución" (Mejía Sánchez 1946: 24).

[14] Scruggs (1994: 370); Landau (1999: 131). An example of a corrido about Sandino is the song "Que se derramen las copas," performed and recorded by Don Felipe Urrutia y Sus Cachorros (accessible via Youtube videos). Felipe de Jesús Urrutia Delgadillo (1918–2014) grew up in a campesino family in northern Nicaragua where Sandino's army was most active. He traveled around Nicaragua working as a cowboy and horse wrangler, attending parties and baptisms along the way. Interviews with him and his family emphasize that he engaged in processes of listening, remembering, and compiling long before he became an active performer with his sons in the 1970s.
[15] Whisnant (1995: 118).
[16] Whisnant (1995: 121).
[17] Gould (1990: 15).

of Nicaraguan society. These tumultuous events rarely emerged in the pages of *Nicaragua Indígena*, with the exception of a 1956 issue that memorialized Anastasio Somoza García following his assassination.

When the Nicaraguan Indian Institute was founded, another movement of Indigenous cultural recuperation was already in process through the work of Nicaraguan poets and folklorists. The writing of poetry and the collecting of folklore often went together in the birthplace of the great poet Rubén Darío (1867–1916). Darío founded the Spanish-American literary movement known as *modernismo* and acquired an almost mystical patrimonial status similar to a patron saint in Nicaragua.[18] Darío absorbed the sound, music, and storytelling of his childhood in Nicaragua, as well as the multilingual literary texts he read voraciously in public and private libraries in Nicaragua and in the many other places he lived in Latin America and Europe.[19] Partly inspired by French modernist and surrealist poetry, Darío revitalized Spanish literary language through a sonorous, metaphorical style that contested the materialism of the new bourgeois as well as the prolix formality of classical writers. As an itinerant journalist who wrote chronicles for Spanish language newspapers, Darío was also a close observer of shifts in modern life and communication, such as the popular collecting of postcards.[20]

Some Nicaraguan folklorists participated in the official realm of Indigenous policy as well as the artistic realm of constructing national heritage. Through the middle of the twentieth century, there was not always a clear distinction between the colonial role of *letrado*, managing legal affairs through learned discourses, and *literato*, a literary writer set apart from legal affairs.[21] Several Nicaraguan folklorists had law degrees, and most published writers had intimate connections to political power. Thirty miles from the center of the capital city of Managua, the town of Granada was a key site of literary production as well as conservative politics and power. The Mexican priests teaching at the Colegio Centroamérica, where the Granada elite sent their children for a classical Jesuit education, influenced the development of discourses of Nicaraguan folklore among some of their students. Folklore

[18] Whisnant (1995). To provide an example of the everyday use of Darío: as a foreigner in Nicaragua, I have often benefited from the recitation of Darío's verses by taxi drivers—a pedagogical project on my behalf and a proud display of Nicaraguan patrimony.
[19] Watland (1965) provides an intellectual biography tracing the books that Darío read throughout his life and his use of libraries and other collections.
[20] Reynolds (2016). Zambrano (2020, 2021) analyzes the music, sound, and listening practices in some of Darío's literary works.
[21] This distinction comes from Ramos ([1989] 2001).

could be used for a variety of political projects. The Jesuits who founded the Colegio Centroamérica in Granada in 1916 had been forced out of Mexico during the throes of the Mexican Revolution.[22] They were not part of the leftist currents in Mexican folklore, arts, and education that developed in the 1920s and 1930s.

The Nicaraguan literary movement known as the Vanguardia emerged in the late 1920s as a nationalist quest closely aligned with Hispanism and Catholicism. One of their younger members who would become well known in Spanish American literary circles was Pablo Antonio Cuadra, from a venerated Nicaraguan family stretching back to colonial times. In 1933, at the age of twenty-one, Pablo Antonio Cuadra accompanied his father Carlos Cuadra Pasos, a powerful conservative senator, to the Seventh Pan-American Conference in Montevideo, Uruguay. The trip gave Pablo Antonio Cuadra the opportunity to travel through the southern cone and meet poets and other intellectuals along the way. He carried with him his first book manuscript, *Poemas Nicaragüenses*, which he left with the Editorial Nascimiento in Santiago de Chile to be published the following year. It was a recuperation of the vernacular orality of the Nicaraguan campesino, captured in playful rhyme and meter (see Figure 3.1).[23]

Analyzing works of the Vanguardia from 1930 to 1943, Juan Pablo Gómez has argued that these writers were responding to two powerful alternatives in the international sphere: on one side, the materialism and imperialism of the United States, and on the other side, Marxism and leftist currents of *indigenismo* such as those promoted by artists and intellectuals in Mexico and Peru. The Vanguardia's response involved a strong embrace of the history and authority of Hispanism and Catholicism, which took on a particular gendered cast.[24] As Gómez writes:

This model of authority and power operated in complicity with a structure of gender. The subjects of action, the protagonists of history, whether it be the conquest, colonial or national history—are men from the cultural group of the conquistadores or their descendants. The power of the men derives from a sacred, divine, Catholic power. The sacralization of power is connected to the principle of cultural authority: the authority of the

[22] Alvarado Martínez (2010).
[23] Solís Cuadra (2008: 34).
[24] Gómez (2015); Gobat (2013).

Figure 3.1 The Nicaraguan poet Pablo Antonio Cuadra at his typewriter. Pablo Antonio Cuadra Papers, Benson Latin American Collection, University of Texas at Austin.

conquistador and the governor proceeds from a genealogical route that leads them toward God.[25]

This centering of patriarchal Catholic masculinity came through even in mundane communications. In correspondence from the Argentine press which published some of Cuadra's work in the 1930s, Susana Calandrelli wrote to Cuadra, "I am grateful for your 'strong friendship in Christ,' as you

[25] "Este patrón de autoridad y poder operó en complicidad con una estructura de género. Los sujetos de la acción, los protagonistas de la historia—ya sea de conquista, colonial o nacional—son hombres del grupo cultural de los conquistadores o sus descendientes. El poder de los hombres deriva de un poder sacro, divino, católico. La sacralización del poder está conectada al principio de autoridad cultural: la autoridad del conquistador y del gobernador procede de una ruta genealógica que los conduce hasta dios" (Gómez 2015: 78).

say; and at the same time I send you mine, no less strong in spite of being feminine. In Christ all friendships are virile."[26]

Gómez's study is focused on the Reactionary period of the Vanguardia writers, when they looked toward the model of the caudillo (such as Somoza or Franco) for a strong political and cultural authority. Though the gendered and spiritual dimensions of this kind of authority were enduring in Nicaragua, the specific political affiliations of Vanguardia members shifted over time.[27] They initially supported Sandino's guerrilla campaign against the US Marine occupation, but the group fragmented and moved in different directions with the rise of the Somoza dictatorship. One of the Vanguardia members, Manolo Cuadra, became an early critic of Somoza and was forcibly confined to Little Corn Island on the Caribbean coast as a mode of exile.[28] Pablo Antonio Cuadra initially supported Somoza, but he became disillusioned with the actual practice of dictatorship (both of Somoza in Nicaragua and Franco in Spain).[29] As Pablo Antonio Cuadra aligned with the opposition and worked as a journalist, Somoza targeted him with various repressive measures in the late 1930s and early 1940s. In 1945, Cuadra went into voluntary exile in Mexico for a period of four years.[30]

In the early 1940s, Vanguardia members looked to folklore as a source of renewal in national culture. Their collecting impulses came together in the work of the Taller San Lucas (Saint Luke Workshop), a Granada-based collective of poets and folklorists founded in 1942. Three members of the Vanguardia took the lead in publishing a cultural journal, *El Cuaderno del Taller San Lucas* (The Notebook of the St. Luke Workshop): Pablo Antonio Cuadra, his younger cousin Salvador Cardenal Argüello, and Ernesto Mejía Sánchez (see Figure 3.2). Other members of the San Lucas cofradía or "brotherhood" included Carlos Cuadra Pasos (father of Pablo Antonio Cuadra), Ángel Martínez, José Coronel Urtecho, Francisco Pérez Estrada, and Ernesto Cardenal. This list reveals intimate family linkages, cross-generational bonds,

---

[26] "Le agradezco su 'fuerte amistad en Cristo,' como dice; y yo a la vez le envío la mía, no menos fuerte a pesar de ser feminina. En Cristo todas las amistades son viriles." Susana Calandrelli to Pablo Antonio Cuadra, 1938, Pablo Antonio Cuadra Papers, Correspondence, Box 2, File 53, BLAC.

[27] See Monte and Gómez (2020) for a trenchant analysis of the connections between historic and contemporary techniques of patriarchy and authoritarian governance.

[28] Delgado Aburto (2002); Minks (2020b).

[29] Solís Cuadra (2008).

[30] Solís Cuadra (2008: 36). Ernesto Mejía Sánchez helped Pablo Antonio Cuadra get connected in Mexico and shared Cuadra's poetry with Jaime Torres Bodet, the director of the Secretariat of Public Education who was mentioned in Chapter 2. Torres Bodet to Mejía Sánchez, July 5, 1949, Pablo Antonio Cuadra Papers, Correspondence, 1935–2002, Box 4, File 9, BLAC.

Figure 3.2 Frontispiece, *Cuaderno del Taller San Lucas*. Benson Latin American Collection, University of Texas at Austin.

and political fluidity, as close relatives ended up on opposite sides of the political spectrum, but then sometimes came back together over the course of their lives. José Coronel Urtecho, for example, had fascist tendencies in the 1930s, but became a supporter of the Sandinistas later in life. His nephew Ernesto Cardenal, a priest and renowned poet, was always more left-leaning and became the Minister of Culture in the revolutionary government of the 1980s.[31]

Between 1942 and 1951, the Taller San Lucas published five volumes of the Cuaderno. At the end of the first volume, they stated in capital letters: "OUR NOTEBOOKS ARE NOT INTENDED AS MAGAZINES. THEY ARE

[31] Ángel Martínez, who is lesser known than the other authors mentioned, was a Jesuit priest, poet, and teacher at the Colegio Centroamérica, a renowned high school in Granada which educated the best known poets and folklorists of the era. Salvador Cardenal Argüello also spoke of the vital impact of this school, where he discovered the convergence of folklore and nationalism through his studies with Mexican Jesuit teachers. See Arellano ([1966] 1986: 76); Barrera Narvaez (1997: 10).

VOLUMES OF A LIBRARY OF NICARAGUAN CATHOLIC CULTURE."[32] This conceptual library was a framework for collecting, codifying, and preserving a specific notion of authoritative heritage: "We aspire to publish for Nicaragua the most complete collection of our literature and popular arts. We possess substantial and invaluable materials in the archives of the Workshop."[33]

For these writers with literary orientations, folklore was a means of rediscovering an orality rooted in Nicaraguan heritage. The literary and historical scholar Pedro Xavier Solís Cuadra, who is also the grandson of Pablo Antonio Cuadra, has emphasized the Vanguardia's quest to bridge "popular and learned language in the face of the decline of the modernist tradition." Their search for national identity, he writes, was connected "to the rich heritage (*acervo*) of the spontaneity and freshness of popular song."[34] Some folklorists in this circle made sound recordings, but in his notes Pablo Antonio Cuadra advocated a methodology of careful transcription from oral recitation:

> Note: to collect these things of life and expressions of the people, aim to be faithful, radically faithful to what is dictated by the people, not correcting anything but rather copying exactly what is said and how it is said. As the case may be, look for the subject who appears most knowledgeable, and have that person dictate what has been heard or sung spontaneously.[35]

In this methodology, which is also an ideology of fidelity and authenticity, there is a slippage between performance and memory. Cuadra appears to emphasize going to the source of popular utterance, but then immediately refers to a local mediator—"the most knowledgeable"—who would recite from memory "what has been heard or sung" to be transcribed by the folklorist. The new folkloric archive that was emerging would be based on aural

---

[32] *Cuaderno del Taller San Lucas*, Vol. 1 (1942: 179). "Nuestros 'cuadernos' no tienen intención de revista. Son tomos de una biblioteca de cultura católica nicaragüense."

[33] *Cuaderno del Taller San Lucas*, Vol. 1 (1942: 179). "Aspiramos publicar para Nicaragua la colección más completa de nuestra literatura y artes populares. Poseemos un cuantioso y valiosísimo material en los archivos del Taller."

[34] Solís Cuadra (2001: 21). See also Arellano (1997: 40–41).

[35] "Nota: para recoger estas cosas de la vida y expresiones mismas del pueblo, procúrese ser fiel, radicalmente fiel al dictado del pueblo, no corrigiendo nada sino copiando exactamente lo que dice y tal como lo dice. Para esto búsquese, según el caso, al sujeto que parezca más conocedor y que a éste dicte lo que ya se ha oído decir o cantar espontáneamente." Pablo Antonio Cuadra Collection of Literary Materials, Binder Cuadernos del Taller San Lucas, BLAC.

embodied memory, but the knowledgeable people who were the sources were usually obscured in the Cuadernos.[36]

Members of the Taller San Lucas were also interested in the dynamic relations among music, language, theater, visual arts, folklore, and history. They included in the Cuadernos musical notation of various songs, and they considered Indigenous pottery as "música palpable" (tangible music).[37] The last volume included plans to support music concerts, radio programs, and an archive for print and recordings. Salvador Cardenal Argüello carried out recording projects in collaboration with the Taller and made plans to produce albums of folk music, setting up an ideology of authenticity through technology. "All the music," he wrote, "will be recorded on a tape recorder (*cinta de magnetefón*) directly from the most pure and autochthonous sources."[38] Recording technology represented a direct channel to cultural essence, obscuring the mediation of researcher and recorder.[39] The Taller did not carry out all these musical plans, but Salvador Cardenal Argüello continued his work recording music throughout the 1950s, 1960s, and 1970s. In 1957 and 1967, Pablo Antonio Cuadra helped Cardenal Argüello to name his radio stations, Radio Centauro and Radio Güegüense, and Cuadra drew the logos for both.[40] Cardenal Argüello promoted both art music and folk music in his radio work (see Figures 3.3 and 3.4).[41]

The editors of the Cuadernos published 500 copies of each volume, 200 of which were sent by Pablo Antonio Cuadra to people and institutions outside of Nicaragua.[42] Correspondence from Argentina asserted the similarity and mutual influence of their projects promoting Hispanic Christianity through folklore.[43] A published accolade from Colombia stated,

[36] Some other Nicaraguan folklorists, for example Ernesto Mejía Sánchez (1946), more often named the person who was the source of collected texts. In the essays published in the *Cuaderno*. the mediation of the writer usually obscured the mediation of the folkloric source in fieldwork.

[37] *Cuaderno de San Lucas* (1951: 79).

[38] *Cuaderno de San Lucas* (1951: 166). "Toda la música ha sido grabada en cinta de magnetofón directamente de las fuentes folklóricas más puras y autóctonas."

[39] Zambrano (2021: 96–103) discusses ideologies of sound fidelity in Nicaragua during this time period, shaped by US advertisements for record players and juke boxes.

[40] Barrera Narvaez (1997).

[41] For more on Nicaraguan art music, see Gordillo (2019, forthcoming) and Gordillo Brockmann (2020a, 2020b).

[42] Arellano (1992: 113).

[43] See letter from the Universidad Nacional de Tucumán to Pablo Antonio Cuadra, April 8, 1943; letter from Instituto de Cooperación Universitario (Buenos Aires) to Pablo Antonio Cuadra, March 27, 1944, Pablo Antonio Cuadra Collection of Nicaraguan Literary Materials, BLAC. Chamosa (2010) discusses the history of the Argentine folklore movement as well as its transnational and ideological connections.

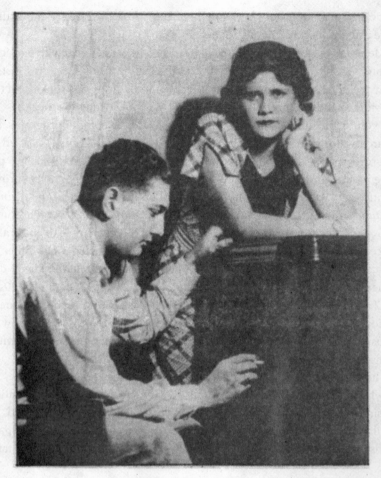

Figure 3.3 Salvador Cardenal Argüello and his wife, Ofelia Vargas, with a radio. Pablo Antonio Cuadra Collection of Nicaraguan Literary Materials, Benson Latin American Collection, University of Texas at Austin.

"Among contemporary publications of our Hispanic America, one would search in vain for something more original and autochthonous than these CUADERNOS . . . It is invigorating and comforting to see in this search for America in oneself, correct responses as profound as these champions of our cultural truth."[44] US destinations of the Cuadernos included the

---

[44] Revista Javeriana (Colombia), cited in *Cuaderno del Taller San Lucas* (1944, vol. 4), back cover.

Figure 3.4 Salvador Cardenal Argüello (left) and Pablo Antonio Cuadra (right) in their youth. Pablo Antonio Cuadra Collection of Nicaraguan Literary Materials, Benson Latin American Collection, University of Texas at Austin.

Pan American Union Library and the Library of Congress in Washington, DC. The Librarian of Congress from 1939 to 1944 was the poet Archibald MacLeish, with whom Pablo Antonio Cuadra exchanged writings.[45]

Another key contact in the United States was the folklorist Ralph Stanley Boggs, who published many articles in Latin American journals and was the husband of the folklorist Edna Garrido from the Dominican Republic. The Taller San Lucas followed Boggs's insistence that true folklore was anonymous and collectively produced through oral transmission. Thus, the songs

"En vano se buscará entre las publicaciones contemporáneas de nuestra América hispana algo más original y autóctono que estos CUADERNOS . . . Es tonificante y confortativo ver en esta busca de América a sí misma, aciertos tan profundos como el de estos campeones de la verdadera cultura nuestra."

[45] In 1944, the US poet Archibald MacLeish, who served as the Librarian of Congress from 1939 to 1944, gratefully acknowledged receipt of a *Cuaderno del Taller San Lucas* as well as Pablo Antonio Cuadra's "Canto Temporal." MacLeish to Cuadra, May 15, 1944, Pablo Antonio Cuadra Papers, Correspondence, Box 6, File 21, BLAC. See White (1993) on the networks and dialogues of Nicaraguan poets with US writers.

of Camilo Zapata—a composer, singer and creator of the "son nica" style in the 1930s—were popular, but they could not be folklore unless they were adapted by the people to the point that they "lost their personal trait."[46] Boggs ultimately affirmed a purist notion of folklore, which "suffers greater suppression and contamination when it comes in greater contact with erudite culture and its grand concentrated and unified social organizations."[47] These ideologies had the consequence of enclosing folklorized subjects, divorcing them from participation in political processes, and leaving the authority of directing political change to the lettered classes.

In the 1940s and 1950s, Cuadra developed a fluid ideology of mestizaje in his essays, in which he negotiated the Indigenous and European influences on Nicaraguan culture. In 1951 he published an artful essay called "El Indio al Pie de la Letra," which might be translated as "The Indian Word for Word," but also plays with the literal meaning, "The Indian at the Foot of the Letter." Cuadra argued for the "rich vitality of that expressive Indigenous substrate" in literature, which he identified as a new kind of consciousness in Nicaragua that had been suppressed in previous eras.[48] Cuadra perceived Indigenous culture as an antidote to the frantic pace of modernity, writing, "The Indian possesses a vital rhythm distinct from the West. That rhythm, burdened by its earthly weight, can serve America as a RESISTANCE, every time that the crazily accelerated movement of 'progress' threatens us with a historic derailment."[49]

Cuadra was also grappling with a deeply felt hybrid subjectivity, as he wrote in *Nicaragua Indígena* in 1954:

> Through a phenomenon very particular to mestizaje, we are accustomed to call "Indian" the type that still conserves the physiognomy which we have more or less arbitrarily determined to be that of the old races.—And we believe that the Indian is that other, without realizing that there is a physiognomy of acts and of feelings, and that if the Indian does not appear on the outside of a person, perhaps it is because the Indian remains within. But we continue being Indians and Spaniards, and history has made it so, sometimes commanded by an invisible cacique [Indigenous leader], other

---

[46] *Cuaderno del Taller San Lucas*, Vol. 4 (1944: 146–147). For a discussion of Camilo Zapata's music in discourses of national culture in Nicaragua, see Scruggs (2002).
[47] Boggs (1943: 86).
[48] Cuadra (1951: 28).
[49] Cuadra (1951: 38).

times commanded by the shadow, from across the seas, of an ancestral conquistador.[50]

Though Cuadra was writing here in collective terms, the union of Spanish conquistador and Indian mother was embodied in his own family line. The family "de la Quadra" was related to the Central American conquistador Juan Vásquez de Coronado, who was the nephew of Francisco Vásquez de Coronado, the famous explorer of the Southwest United States. In the early nineteenth century, Cuadra's great-grandfather, Dionisio de la Quadra, had to defend his mixed Spanish and Indian ancestry to acquire an official position under the Spanish system of "limpieza de sangre."[51] Cuadra later commented on Dionisio's royal appeal: "His defense of mestizaje in this process was a defense of America, of the originality and independence of America."[52] Mixture, here, was tied to American authenticity.

Cuadra demonstrated a plurality and ambivalence in Nicaraguan discourses of mestizaje, and in the heterogeneous formation of Nicaraguan subjectivities. However, this plurality of Nicaraguan mestizaje did not extend to African heritage or to Caribbean/Atlantic Coast cultures. As Sergio Ramírez has written, the subject of Africans and African heritage did sometimes appear in the poetry of the Vanguardia, but the culture of silence around African ancestry in the Pacific region subsumed these literary portrayals.[53]

Both Indigenous and Afro-descendant peoples of the Atlantic Coast remain in the margins of Pablo Antonio Cuadra's imaginaries of national

[50] Cuadra (1954: 18). "Por un fenómeno muy propio del mestizaje acostumbramos llamar 'indio' al tipo que aún conserva la fisonomía, que más o menos arbitrariamente nos hemos fijado, de las viejas razas.—Y creemos que el indio es ese, ese otro, sin fijarnos que hay una fisonomía de los actos y de los sentimientos y que a quien no se le sale el indio hacia fuera, tal vez es porque se le queda dentro; pero que seguimos siendo indios y españoles, y que la historia la hemos hecho, a veces comandados por un invisible cacique, a veces comandados por la sombra ultramarina de un ancestral conquistador."

[51] This legal evaluation of "cleanliness of blood" was initially developed in the fifteenth century to restrict those of Jewish and Arabic ancestry from government and religious posts in the Iberian peninsula.

[52] Quoted in Solís Cuadra (2008: 15). The Nicaraguan literary scholar Jorge Eduardo Arellano also traces his family line to Dionisio de la Quadra, an example of the densely overlapping social, intellectual, and genealogical networks in the analysis of Nicaraguan literary movements, history, and heritage. See Arellano (2017).

[53] Ramírez (2007: 18, 24). Sergio Ramírez is the acclaimed Nicaraguan novelist who participated in the Sandinista Revolution and served as Nicaragua's Vice-President from 1985 to 1990. Ramírez's nonfiction book *Tambor olvidado* (2007) is one of the few works of any discipline to address the impact of African histories in Pacific Nicaragua. He takes the title from the poetry of Luis Alberto Cabrales, who wrote about the African lineage in his own mixed ancestry in his poem "Canto a los sombríos ancestros." Cabrales was associated with the Vanguardia, an important reminder about the potential for heterogenous ideologies. Romero Vargas (1993) made an earlier intervention tracing African histories in Pacific Nicaragua.

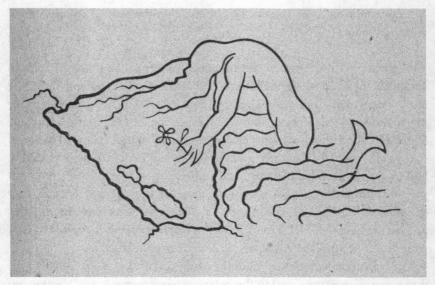

Figure 3.5 Illustration in *El Cuaderno del Taller San Lucas*, 1944, Vol. 4, p. 37. The Escondido River "opens all its arms, like an Indian god, to embrace the sea in many ways" (Carlos Bravo). Benson Latin American Collection, University of Texas at Austin.

heritage and civilization. The majority of writers from the national centers in western Nicaragua used the texts of foreigners as sources to describe the Atlantic Coast of Nicaragua. Pablo Antonio Cuadra had, at least, traveled to the Atlantic Coast in his work as a journalist, and photos of the coast from his personal archive appeared in *Nicaragua Indígena*.[54]

Another writer from western Nicaragua who traveled to the coast was Carlos A. Bravo, known for his use of landscape in narrative writings.[55] In his essay "To the Atlantic Coast among the Clouds," Bravo described his reflections on the coast while traveling there by plane. He offers rich details about the sounds of rivers and birds, creating a cartography with their names. He writes that the Escondido River "opens all its arms, like an Indian god, to embrace the sea in many modes," while a drawing shows a gigantic siren with her fingers and hair forming the rivers moving into the mainland (see Figure 3.5). For Bravo, nature on the eastern coast was full of sound: "There

[54] Ramírez (2007: 17) notes that Cuadra wrote his poem "El Negro" (published in *Poemas Nicaragüenses* in 1933) in the Creole (Afro-Caribbean) towns of Bluefields and Pearl Lagoon.
[55] Arellano ([1966] 1986: 108).

are thousands of sounds. Sometimes it seems that all are quiet and then one hears a creature that may be the ugliest of the forest, but it has the divine gift of song." This essay almost gives the impression that the Atlantic Coast is not inhabited by humans, only rivers and animals. Only when he describes the sky above Hendy Creek, Bravo mentions, "They immortalized the last Miskitu chief—an inexpressive Indian—by giving his name to one of the melancholy tributaries of the most beautiful river in Nicaragua."[56] As in western Nicaragua, sadness is the dominant emotion linked to Indigenous peoples in these representations, which inscribed landscapes and soundscapes with ontologies of difference. The distinct modes of interpreting Indigenous cultures from eastern and western Nicaragua calls for closer examination, in their alternate representation as primitivism *or* patrimony.

Primitivism or Patrimony

The Nicaraguan National Indian Institute located "Indians" and the "Indian problem" on the Atlantic Coast, while the existence of politically active Indigenous communities in Pacific Nicaragua was obscured. This division followed a long history of regional differences in the construction of race and nation in what became Nicaraguan territory at the end of the nineteenth century. Under Spanish colonialism in western Nicaragua, certain Indigenous communities maintained some autonomy through collective political structures, but these were greatly weakened by the early twentieth century. Nicaraguan officials and intellectuals consolidated a vision of the essential mestizo race, descended from distant unions between Spanish fathers and Indian mothers. Promoters of this vision used the Atlantic Coast as a foil, the radical "other" that illustrated the unity of race and culture in western Nicaragua.[57] For Nicaraguan indigenistas of the mid-twentieth century, the "Indian problem" was the perceived backwardness of Atlantic Coast peoples and their lack of integration into the nation-state.

Though named in official discourse *la Costa Atlántica* or simply *la costa*, the eastern littoral was culturally and geographically part of the Caribbean. Prior to its incorporation into the Nicaraguan state in the late nineteenth century,

---

[56] Bravo (1944: 38). The poet Manolo Cuadra had more intimate experience on the Caribbean coast because he was exiled by Somoza on Little Corn Island. See Cuadra (1937); Delgado Aburto (2002); Minks (2020b).

[57] Wolfe (2007: 162).

this region had been subject to the indirect colonialism of England in the seventeenth and eighteenth centuries, and to a US economic enclave beginning in the late nineteenth century. As early as the 1630s, Indigenous people living near the coast had mixed with escaped African slaves and became known as Miskitu—a term that later included other Indigenous communities that spoke the same language.[58] While there were African descendants in western Nicaragua under Spanish colonialism, their numbers were much greater on the eastern coast, due in part to English plantation settlements, and in part to the arrival of formerly enslaved people who had escaped from other colonies. By the early eighteenth century, certain communities of free people of color came to be known as "Creoles" on the Caribbean coast. Though their mixed lineages included European, Indigenous, and African ancestry, Creole cultural practices and forms of identification were predominantly Anglo- and Afro-Caribbean. During the course of the nineteenth century, Creoles displaced Miskitu people from a position of regional power and maintained relatively autonomous communities on the fringes of the British empire.[59] In the late nineteenth and early twentieth centuries, an influx of West Indian and, to a lesser extent, Chinese immigrants mixed with eastern coast communities.[60] The coast was forcibly annexed by the Nicaraguan nation-state in collaboration with the US Marines in 1894, followed by periodic state attempts at cultural assimilation and national integration of coast communities.

The eastern coast became a key site of intervention for the Inter-American Indian Institute and the Nicaraguan state. In 1944, John Collier and Manuel Gamio helped to launch a major health project in Miskitu communities along the Río Coco, which involved an international team of researchers headed by Lieutenant Michel Pijoan of the US Naval Medical Institute. While they professed to support Indigenous communities, officials took a strongly integrationist and assimilationist approach, in this case promoting "modern" and "scientific" medical procedures over the "old magical and barbarous practices of the *sukias*," traditional Miskitu healers.[61] The perceived need to incorporate this region into the Nicaraguan nation-state resulted in another international development project in the mid-1950s. A pilot project in Spanish-based education was launched in the Río Coco region with support from the Nicaraguan Ministry of Education, UNESCO, and

58 Offen (2010).
59 Gordon (1998).
60 Pineda (2001, 2006).
61 Editorial, *Nicaragua Indígena* (1947: 2).

a related international organization based in Pátzcuaro, Mexico.[62] The Río Coco project was aimed not only at linguistic and cultural assimilation into the nation-state; it was also a "civilizing mission" specifically mandated by President Luis Somoza Debayle.[63]

In portraying Indigenous culture on the Atlantic Coast, Nicaraguan indigenistas faced the paradox that Atlantic Coast peoples were supposedly primitive, but many spoke English (rather than Spanish) as a second or even first language, worshipped in Moravian Christian churches (founded by Germans in the mid-nineteenth century), and worked for North American companies. People who identified as Creole or Garifuna were virtually ignored, without any consideration that they may have claims to indigeneity. Whereas Indigenous Miskitu, Sumu, and Rama people on the Atlantic Coast were viewed as a "problem" for national integration and progress, Creole and Garifuna people were completely excluded from the narrative of cultural diversity that was being constructed. The alignment of Creole and Garifuna cultures with Blackness and Afro-Caribbean diasporic networks erased their Indigenous heritage and placed them outside the bounds of Nicaraguan mestizaje.

Music, dance, and artisanship were areas of Indigenous culture that were supposed to be promoted by the inter-American model of indigenismo, but expressive culture from the Atlantic Coast was largely absent from the pages of *Nicaragua Indígena* and other national publications of the period, in marked contrast to Pacific regional folklore. Margarita Gamio de Alba, Manuel Gamio's daughter who headed a III project on Central American Indigenous women in the 1950s, wrote a piece on Miskitu women that was republished in *Nicaragua Indígena* in 1957. Gamio de Alba explains that Miskitu are the product of mixtures between Black, Spanish, Carib, Sumu, Syrian, and Chinese people, but "their culture remains predominantly Indigenous."[64] This in itself was not paradoxical, since the III located indigeneity in cultural rather than racial characteristics. But under the section "Intellectual Manifestations," she wrote of the Miskitu:

---

[62] The *Centro Regional de Educación Fundamental para América Latina* (CREFAL) is an international organization founded in 1950 in Pátzcuaro, Mexico (where the III was founded ten years earlier) as a joint initiative of UNESCO, the Mexican government, and the Organization of American States. The acronym currently stands for *Centro de Cooperación Regional para la Educación de los Adultos en América Latina y el Caribe.*

[63] Editorial, *Nicaragua Indígena* (1957: 5).

[64] Gamio de Alba (1957: 59).

They lack intellectual characteristics and special cultures. They are primitive and they live from what the land offers them. They don't possess a creative art. They don't weave baskets or make objects of leather. The *pipanti* (*pilpan*, canoe) and their house are their maximum creation.[65]

The Mexican tendency to locate Indigenous culture in material collections clearly did not work in this context. The overall ambivalence of the Miskitu position in cultural hierarchies was evident in Gamio de Alba's closing statement: "We can say that the Miskitu are absorbing western civilization as permits their economic situation and proximity to civilized populations, but their level of life is still very primitive."[66]

The representation of Miskitu oral communication was also ambivalent in these discourses, exemplified by the memoirs of General Isidro Urtecho, a great-uncle of Vanguardia member José Coronel Urtecho. Unlike most Pacific intellectuals, Isidro Urtecho spent a great deal of time in eastern Nicaragua through his role as Inspector General of the Atlantic Coast. In his memoirs (written in 1906 and published in 1968), he described in detail political meetings in the region, demonstrating the outstanding diplomatic skills of coast leaders. He criticized the perception that the Indigenous people were *monos* (monkeys) and affirmed that they were natural orators—"Ciceros of the Mosquitia"—with a great deal of political capacity. However, while Isidro Urtecho heard rationality in the political discourse of Miskitu people, he heard only repetitive, uncontrolled voices in their music. He wrote:

They have their fiestas, their songs, their music, their dances. They convert any event into a fiesta and this consists, like all fiestas, in eating, drinking, singing, and dancing; except that these acts have a savage crudeness. They sit in a circle, "al natural," they drink an intoxicating fermented chicha, they eat the most appetizing delicacy for them, a kind of paste made of plantain, they sing without any changes of the voice, always with a repetitive voice that leads one to despair, and they dance alone and together, jumping, without order, to the beat of a drum, which is made by hollowing out a piece of tree with fire and covering its ends with animal skins which they hunt.

---

[65] Gamio de Alba (1957: 59). "Carecen de características intelectuales y culturas especiales. Son primitivos y viven de lo que la tierra les ofrece. No poseen un arte creativo. No tejen canastos o hacen objeto de piel. El *pipanti*, y su casa son su máxima creación."
[66] Gamio de Alba (1957: 60).

The fiesta is concluded with all the men and women, confused, toppling to the ground.[67]

Urtecho's commentary shows the typical prejudices of the era, but also the cross-cultural diplomatic abilities of coast people, who could carry out political negotiations using the techniques recognized by the dominant power. In other moments, they still maintained their collective ceremonies and celebrations based on other cultural practices. Urtecho heard culture in the intercultural field of political discourse, and he heard savage nature in the intracultural field of ritual.

A 1959 report to the IV Inter-American Indian Congress provides a rationale for Nicaraguan indigenistas' reluctance to engage with music and folklore in the eastern region: the coast's divergent cultures and historical ties with England made it impossible to claim as national heritage. While the expressive culture of Atlantic Coast people was either ignored or considered outside the bounds of the nation-state, the natural landscape of the Atlantic Coast *was* represented as national heritage. In that 1959 report, Eudoro Solís, the Nicaraguan delegate to the III congress and his country's poet laureate, wrote of the "reincorporation" of the Mosquitia, part of the dominant discourse that assumes the Atlantic Coast was Nicaraguan territory prior to the late nineteenth century. In a brief historical account, which precedes more detailed discussion of the Río Coco educational project, Solís described the past British governance of the region in collusion with the Miskitu king, as opposed to the "democratic and legitimate Authority" of Nicaraguan leaders. The military annexation of the coast in 1894 is described significantly in terms of musical sound, with the imagined voice of the nation springing forth from nature:

And beneath the Nicaraguan sky which showed its best colors, [General Rigoberto Cabezas] raised the flag of Nicaragua and the national hymn was heard in the throats of the birds, in the Mediterranean voice of the rivers

---

[67] Isidro Urtecho was writing about events that he observed in 1887 in Bluefields (Urtecho [1906] 1968: 48). "Tienen sus fiestas, sus cantos, su música, sus danzas. Cualquier acontecimiento lo convierten en fiesta y esta consiste, como toda fiesta, en comer, beber, cantar y bailar; solo que estos actos tienen una rudeza salvaje. Se sientan en rueda, al natural, se bebe la chicha fermentada que embriaga, se come el manjar más apetitoso entre ellos, una especie de engrudo, compuesta con masa de guineo, se canta sin modulaciones de voz siempre con una monotonía que desespera, y se baila ya solo, ya acompañado, a brincos, sin concierto, al golpe de un tamboril, que se hace ahuecando a fuego un pedazo de árbol a propósito y cubriendo sus extremos con pieles de animales que cazan. Concluye la fiesta rodando todos, mujeres y hombres confundidos, por el suelo."

and in the epic song of the forest. Rigoberto Cabezas, founder of journalism in Nicaragua, achieved the geographic integration of the Atlantic littoral and signaled to Nicaraguan thinking the route of a new world, without boundaries, because the Mediterranean does not have boundaries, to begin the spiritual unity, the erudite [letrada] attention that makes peoples greater and arms them with a universal conscience.[68]

Solís's representation of the national hymn resounding from nature accomplishes the ideological work of naturalizing Nicaraguan sovereignty on the Atlantic Coast. His reference to the "Mediterranean voice" evokes the notion, elaborated by other writers, that the literary and artistic products of America were comparable to the achievements of ancient Greece in their mixture of civilizations. Solís's use of the adjective letrada is also significant because the Nicaraguan indigenistas were above all letrados—lettered intellectuals who were simultaneously poets, politicians, lawyers, journalists, and folklorists with a mandate to write their nation into orderly being, within a discourse of democratic civilization but upholding starkly unequal social structures.[69]

In a later publication, the Nicaraguan lawyer, government official and scholar Emilio Álvarez Lejarza criticized the Vanguardia for their derogatory references to Indians, but considered the Indigenous people of the eastern coast, the Mosquitia, to be outside of the nation because of their long-standing affiliations with English missionaries. He wrote:

> The Nicaraguan always looks with distrust at these English missionaries because they taught the Indians to sing "God Save the King," at the beginning of classes. The Indian interprets this song as if the King of England will return to be his Protector, and every day our hope for spiritually nationalizing the Mosquitia become more distant.[70]

[68] "Y bajo el cielo nicaragüense que se puso sus mejores colores, izó la bandera de Nicaragua y se escuchó el himno de la patria en la garganta de los pájaros, en la voz mediterránea de los ríos y en el canto épico de la selva. Rigoberto Cabezas, fundador del diarismo en Nicaragua, logró la integración geográfica del Litoral Atlántico y señaló al pensamiento nicaragüense la ruta de un mundo nuevo, sin linderos, porque lo mediterráneo no tiene linderos, para comenzar la unidad espiritual, la atención letrada que hace más grande a los pueblos y los arma de una conciencia universal" (Solís 1959: 24).

[69] Rama ([1984] 1996).

[70] This article was published in Nicaragua Indígena in 1969, as well as in the Revista Conservadora in 1971 (Álvarez Lejarza 1971: 43). "El nicaragüense mira siempre con desconfianza a estos misioneros ingleses porque enseñaban a los indios a cantar el 'God Save the King', al abrir las clases. El indio interpreta este canto como que volverá el Rey de Inglaterra a ser su Protector y se aleja cada día más nuestra esperanza de nacionalizar espiritualmente la Mosquitia."

Embedded here is a sense that Indigenous people on the Caribbean coast used their history of relations with England as a tool for resisting the nationalism of the Nicaraguan state.

As we have seen, in both Nicaraguan and inter-American indigenismo, contemporary Indians were made most visible on the Atlantic Coast, but their music and other expressive practices were largely silenced. The politics of Indigenous communities in the Pacific region were obscured, but their expressive practices received a great deal more attention from Nicaraguan indigenistas. *Nicaragua Indígena* signaled the folkloric orientation of the 1950s through the republication of two short pieces by Rubén Darío.[71] Darío lamented the neglect of folklore in Central America in his time, and he collected descriptions of Indigenous performance from written sources as well as his own youthful memories (he left Nicaragua for Chile at the age of seventeen and spent most of his life abroad, moving between Latin America and Europe). In an essay on "popular representations and dances," Darío discussed theatrical performances involving music, dance, and dialogue, and he emphasized the marimba as an icon of indigeneity (and sorrow) in Nicaragua:

> The marimba manifests the sentiment of the euphonious harmony of the Indian. In that rough instrument are all the sad echoes of the mountain, the songs of the primitive hut, the softness of the country in good weather, or the cry of indomitable love and the lament of deepest bitterness. The marimba seems to be invented by some formidable and savage Pan of the Western world, errant knower of sadness, anxiety, pains and victories of the tribes, father of Native American poetry.[72]

Listening to the marimba, Darío heard Indigenous heritage as both nature and culture. The diatonic marimba endured in Nicaragua (and still endures) long after being replaced by the chromatic marimba in most of Central America. Darío's essay was reprinted in *Nicaragua Indígena* at a time when middle-class mestizo Nicaraguans were laying claim to Indigenous dance

---

[71] Darío (1954a,1954b).

[72] "La marimba manifiesta el sentimiento de la armonía eufónica en el indio. En ese rudo instrumento están todos los tristes ecos de la montaña, las canciones de la choza primitiva, la suavidad del campo en el buen tiempo, o el grito del amor indómito y el lamento de las más hondas amarguras. La marimba parece ser inventada por algún formidable y salvaje Pan del mundo de Occidente, errante conocedor de las tristezas, ansias, duelos y victorias de las tribus, padre de la nativa americana poesía" (Darío 1954b: 23).

and festival as regional and national heritage, but the specific activity of marimba playing continued to be associated with the stigmatized status of Indian.[73]

Even more than the iconic sound of the marimba, indigenistas found the roots of Nicaraguan culture in patron saint festivities and street theater performed most ardently by people of Indigenous descent in the Pacific region. In their descriptions of these performances, folklorists brought out the importance of music as a medium of collective mobilization that resounded through public space. Both music and dance were interpreted as evidence of specific forms of mixture that characterized the Nicaraguan nation. Leopoldo Serrano was a lawyer and magistrate who became a founding partner in the Center of Folklorist Studies of Diriamba, a rich cultural haven for traditional performance. In 1955 Serrano published an article in *Nicaragua Indígena* chronicling the festivities of San Sebastian—the patron saint of Diriamba. He explains the formation and conservation of popular performance in terms of racialized and stylistic mixture:

> But the people, more than anyone, have kept that tradition; the clever conquistador made dark people, Indian or mestizo, the custodian of those popular dances; those people kept the music, the dialogue, he taught them the dance; and that people faithful to tradition, with the attachment of that .which is exclusively their own, learned, and sang and danced and recited and, with the ear attuned to the throbbing of the race, they heard and interpreted the autochthonous music, and this music was mixed with their dialogues, with dance steps, and with it, thus, [the people] sang and danced; and that's why this music is of the people and these representations and these dialogic dances, mixtures of zarzuelas and comedias, they continue conserving them, faithful to their ancestors.[74]

In Serrano's view, popular performance associated with saints' days had roots in Spanish tradition, but through the aurality and physicality of the "dark races," these performances came to mix cultural forms and created something uniquely Nicaraguan. Serrano continued, "The peoples in love with

[73] T. M. Scruggs notes the common characterization of marimba and other Indigenous music as melancholy; he suggests this perception may have been related to a defensive, reserved demeanor around mestizos, and to mestizo writers' assumptions that Indigenous culture was in decline (Scruggs 1994: 285–286).

[74] Serrano (1955: 53). Original text is in the next footnote.

their past are prolonged in the future in diverse manifestations; and art is one with them. Is not art perhaps the very soul of the people?"[75] This notion of conserving culture seems to be more fluid and future-oriented than dominant US approaches to Indigenous culture at the time. In Nicaragua, performance became a medium and metaphor of mestizaje, which acknowledged Indigenous heritage but claimed a shared cultural mixture, since "the fusion of races in the violence of conquest is not only material, but also spiritual; and art is the favorable field for the languages to intermingle."[76]

These and other folkloric writings of the time created an abstract discourse of the Nicaraguan national imaginary that was detached from the everyday realities of Indigenous communities across Nicaragua. Gould argues that most of the Nicaraguan indigenistas of this era wrote from national centers and had little interaction with Comunidades Indígenas. The intellectuals who did have contact with Indigenous communities usually took the side of non-Indian landowners.[77] In the 1940s and 1950s, the folkloric imaginary of the mestizo/Indo-Hispanic race was not flexible enough to include expressive practices of the Atlantic Coast at all. Nevertheless, I argue, these writings shifted the dominant discourse away from Hispanism and opened up more heterogeneous ideologies of national heritage. This, in turn, set the stage for revolutionary reimaginings of Nicaraguan folk and popular culture.

Indigeneity, Revolution, and Counterrevolution

In the 1960s and 1970s, new transnational Indigenous movements were taking shape with Indigenous leaders at the helm. Currents of liberation theology moving throughout Latin America took a distinctive form on the

[75] "Pero el pueblo, más que nadie, ha guardado esa tradición; a ese pueblo oscuro, indio o mestizo, le dió el avispado conquistador la guarda de esos bailes populares; a ese pueblo le entregó la música, le dio el diálogo, le enseñó el baile; y ese pueblo fiel a su tradición, con el apego de lo que le es propio y exclusivo, aprendió, y cantó y bailó y recitó y, con el oído puesto en el palpitar de la raza escuchó e interpretó la música autóctona y esta música la entremezcló con sus diálogos, con pasos de bailes y con ella, entonces, cantó y bailó; y por eso esa música es del pueblo y estas representaciones y estos bailes dialogados, mezclas de zarzuelas y comedias, las siguen conservando, fieles a sus antepasados. Los pueblos enamorados de su pasado se prolongan en el futuro en diversas manifestaciones; y el arte es una de ellas. El arte, no es acaso el alma misma del pueblo?" (Serrano 1955: 53).

[76] "La fusión de las razas en la violencia de la conquista no solo es material, sino que espiritual; y el arte es el más propicio campo para que las lenguas se entremezclen" (Serrano 1955: 58).

[77] Gould (1998: 199). An exception was Alfonso Valle, who "claimed Sutiavan roots" and served as a lawyer (with some success) for the Sutiavas during their struggles to recover land rights outside of León in 1958 (Gould 1990: 101). Valle contributed several articles to Nicaragua Indígena in the late 1950s and early 1960s.

Atlantic Coast of Nicaragua, where Catholic and Moravian church members, especially in Miskitu communities, promoted Indigenous-centered narratives of the Bible and developed increasing pride in their histories and autochthonous cultures. In the mid-1970s, Miskitu leaders participated in early meetings of the World Council of Indigenous Peoples, founded in Canada by George Manuel (Shushwap Tribe, British Columbia), who also traveled to Nicaragua to meet with Miskitu leaders. Carlos Mejía Godoy, a composer of politically committed popular music from western Nicaragua, included a Miskitu text in his *Misa Campesina*. A few young Miskitu studying in universities of western Nicaragua became involved in the underground Sandinista movement. Young Sandinista guerrillas from urban mestizo backgrounds developed closer relationships with other Indigenous communities while hiding in the mountains of the northern central region.[78]

The Sandinista movement focused on refiguring class hierarchies more than ethnic hierarchies, and prioritized unity over addressing Indigenous demands. But class and ethnic hierarchies were inextricably linked in Nicaragua, and the revolutionary vanguard understood that even outside of membership in recognized Comunidades Indígenas, poor people of mixed descent were often racialized as Indian. Jaime Wheelock Román, a key leader of the Sandinista insurrection, published his book *Indigenous Roots of the Anticolonialist Struggle in Nicaragua* with a Mexican press in 1974, five years before the triumph of the Revolution.[79] He lambasted the Nicaraguan writers of the 1930s and 1940s (including Pablo Antonio Cuadra and José Coronil Urtecho) who promoted a vision of the past as a "colonial peace" with fraternal, symbiotic relations binding together the dominant class, Indians and peasants, and the land. The book drew on colonial archives and chronicles as well as nineteenth-century histories to reveal the brutality of Spanish colonization of Indians in the territory that became Nicaragua. Indigenous peoples of the eastern coast play a central role in Wheelock's narrative because of their fierce resistance to Spanish colonizers, which kept the region outside of Spanish control. But Wheelock reproduced earlier Nicaraguan ideologies of Indigenous peoples as more primitive on the eastern coast than in the western part of the country. He also reproduced the rhetoric of the

---

[78] See Hawley (1997); Meringer (2010); Sanders (1977); Hale (1994). Gordillo (2021) analyzes the musical histories of the Central American vernacular masses which grew out of liberation theology movements, including little-known connections between the popular composer Carlos Mejía Godoy and the Capuchin priest who was especially influential on the Atlantic Coast, Gregory Smutko.

[79] Wheelock Román (1974).

"reincorporation" of the eastern littoral into Nicaragua in 1894, even after he exhaustively detailed how the region was never colonized by Spain and remained outside of national control after Nicaraguan independence.

Music and folklore research contributed to the revolutionary movement from the 1950s onward. Ernesto Mejía Sánchez, one of the founders of the Taller San Lucas, was suspected of involvement in the assassination of President Anastasio Somoza García in 1956 (the actual shooting was carried out by another poet, Rigoberto López Pérez). Mejía Sánchez was already living in Mexico and was essentially exiled there after the assassination.[80] Salvador Cardenal Argüello, another founder of the Taller, continued his work recording and compiling music from across Nicaragua, developing a broader national consciousness that moved beyond the earlier privileging of Masaya, Granada, and León. In 1977 he released a landmark set of LP records, *Nicaragua: Música y Canto*, which contributed to the burgeoning popular consciousness that fueled the revolution. His grandchildren, Salvador and Katia Cardenal, formed a Nueva Canción duo—they called their version *volcanto*—while still in their teens.[81] Their Duo Guardabarranco became influential in networks of protest music across Latin America.

The elder Salvador Cardenal Argüello never made field recordings on the Caribbean coast, but he did record some Miskitu musicians in his studio in Managua and included them in his 1977 anthology—a significant departure from earlier folklorists' neglect. In 1978 the same private foundation that supported the anthology of recordings also republished a collection of writings by the Taller San Lucas. It was no longer possible to speak of Nicaraguan folklore only with reference to the Pacific regions. The editors of the new anthology added texts of Creole and Miskitu folklore to the earlier collections.

The triumph of the Revolution in 1979 led to literacy campaigns across the country that included music and folklore research. On the Caribbean coast, communities insisted that their literacy programs be conducted in regional

---

[80] Over the course of his career as a professor at the UNAM in Mexico City, Mejía Sánchez published collections that moved across genres and borders, representing not only folkloric tradition, but also literary modernism. He edited seminal anthologies of Rubén Darío's poetic and fictional works, and of José Martí's letters from New York to Latin America. The edition of Martí's letters is particularly resonant with the folklorist's approach, as it provides comparative data for different versions of Martí's articles and letters sent to newspapers across Latin America. For an aural experience of Mejía Sánchez's voice, the Library of Congress has an online recording of him reading from his own poetry in Mexico in 1960 at https://www.loc.gov/item/93842681/.

[81] See Scruggs (1999, 2002). See also the documentary film, *Si Buscabas*, by Cierto Güis Productions, at https://www.youtube.com/watch?v=BTLotYL8ftU.

languages. The translation of revolutionary discourses into Indigenous languages led to a transformation of meaning, combining the new revolutionary currents with the earlier currents of liberation theology as they had been adapted on the coast.[82] When the Sandinistas promised power to the people, a plurality of "peoples" responded to the call on the Caribbean coast, but they were not granted leadership roles. The patriarchal ethnocentrism of the Sandinista leadership, together with the threat of a US-backed counterrevolution, increased tensions even further.[83] The civil war known as the Contra War involved multiple factions fighting against the Sandinistas for different reasons, though they sometimes collaborated to benefit from US arms and assistance. After several years of violence, the Sandinista government reconsidered their approach to the Atlantic Coast and moved toward peace talks and concessions. Two autonomous regions were created in 1987, the North Atlantic and South Atlantic Autonomous Regions.

Both the Miskitu insurrection and the discourses of autonomy increased the visibility and audibility of Indigenous cultural movements on the Caribbean coast. In 1992—the 500-year anniversary of Columbus's arrival to the Americas—transnational discourses of Indigenous rights also helped to increase the visibility of Indigenous communities in western Nicaragua. In 1993 the Inter-American Indian Institute carried out its eleventh congress in Managua, Nicaragua's capital city. The III publication *América Indígena* dedicated an entire volume to studies about Indigenous law and culture on both sides of Nicaragua. But in the face of new Indigenous movements, the III was losing its claims to relevance. The congress in Managua was the last congress of the Inter-American Indian Institute, and after some attempts at reform and reorganization, it was dissolved in 2009.

In recent decades, Indigenous folklore has increasingly become the domain of Indigenous cultural workers in Nicaragua—teachers, anthropologists, poets, and journalists (among others) who carry out research in their own communities. On the Caribbean coast they have disseminated their work in publications such as the cultural journals *Tininiska* and *Wani*, as well as community radio and television, which reach a large regional audience. Folkloric performance has played a prominent role in the Sihkru Tara, a meeting inspired by a traditional spiritual event bringing together Miskitu people from Nicaragua and Honduras. This event, both political and cultural, has

[82] Freeland (1995).
[83] Hale (1994); Gordon (1998).

typically coincided with the UN International Day of the World's Indigenous Peoples.[84]

The indigenista texts still circulate, as well. In 1957, Elba Sandoval Valdívia published a study of Miskitu "customs and folklore" in *Nicaragua Indígena*. The very same text was republished in 1999 in a UNESCO publication titled *Nuestra Cosmovisión: Creencias, Prácticas y Rituales* (Our Cosmovision: Beliefs, Practices, and Rituals).[85] This is a sign of the endurance of old paradigms of folklore in later regimes of cultural heritage, which often position Indigenous cultures in the tightly constrained categories of official recognition.

Grassroots Indigenous movements are not isolated primordial cultures, but rather the products of transregional and transnational interactions that prompt people to use history and culture strategically in particular moments.[86] In this sense, Indigenous movements have run parallel to, and sometimes intersected with, indigenista movements. We must be vigilant to avoid mapping old concepts of authenticity onto the former while dismissing the impact of the latter. Both Indigenous and indigenista movements have shaped contemporary discourses of Indigenous heritage.

Traces of Heritage

In this chapter, I have focused on Nicaraguan discourses about Indigenous culture and folklore from the 1930s to the 1960s, as well as the new directions they took from the 1970s onward. A cross-regional analysis reveals how the early work of Nicaraguan letrados valued some forms of Indigenous culture more than others as national heritage. However, the deeply felt heterogeneity of discourses of mestizaje created some openness in their ideological structures.

Critical social-historical work can be a labor of listening, especially when spaces for voicing become constricted. It can involve the careful indirection of poetry to think about the present and the future, through the echoes of the past. As Ochoa Gautier has written, "The question that emerges for a decolonial history of the voice is not only how to identify the constitution

---

[84] Matamoros Mercado (2008); Minks (2013).

[85] Sandoval Valdivia (1957, 1999).

[86] See Juan Eduardo Wolf's (2019) parallel argument regarding Afro-descendent movements in Chile.

of an alterity of the acoustic as part of the political theology of the state but also the presence of different modes of relating alterity and the voice that do not fit such a paradigm."[87] In the Nicaraguan case, part of the alterity of the acoustic is the historical tendency to hear the Caribbean coast through representations of nature and perceptions of human savagery—a key colonial trope of racialization. These auralities were problematized, often in the very same texts, by transnational connections to British cultural heritage—the English language and the singing of "God Save the King." Afro-Caribbean culture was placed irredeemably outside the Nicaraguan nation, following a pattern in many places of the Americas where national intellectuals have viewed and heard Blackness as external to indigeneity, notwithstanding the cultural and territorial claims of a wide range of peoples with deeply rooted histories and identities.[88]

Nevertheless, at certain historical moments, other relations between alterity and the voice emerge, as in the text of Isidro Urtecho about Indigenous rationality and political subjectivity. This recognition of political subjectivity among Miskitu people has to do with "transformations of the sensorial, juridical regimes, and the redefinition of the public sphere."[89] While these relations among law, culture, and ontology were initially articulated in the colonial period, they have continued to undergird modes of inclusion and exclusion in the nation. However, these were never closed structures with inevitable consequences, partly because of the heterogeneity of cultural patrimonies within and across family histories. A homogenized concept of the patriarchal family was a model for the modern nation-state, but actual families were always more heterogeneous and fluid.[90] The patrimonial discourses of Pablo Antonio Cuadra reveal this heterogeneity in his quest for understanding the nation as a dual heir to Spain and to the Indigenous. Cuadra's recognition of Indigenous heritage, and the archival projects to which he contributed, signaled a subtle ideological shift—not so much a radical challenge as a destabilization of cultural and racial hierarchies.

Cuadra's musings about his own intimate subjectivities join together the public patrimony and the private, which brings us back to archival theory. Derrida's genealogy of the archive posits the externality of a physical location for storing records (beyond the human mind and body) which is also a site

---

[87] Ochoa (2014: 20–21).
[88] Goett (2006, 2017); Hooker (2005); Anderson (2009); Birenbaum Quintero (2018); Wolf (2019).
[89] Ochoa (2014: 149).
[90] Bauman and Briggs (2003).

Figure 3.6 Pablo Antonio Cuadra (left) and Salvador Cardenal Argüello (right) later in life. Pablo Antonio Cuadra Collection of Nicaraguan Literary Materials, Benson Latin American Collection, University of Texas at Austin.

of power.[91] Bernard Gordillo's discussion of Nicaraguan archives suggests the fragility of these physical locations, subject to destruction by fire and earthquake, as well as mismanagement and loss.[92] As Derrida commented in a discussion of South African archives: "Because of this exteriority, what is kept in the archive, of course can be erased, can be lost, and the very gesture which consists in keeping safe—in a safe, so to speak—is always, and from the beginning, threatened by the possibility of destruction." Derrida's larger project was an exploration of the relations between the external archive and the internal subconscious, especially the sites of repression in both: "And, in this economy of repression, nothing is lost . . . What is forgotten or repressed is kept safe somewhere else, and then, in some situation, the repressed can of course come back."[93]

[91] Derrida (1995, 2002).
[92] Gordillo (2019: 9–10).
[93] Derrida (2002: 42).

A key mechanism for processes of repression and recovery is the trace. Each time we write or speak, "we leave a trace which becomes independent of its origin, of the movement of its utterance—the trace is at the same time the memory, the archive, *and* the erasure, the repression, the forgetting of what it is supposed to keep safe."[94] But "it is impossible to close the archive."[95] The archival impulse depends on an orientation toward the "future to come." This future orientation and the targets of preservation shift over time, and they are not limited to official archives. They are located in home and family collections, in lost and found objects, in forgotten and remembered stories, and in bodies and minds which are mobile. The project of recuperating archival knowledge calls us to listen to and through these traces; to position writers in their own cultural contexts vis-à-vis those they wrote about; and to follow their networks of social and institutional relations. In doing so, we can begin to perceive the heterogeneity of social and national constructions, and to imagine a plurality of possible futures.

[94] Derrida (2002: 54, italics added).
[95] Derrida (2002: 46).

4

Indigenous Collections and Integrative
Arts in Chile

In February of 1941, the Chilean composer Domingo Santa Cruz was visiting Washington, DC, under the sponsorship of the US State Department.
With the growing crisis of World War II, musical diplomacy had become a
key area for the US State Department in its efforts to strengthen alliances
with Latin American nations.[1] On this trip Santa Cruz traveled with his wife,
Filomena Salas, and with the Chilean intellectuals Eugenio Pereira Salas
and Carlos Humeres, all of whom were active in Chilean musical circles (see
Figure 4.1).[2] One afternoon, Santa Cruz was shepherded into the Library of
Congress where Charles Seeger happened to be working in the Archive of
American Folk Song. Seeger was in his final days directing the Federal Music
Project of the Works Progress Administration, the Depression-era program
which worked closely with the Library of Congress and contributed new
collections to state and federal archives, as we saw in Chapter 1.[3]

When they met in the Library of Congress, Seeger and Santa Cruz immediately hit it off. Santa Cruz wrote in his memoir that Seeger seemed like an
older brother or young uncle; he had the air of an English lord.[4] (Santa Cruz
had an Irish ancestor and thought his "Saxon" heritage helped him adapt
quickly in his US travels.) Santa Cruz and Seeger had a long talk over lunch
the next day and continued to deepen their friendship through subsequent
meetings, family relations, and especially long letters that passed back and
forth across the continent, some years frequently, other years less so, for at
least thirty-six years. Santa Cruz later wrote of his 1941 trip to the United

---

[1] Campbell (2012).

[2] The prominent Peruvian indigenista Luis E. Valcárcel also traveled with the Chilean representa-
tives under the sponsorship of the US State Department ("Visitors from Hispanic America," *Hispanic
American Historical Review*, 1941). Valcárcel became the director of the Peruvian branch of the Inter-
American Indian Institute, and later the Minister of Education (de la Cadena (2014: 70–71, 80).

[3] In 1935 Seeger began working on music and folklore projects with the Resettlement
Administration based in Washington, DC, and then directed the Federal Music Project of the Works
Progress Administration (WPA) from 1938 to 1940 (Gough 2015; Pescatello 1992).

[4] Santa Cruz (2008: 610).

Indigenous Audibilities. Amanda Minks, Oxford University Press. © Oxford University Press 2024.
DOI: 10.1093/oso/9780197532485.003.0005

Figure 4.1 Chilean university representatives and their wives, among others, visiting the Pan American Union, Washington, DC, January 30, 1941. Domingo Santa Cruz is standing, third from right. *Iconografía musical chilena: investigaciones* / Samuel Claro Valdés [et al.]. 1a. edición. Santiago: Ediciones UC (Pontificia Universidad Católica de Chile), 1989.

States, "They discovered us with surprise. We weren't black or mulatto, or of apparent indigenous ancestry. We had education equal to theirs, and our ecumenism placed us above the average cultural level of the North American intellectual."[5] In the 1940s, the close friendship between Seeger and Santa Cruz helped to fuel new Chilean institutions for folklore research, which ultimately moved discourses of Chilean cultural heritage well beyond Santa Cruz's vision.

---

[5] Santa Cruz (2008: 608). One wonders how Santa Cruz conceptualized the "we" in this statement. See Wolf (2019: 23–36) on the shifting national interpretations of race, culture, and music in Chile.

In this chapter I use the relationship between Seeger and Santa Cruz as an entry point to examine the role of Indigenous and art music collections in the intersecting networks of national and international institutions. Chile was never a prominent actor in indigenista discourses, but partly for that reason it presents a valuable case for examining the development of Indigenous music collections in the middle of the twentieth century. The Universidad de Chile was founded in 1842 by the revered Venezuelan-Chilean poet and statesman, Andrés Bello, who emphasized the rationalizing function of the university in consolidating and maintaining the nation-state.[6] In newly independent countries across Latin America, Chile was a model for legal frameworks as well as universities in the nineteenth century. In the first decades of the twentieth century, Chile did not follow the trends of Latin American countries that explored Indigenous and Afro-descendant cultural symbols as emblems of populist nationalism. Rather, the Chilean intellectual elite aimed to continue the *belles lettres* approach to knowledge which aligned them with the cultural heritage of Europe, with especially close ties to France as well as Spain.

Chilean intellectuals with an interest in Indigenous music initially sought to locate Indigenous heritage in colonial and scientific archives in Europe. However, in the 1930s and 1940s, new practices of documenting Indigenous music led to new archives and new modes of musical creation in Chile. The empirical materiality of these collecting projects also contributed to new discourses of heritage. Even in the face of enduring Eurocentric perspectives, music archives provided evidence of what Mariana León Villagra and Ignacio Ramos Rodillo have called "los sonidos de un Chile profundo"—the sounds of Chile in all its cultural depth. These archives manifest the cultural diversity embedded in Chilean history, and today they are important sources for reactivating a plurality of social memory.[7]

Archival collections are an outcome of the mediating interactions that tied together actors, institutions, and states within and across borders. The following intertwined stories consider Chilean music collections in relation to a variety of networks. Francisco Curt Lange first built an inter-American network for music research in Uruguay in the 1930s, prior to the collaboration of Seeger and Santa Cruz through the Pan American Union in the

---

[6] Ramos ([1989] 2001: 24). Claire Fox (2013: 26) suggests that Latin Americans involved in the cultural programs of the Pan American Union followed Bello's idealization of Enlightenment thought as well as his model of liberal statemen-humanists.

[7] León Villagra and Ramos Rodillo (2011: 38).

1940s. The works of the Chilean composer, artist, and ethnographer Carlos Isamitt were especially prominent in Lange's publications as well as in the music projects of the Inter-American Indian Institute in Mexico. I trace the interrelations between these actors as well as the work of Argentine researcher Isabel Aretz in the pivotal year of 1941. Aretz would later go on to found the Inter-American Institute of Ethnomusicology and Folklore (INIDEF) in Venezuela in the 1970s. The work of Violeta Parra provides a counterexample of collections made primarily outside of institutions, which still have institutional resonances, especially through rediscovered collections. Chilean researchers are engaged in a range of revisionist projects focused on the music and histories of people who were excluded from official institutions.[8] This involves the recovery of sources that had been obscured, or a reexamination of sources that had been made to speak in the voice of a hegemonic scholar—a "ventriloquism," in the analysis of Fernanda Vera.[9] At the end of this chapter I explore the social force of new projects of recuperation.

Inter-American Mediations: Seeger, Santa Cruz, Lange

Charles Seeger was a composer and musicologist who was among the founders of the Society for Ethnomusicology and a builder of disciplines, institutions, and relationships. He is also known in broader historical memory as the husband of Ruth Crawford Seeger, a groundbreaking modernist composer, and the father of world-famous folk singer Pete Seeger. Charles Seeger was born in Mexico City in 1886, part of the upscale sector of a Yankee colony with close relations to the regime of Porfirio Díaz. Seeger's father published a bilingual newspaper with a subsidy from Díaz that promoted US businesses in Mexico, and he was especially involved with developing train and bus lines through US investment.[10] During his childhood years in Mexico, Seeger studied guitar and learned about Mexican popular and folk music. The family periodically moved back and forth between Mexico City and their house on Staten Island, New York, until the Mexican Revolution. Although Seeger was sheltered from the social strife of the time,

[8] Chávez Cancino (2021, 2022a, 2022b); Izquierdo König (2011a, 2011b); Karmy Bolton (2019); Karmy (2021a, 2021b); Masquiarán Díaz (2011); Peña Queralt (2010); Ramos Rodillo and Donoso Fritz (2023).

[9] Vera (2015: 75–76).

[10] Schell (2001: 15).

these years shaped his enduring conception of American music as "of the Americas," not limited to the United States.[11]

While living in New York in the early 1930s, Seeger maintained close relationships with several members of the Pan American Association of Composers, founded in 1928, the same year the Archive of American Folk Song was established at the Library of Congress. The association developed from conversations among Carlos Chávez, Henry Cowell (Seeger's former student), and Edgard Varèse.[12] Their aim was to sponsor concerts of modernist music by composers from across the Americas, showcasing and promoting artistic independence from Europe; music critics of the day called them "ultramodern."[13] In addition to the organizers, the list of seventeen founding members of the group included the Chilean composer Acario Cotapos, the Mexican composer Silvestre Revueltas, the Uruguayan composer Eduardo Fabini, and the US composer Ruth Crawford, who would become Charles Seeger's second wife. Cotapos was proclaimed by critics to be "the Chilean futurist" and "the Schoenberg of South America." Cotapos also served as a diplomat in the Chilean Consulate of New York—a form of state patronage to support his creative work abroad (a common practice for Latin American writers and artists beginning in the late nineteenth century).[14]

At the other end of the continent, Domingo Santa Cruz studied law, initially following in the footsteps of his father, who had served in elected and appointed positions in the Chilean government. As a young man he attained a diplomatic position in Spain and first embarked to France in 1922 (this was a conventional diplomatic appointment; he had not yet developed a strong identity as a composer). There he fell in love with Wanda Morla Lynch, a daughter of the long-time Chilean ambassador in Paris. Her mother, Luisa Lynch, was a prominent feminist writer immortalized in an 1888 bust by the French sculptor Auguste Rodin, titled "Madame Vicuña." Santa Cruz and Wanda Morla Lynch traveled to Germany during their courtship and spent time with the Chilean piano prodigy Claudio Arrau, who was launching his career as an international superstar. During that visit Arrau introduced Santa Cruz to the early atonal and twelve-tone music of Arnold Schoenberg.[15] Wanda Morla Lynch married Santa Cruz and moved with him to Santiago,

---

[11] Pescatello (1992).
[12] Sachs (2012: 154); Paraskevaídis (2004); Root (1972: 51); Hess (2013a).
[13] Merino (1983: 20).
[14] Merino (1983: 20–21, 30).
[15] Santa Cruz (2008: 114).

where their first child, a son, was born. She tragically died in 1926 at the end of a difficult pregnancy, along with their newborn daughter. This dual loss led Santa Cruz to leave his diplomatic career in order to pursue his first love, music.[16] In his compositions, Santa Cruz was later described by Nicholas Slonimsky as the "Chilean Hindemith," a term that captured his modernist and neoclassicist orientations but obscured the ways his work also aimed to articulate Chilean identity through geographic references and a transcendent national spirit.[17]

Santa Cruz had played a key role in founding the Sociedad Bach in 1924 to promote art music in Chile, especially through public choral programs and through German Baroque and Classical music.[18] The activities of the society were intended to supplant Italian opera and other Romantic idioms, which had reigned supreme in Chile. Santa Cruz had political connections and cultural clout, at least among the upper echelons of Chilean society. He drew on his legal knowledge and connections to develop a new state-supported institutional structure for the arts. As in the United States, 1928 was a pivotal year for arts organizations in Chile. That year, Santa Cruz orchestrated a reform of the National Conservatory which pushed out the predominantly Romantic and Italian-influenced musicians and composers. This new structure had direct government support and operated as a semi-autonomous entity at the Universidad de Chile. Santa Cruz and his allies continued the earlier project of forging a rational, lettered citizenship, and they also joined this project with the new disciplinary and generic specializations of the twentieth century. As the result of Santa Cruz's reform, prominent Chilean musicians who had earned their living from composing, teaching, and performing a wide range of music in the late nineteenth and early twentieth centuries were subsequently erased from Chilean musical history and institutional archives.[19]

When Seeger and Santa Cruz met in Washington, DC, Seeger was transitioning to a new position as the director of the Music Division in the Pan American Union. The Pan American Union (PAU) was established by the US government in 1890, with headquarters in Washington, DC, although

---

[16] See Merino (1979); Santa Cruz (2008: 216, 218). A collection of Wanda Morla Lynch's letters was published in 2013 (Díaz Navarrete 2013; see also Miranda 2016). Santa Cruz later married Filomena Salas, a leading music educator in Chile whose son from a previous marriage, Juan Orrego Salas, also joined inter-American musical networks and became well known as a composer and director of the Latin American Music Center at the University of Indiana (Merino 2000; Herrera 2017).

[17] Slonimsky (1945: 163), quoted in Hess (2013a: 129). See also Merino's (1979) analysis of Santa Cruz's oeuvre.

[18] Santa Cruz (1950).

[19] Izquierdo König (2011a, 2011b).

it had some historical connections to earlier international meetings based in Latin America. The PAU focused on international commerce and also engaged in cultural discourses in an attempt to facilitate deeper relationships and trust. The PAU sponsored Latin American music concerts beginning in 1924 and presented many guest soloists from Latin America and the Caribbean.[20] The eclectic music performances were intended to promote international understanding, including US military bands performing the music of Latin American composers. As Alejandro García Sudo has noted, these performances were a distraction from US military interventions in Latin America at the time, but they were also carried out in collaboration with Latin American elites and aspiring artists, representing heterogeneous interests.[21]

PAU cultural programs took on new importance under the Good Neighbor policy of President Franklin Delano Roosevelt in 1933, when the United States shifted from overt military occupation to indirect political and cultural influence in Latin America. By the late 1930s, the buildup of the Second World War increased the stakes for cultural diplomacy. In 1938, the Eighth International Conference of the American States in Lima, Peru, passed a resolution promoting the value of music in international exchange, recognizing both the work of Francisco Curt Lange in Uruguay and the work of the PAU in Washington. Though Seeger would later trace the origins of the PAU Music Division to the Lima conference, the Chilean historian Eugenio Pereira Salas traced its origins to the US State Department and the conference on Inter-American Relations in the Field of Music in Washington in October 1939.[22] Musical exchange had become a tool of national security and international diplomacy, and US powerbrokers wanted that tool to be based in the US capital. Pereira Salas and Santa Cruz participated in the US-backed projects but pursued their own agendas in them.

There were other threads of influence within the Music Division coming from different ideological frameworks. Claire Fox has argued that the cultural programs of the Pan American Union unfolded with "relative autonomy" and served as a meeting ground between the cultural currents of Latinoamericanismo in the South and the social scientific and political currents of Latin American Studies in the North.[23] Seeger had moved

---

[20] Pereira Salas (1943) includes a list of performers; see also *Bulletin of the Pan American Union* (1934).

[21] García Sudo (2019).

[22] Pereira Salas (1943). See also Campbell (2012).

[23] C. Fox (2013: 11–12).

decisively toward the left in the 1930s, when his work in the WPA led him to appreciate musical creativity across classes and ethnic groups. Fox suggests that Seeger brought a wider range of musics into the PAU than had previously been supported. Whereas classical music had been privileged as the cultured backdrop for diplomacy, "Seeger introduced previously neglected indigenous, African diasporic, proletarian, and folk music" to PAU programs.[24] Seeger and Santa Cruz critiqued the stereotyping of Latin Americans and Latin American music which was especially pronounced in the Disney films produced under the Good Neighbor program.[25] Seeger also advocated for equitable pay for Latin American musicians and intellectual property rights for Latin American composers. His cosmopolitanism and chivalrous manner facilitated close relationships with Latin American elites who moved through artistic as well as cultural policy networks.

Seeger's PAU activities built on earlier networks and relationships. Leonora Saavedra has examined the fascinating intellectual and social relations between Seeger and the Mexican composer Carlos Chávez in the 1930s, recovering the texts of some of their letters between 1932 and 1945. Working for the PAU in 1943, Seeger wrote to Chávez: "I am especially pleased to print the facsimile of the Piano Sonatina. This is the first work of yours that I became familiar with, and I remember with pleasure your playing it with me in the little room in Greenwich Village some years ago."[26] In this case, Seeger's bureaucratic activities of copying, printing, and circulating music at the PAU were grounded in social relations and informal music-making, probably during Chávez's residence in New York between 1926 and 1928.

Pablo Palomino points out the imperialist underpinnings of the PAU Music Division: its initiatives originated in the United States, with funding that was intended to serve US political and economic interests.[27] Palomino also notes that the creation of an inter-American music center in the PAU Music Division was an affront to the international programs that Francisco Curt Lange had already launched in Uruguay. After emigrating from Germany, Lange had leveraged his classical music background to become the director of the recording collection at SODRE (Official Service of Electric

---

[24] C. Fox (2013: 50). See also Pernet (2007: 145).

[25] Poveda (2019, 2021) analyzes the role of music in Disney's animated films about Latin America produced in the early 1940s, including some representation of Chilean music. Poveda notes that Chile was a key object of US propaganda, but Chilean music did not fit easily into the tropical, exotic portrayals of the Disney films (Poveda 2019: 129).

[26] Quoted in Saavedra (1999: 56).

[27] Palomino (2015, 2020).

Broadcasting), a governmental entity of Uruguay. In 1934 Lange began to promote his ideas of "musical Americanism."[28] Lange wanted to increase musical dialogue among Latin American countries, which had been largely isolated from each other as elites of each country were oriented more toward Europe. A key venue for dialogue was the publication he launched in 1935, the *Boletín Latino Americano de Música*. The *Boletín* brought together articles on art music, folk music, Indigenous music, and sound technologies, along with a supplement that contained musical scores.[29] In Palomino's words, Lange's agenda was a "modernizing intellectual project" that aimed to institutionalize networks for advancing music research, education, and composition across the hemisphere.[30]

This understanding of Lange's work resonates with Jorge Pavez Ojeda's analysis of German intellectuals in Chile in the early twentieth century. Pavez traces a loose network of German intellectuals across the Americas (including Franz Boas) who promoted new paradigms of inductive research in the name of science. In Chile, the German émigré Rodolfo Lenz helped to found the "Sociedad de Folklore Chileno de Santiago de Chile" in 1909, possibly the first folklore society in Latin America.[31] The Society of Chilean Folklore was a key site for the "patrimonialization of the ethnic" in Chile, where elite intellectuals had identified much more with European heritage.[32] Christian Spencer, Antonieta Contreras, and Gabriel Rammsy have argued that the Society of Chilean Folklore also integrated the English approach to popular antiquities through a concern for the material object of collections. It was, they write, the first inclusive approach to documenting oral heritage (*acervo oral*) "from below"—from the people themselves.[33] Lenz was part of the German-influenced secularization and empirical study of Indigenous culture, which had previously been the topic of writings by missionaries and travelers in the colonial and early national periods. This new scientific approach did not overcome racism, but articulated it in different ways.[34] Lenz's

---

[28] Gordillo points out several earlier uses of the term "americanismo musical" by Latin American composers (Gordillo 2019: 42, 51–53).

[29] The ideologies behind the music research in the *Boletín Latino Americano de Música* were diverse. Ríos (2020: 41) discusses the contribution of the Bolivian musical intellectual Antonio González Bravo, who argued that the Andean siku ensemble expressed the "'communist' values of ancient and contemporary Andean indigenous societies."

[30] Palomino (2020: 171).

[31] Carvalho-Neto (1976).

[32] Pavez Ojeda (2015: 60).

[33] Spencer, Contreras, and Rammsy (2019: 2).

[34] At the same time that Lenz aimed to counter the racist dismissal of Indigenous Mapuche culture by Chilean elites, he presented the work of the Mapuche writer Manuel Manquilef in ways that

folkloric inscriptions, however, would resurface with surprising effects, such as in Violeta Parra's discovery of folklore, as I discuss later.

Collections of texts, artifacts, and sound recordings were a central focus of these modernizing scientific projects. Lange's interest in collections was shaped by German comparative musicology, as well as his work in Uruguayan institutions.[35] Although Indigenous music was not a major focus of Lange's work, in a 1936 publication he promoted documenting Indigenous music for the sake of its preservation and study, as well as its use in art music compositions.[36] Lange argued that new collections of Indigenous music and arts should not be deposited in archaeological museums, because they were living arts rather than the remnants of extinct cultures. He advocated for the university to become a center for this kind of "scientific labor."[37] Lange considered the classical musician's highly trained ear to be useful for field transcriptions that adapted conventional music notation, but he expressed concern about errors and the difficulty for others to adequately interpret and reproduce aural transcriptions from fieldwork. He considered the recording device to be an essential tool for capturing some aspects of musical performance and for helping to fill in memory gaps of the researcher. He was not overly celebratory of recording technology, however, because of its sonic limitations, problems of preservation, and the funding and skill required to use recording devices.

By 1941, the music specialists advising the new cultural initiatives in Washington were familiar with Lange's publications. Their focus on collections reflected pre-existing shared interests, in addition to the influence of Lange's writings. The PAU had a history of collecting music scores even before Charles Seeger's tenure there, with the aim of promoting international exchange and understanding.[38] Seeger was oriented toward collections work through his employment in the Federal Music Project,

reproduced racial hierarchies and maintained his own position of scientific authority (Mallon 2010; Crow 2013; Pavez 2015).

[35] Palomino (2020: 143).

[36] This was a paper Lange had presented in 1936 during a visit to Peru, in which he focused on the Peruvian context while also drawing broader conclusions (Lange 1936). The richly suggestive title can be loosely translated as "Systems of Folklore Research and the Use of Folkloric Collections [*acervo folklórico*] in Art Music." Hess (2013a: 130) and Gordillo (2019: 94) discuss how Lange later critiqued musical nationalism that used specific vernacular elements. Gordillo demonstrates that by 1939, Lange preferred a universalistic approach that fused a generalized folkloric sensibility with European styles.

[37] Lange (1936: 152).

[38] García Sudo (2019: 354).

which brought him into close collaboration with the Library of Congress and its Archive of American Folk Song. His wife, Ruth Crawford Seeger, had spent countless hours working with field recordings in the Archive and at home, creating transcriptions and arrangements for publication. Carleton Sprague Smith, another key player in inter-American cultural exchanges, was director of the Music Division of the New York Public Library. Smith emphasized the importance of Latin American music libraries after his 1940 tour of South America, sponsored by the US State Department as a means of developing recommendations for cultural diplomacy.[39] US interest in Latin American collections was also a continuation of institutional trends since the nineteenth century, following the Mexican American War and the Spanish American War. These collections served the US public's fascination with the countries that many people now viewed as America's backyard. In US institutions, Latin American collections had concrete political and economic incentives as a resource for the cultivation of expert knowledge during the rise of US power on the international stage.[40]

Despite Seeger's efforts to avoid encroaching on Lange's work, in the early 1940s the leadership and priorities for inter-American music affairs were largely co-opted by US funding in Washington.[41] Yet there were multiple interests on either side of the North/South divide. In the correspondence between Seeger and Santa Cruz, Santa Cruz openly criticized the instrumentality of US cultural exchange at the same time that he used US-based resources for his own institutional plans. Latin American music intellectuals were by no means a unified group. Lange's networking was impressive, especially given the challenges of transnational communication and travel at the time, but he often alienated people with his brusque personality and single-minded focus on his own vision for musical Americanism.[42]

In October of 1942, Santa Cruz wrote to Seeger about his impressions of Lange, recognizing his foundational work and defending him against accusations of Nazi sympathies (a suspicion often directed toward German émigrés at the time):

[39] Palomino (2020: 177); Smith (1940); Shepard (2006).

[40] Salvatore (2005, 2014); Palomino (2020); Delpar (1992).

[41] In 1952, an OAS committee requested more information on why support for Lange's initiatives dissipated after the 1938 inter-American conference attesting to their significance. This resulted in a defensive report, presumably authored by Seeger, arguing that the PAU provided some support for Lange while avoiding direct overlap with his work. See "Report to the Committee for Cultural Action on the Relations between the Instituto Inter-Americano de Musicología and the Pan American Union," January 19, 1953, Music/Francisco Curt Lange File, CML.

[42] See Palomino (2020: 167).

I have the impression that Curt Lange is effectively the victim of internal intrigues owing in great part to the rather brusque and authoritarian manner in which he treats things. This man has done well, with whatever end that has been achieved in bringing us closer, and he connected musical activities in America when no one else was thinking of it. Where he was mistaken was in believing that Uruguay, for its geographic situation and more than anything for him being the head, could be constituted as a kind of General Management of Latin American music. Within his country he sinned by being impulsive, and outside it by being undiplomatic, but we have no reason to suppose him to be a Nazi sympathizer, at least until the moment in which I am writing you. Curt Lange will come to Santiago, invited by us, for the festivities of the Centenary of the University, and I will tell you later my impression of what I converse with him about. I have written him letters with a tremendous frankness and he has not gotten angry, which I believe is a good sign.[43]

Five years later, Santa Cruz was more ambivalent in his assessment of Lange:

Some months ago Lange was desperately suggesting to me in all tones that I procure a paid invitation for him. That was not possible for a thousand reasons, but he came anyway and he stayed a month in Santiago. He met [Hermann] Scherchen [a German conductor], they talked about Twelve Tones (of whose clan I see there exists a true network that Scherchen highlighted: Kollreuter, Santoro, Paz, Lange, Hoffman in Lima).[44] I acquired some pesos for him and we left him in liberty. He gave three very bad lectures and he left. He is a man who provokes the most varied reactions: one appreciates him and admires his activity and his enthusiasm, and at the same time we consider him not much of a musician, more worried about

---

[43] Here I maintain the hyphens that Santa Cruz used in his letter: "Tengo la impresión de que Curt Lange es efectivamente víctima de intrigas internas debidas en gran parte a la manera un tanto brusca y autoritaria con que trata las cosas.—Este hombre ha hecho bien, con cualquier fin que haya sido logró acercarnos y relacionó las actividades musicales en América cuando nadie pensaba en ello.— En lo que se equivocó fue en creer que el Uruguay por su situación geográfica y más que todo por ser él la cabeza, podía constituirse en una especie de Dirección General de la música latino-americana.— Dentro de su país pecó por impulsivo y fuera de él por poco diplomático, pero no tenemos nosotros ninguna razón para suponerlo un simpatizante nazi, por lo menos hasta el momento en que yo le escribo.—Curt Lange vendrá a Santiago invitado por nosotros a las festividades del Centenario de la Universidad y yo le diré después a Ud. la impresión que me forme de lo que converse con él.—Yo le he escrito cartas de una franqueza tremenda y no se ha enojado, lo que creo que es un buen síntoma." Santa Cruz to Seeger, October 27, 1942, Seeger Family Collection, LoC Music Division.

[44] See Hess (2013b) for discussion of Paz, Kollreuter, and Santoro.

imaginary organizations and his dream of Americanist hegemony through Montevideo. Lange is a problem everywhere and above all in Uruguay. I am happy that he arrived to see us and attained first-hand knowledge about everything we have already created and have in process.[45]

In spite of his irreverent portrayal of Lange, Santa Cruz still seemed to value his efforts. Above all, Lange's interest in visiting Chile and publishing Chilean articles and compositions helped to validate the international importance of Chilean music institutions. Santa Cruz's letter also reveals his own international alignments at the time. His discussion of Argentine and Uruguayan institutions often seemed competitive and territorial, here expressed in his concern over "Americanist hegemony through Montevideo." Recognizing these shifting tensions and solidarities should not minimize the political machinations of US imperialism, but creates a more complex portrait of hemispheric politics than a North/South dichotomy.

Seeger and Santa Cruz were most optimistic and energetic about their collaboration from 1941 through 1945, with Seeger gathering Chilean music for US institutions and projects, and Santa Cruz acquiring equipment to advance the reproduction of art and folk music through emerging print and audio technologies. An important outcome of the PAU collaboration was the donation of recording and copying equipment to the Universidad de Chile. The program was influenced by the trip to the US Library of Congress made by Domingo Santa Cruz, Filomena Salas, and Eugenio Pereira Salas in 1941. At the end of July 1942, Santa Cruz wrote to Seeger with excitement about the possibilities that would be enabled by new recording equipment. He envisioned this equipment as the foundation for a new unit in the Universidad de Chile library. An associated recording archive would serve as a teaching resource in the "reformed Conservatory" and would facilitate the development of a new folklore department. Santa Cruz was planning for the

---

[45] "Desde hacía meses Lange estaba desesperado sugiriéndome en todos los tonos que le agenciara una invitación pagada. Eso no se pudo por mil razones, pero llegó de todos modos y se quedó un mes en Santiago, conoció a Scherchen, hablaron de los Doce Tonos, (de cuyo clan veo que existe una verdadera red que Scherchen puso en evidencia: Kollreuter, Santoro, Paz, Lange, Hoffman en Lima). Yo le conseguí unos pesos y lo dejamos en libertad. Dió tres conferencias muy malas y se fue. Es un hombre que provoca las reacciones más variadas: uno lo aprecia y admira en su actividad y su entusiasmo y al mismo tiempo lo sentimos poco músico, más preocupado de organizaciones imaginarias y de su sueño de hegemonía americanista a través de Montevideo. Lange es un problema en todas partes y sobre todo en el Uruguay. Me alegro que haya llegado a vernos y haya conocido de cerca todo lo nuestro ya formado y caminando." Santa Cruz to Seeger, October 12, 1947, Seeger Family Collection, LoC Music Division.

folklore director to be Carlos Lavín, whom he described as "our composer and eminent folklorist who just arrived from Europe after twenty years of absence and according to [Carlos] Isamitt, is the man who knows the most about folkloric materials here."[46] Santa Cruz's language attests to the value he placed on European experience, and also points to the role of archives as a reservoir of folkloric knowledge.

At first glance, it may seem strange that Santa Cruz privileged Lavín's authority over Carlos Isamitt's. Lavín had been out of the country for two decades while Isamitt was studying a range of folk and Indigenous arts across Chile. The Chilean government initially sent Lavín to Europe to expand his studies of Mapuche music by investigating colonial archives. This official mission was in keeping with a tendency among powerholders in Chile (as in many places) to valorize Indigenous heritage only from the distant past. Lavín had made aural transcriptions of live Mapuche music in Chile, but he was especially interested in the wax cylinder recordings made in 1911 by the German Capuchin missionary, Felix de Augusta, which were held in the Berlin Phonogram Archive.[47] Lavín was a self-taught composer who drew on Mapuche music in his Impressionist-influenced compositions, primarily while he was living in France. Isamitt met Lavín during his own sojourn in France in the mid-1920s, when he was representing Chile in an international arts exhibition in Paris, as well as visiting museums and studying pedagogies at art schools.[48] Both within and beyond Chile, it was Isamitt who became best known in the 1930s and 1940s as a composer who drew source material from his own documentation of Mapuche music. But this view was also limited. Recent Chilean research has presented a broader interpretation of Isamitt's approach, which integrated pedagogy, the arts, and Chilean cultural diversity.

Carlos Isamitt's Integrative Arts

In the early years of the twentieth century, Carlos Isamitt studied painting and musical composition in Santiago while working as a primary school

[46] Santa Cruz to Seeger, July 31, 1942, Seeger Family Collection, LoC Music Division.

[47] Salas Viu (1967) discusses Lavín's research in the Berlin Phonogram Archive. See Rekedal (2015: 57–58) on the role of Capuchin written records in the nineteenth century Chilean conquest of Mapuche territory.

[48] This was the International Exhibition of Modern Decorative and Industrial Arts, a mostly European-oriented world's fair held in 1925.

teacher and director beginning at the age of sixteen. Growing up in a rural area outside Santiago, Isamitt had moved alone to the city at the age of twelve to study education. Freddy Chávez Cancino has analyzed how Isamitt's philosophies were shaped by the Abelardo Núñez Normal School in Santiago. This teacher-training school instilled an approach that was "sensitive to the troubles of the world of the worker and of labor exploitation, especially tied to the emerging industrialization promoted by a dominant class incapable of perceiving the social problems affecting workers." Isamitt launched his teaching career in an urban school populated by the children of "peasants, laborers, and artisans."[49] He sought new materials and methods for teaching the arts in an integrative way to marginalized Chilean youth. This quest prompted Isamitt to begin traveling to different regions of Chile to study the popular arts. Carlos Isamitt's son Dionis has explained his approach this way:

> When he was in the Abelardo Núñez school [for teacher training], he had access to a tremendous library. He was interested in everything in the world. But . . . he had the firm conviction that the only form of learning was to go to the people, and for that he had to leave the library, the academy, the city and go where they lived . . . where every human being lived his life, and to accompany him, not as a reference or for questioning, but rather for seeing him, accompanying him in his life.[50]

Though this practice was often interpreted as folkloric research, it was an early manifestation of a popular pedagogy based on local ontologies, aesthetics, and political advocacy.[51] It was also related to an "artistic popular anthropology," with which Isamitt identified in his European travels.[52]

Isamitt's documentation of Chilean cultures took a new turn in 1930, when he embarked on an attempt to study Mapuche music in intimate social and ceremonial contexts in the Araucanía region. He was familiar with Mapuche arts and had facilitated an opportunity for his friend and former composition teacher, Pedro Humberto Allende, to make a gramophone recording of

---

[49] Chávez Cancino (2021: 17).

[50] Quoted in Chávez Cancino (2021: 17). "Cuando él estuvo en la Abelardo Núñez (la escuela normal), tuvo acceso a una tremenda biblioteca. Se interesó por todas las cosas del mundo. Pero . . . tenía la firme convicción de que la única forma de aprender, era ir al hombre y para eso debía salir de la biblioteca, de la academia, de la ciudad e ir donde se vivía . . . donde cada ser humano vivía su vida y acompañarlo, no de referencia, de preguntarle, sino que mirarlo, acompañarlo en su vida."

[51] Chávez Cancino (2019, 2021, 2022b).

[52] Comité Editorial, *Revista Musical Chilena* (1966: 8).

Mapuche music in Santiago in 1928.[53] In 1930, the Universidad de Chile sent Isamitt and Allende to collect Mapuche songs in situ, to be presented to a Congress of the League of Nations in Bern, Switzerland. Personal and institutional trajectories came together in this project, which was also shaped by international networks.

In the colonial and early national periods, Mapuche people had fiercely resisted Spanish and then Chilean encroachment and governance.[54] In 1930, the Mapuche communities in southern Chile also resisted the presence of outsiders such as Isamitt and Allende. After a month of failed attempts, Allende gave up on the project and returned to the capital, while Isamitt continued trying to develop trust and communication. He eventually learned to speak Mapuzugun fluently and came to be accepted among Mapuche people as a close friend, co-creator, and political ally.[55] From around 1931 to 1937, Isamitt spent about half of each year in Mapuche communities near Quepe and Toltén. He documented Mapuche songs through aural transcription, and he documented Mapuche instruments, people, and scenes through his skills as a visual artist. Soon after his first extended fieldwork, Isamitt began to develop innovative musical compositions that included melodies and texts of Mapuche songs, which were revoiced by classically trained singers in performances of Isamitt's work.

Santa Cruz was generally critical of nationalist music that incorporated folkloric sources, but he admired Isamitt's vanguardist techniques, which included serialism. In October of 1932, Santa Cruz wrote about Isamitt's early Mapuche work in the first issue of *Aulos*, a music journal that Santa Cruz founded to promote musical discussions within Chile and abroad. There, Santa Cruz reviewed Isamitt's presentation of Mapuche songs in an intimate salon setting sponsored by the Friends of Art Society in Santiago. As part of the presentation, the songs were performed by the classically trained vocalist Adriana Herrera de López and the pianist Judith Aldunate. According to Chávez Cancino, this must have been the first version of the work that would become Isamitt's *Friso araucano*, a symphonic composition with vocals in Mapuzugun.[56] In these kinds of performances, Isamitt worked with the performers to evoke Mapuche aesthetics, for example by limiting vocal

---

[53] Chávez Cancino (2021: 25).

[54] Rekedal (2015, Chapters 2–3) provides a valuable summary of this history while drawing connections to Mapuche ritual and performance.

[55] See the compilation of Isamitt's writings in Chávez Cancino (2022b).

[56] Chávez Cancino (2022a).

vibrato and learning to sing with an upward glissando at the ends of certain phrases. Santa Cruz's review of this first performance described Isamitt's fieldwork with wonder, at the same time revealing his own elite artistic biases, which were completely contradictory to Isamitt's project. He wrote, "Isamitt, with his eternal smile and his fleece hat, has gone from 'ruca' to 'ruca' (house to house) with a friendly attitude; he studied the language, learned the songs, and played them on a violin, with the admiration of those poor people who never had a precise instrument."[57] Santa Cruz did not seem to appreciate the Mapuche musicality that contributed to Isamitt's innovative sonorities, but instead attributed those sounds to Isamitt's originality and artistic genius.

In contrast to Santa Cruz, Isamitt valued Mapuche music as revelatory aesthetic expression that followed different cultural norms. In the same debut issue of *Aulos*, Isamitt published the first segment of a Mapuche music ethnography, joining musical analysis and cultural description.[58] Isamitt critiqued the neglect and denigration of musical folklore in Chile, and argued that comparative and theoretical studies were not sufficient. He seemed to consider documentation and collection to be of utmost importance, writing, "Today the search for all our popular artistic patrimony remains, as a necessity that must be satisfied."[59] He was not a salvage ethnographer, seeking to unearth past practices of Mapuche people, but rather he insisted on hearing and viewing them in the present. Isamitt argued that careful collection of Mapuche songs would enable them to be incorporated into "our historical and artistic treasury" (*nuestro haber histórico y artístico*). Together with criollo folklore (rooted in Hispanic Chilean heritage), these songs should "form the basis of music teaching in the schools, oriented toward a nobility and a real love for our land, which unfortunately are still far from being achieved."[60]

Isamitt's writings illustrate the long labor of developing trust, which he continually emphasized was crucial to his documentation work in Mapuche communities. He notes that many studies of Mapuche song were misleading because Mapuche people tended to sing with a restricted range and sonority when asked to perform for non-Indigenous strangers (*winka*).[61] When

---

[57] Santa Cruz (1932: 23).
[58] The original sources are Isamitt (1932a, 1932b, 1932c, 1933). These and other ethnographic writings of Isamitt have been compiled in Chávez Cancino (2022b).
[59] Isamitt (1932a: 8).
[60] Isamitt (1932c: 3).
[61] This critique indirectly applied to his friend and teacher, Pedro Humberto Allende, who said in a 1930 talk (later published in English in the Pan American Union Bulletin), "Vocal music, unaccompanied, is characterized by the small number of different notes used; these are all in the lower register" (Allende 1931).

Isamitt first arrived in Mapuche territory, he was excluded from close observation and listening; people would stop singing in his presence, or they would tell him to go away. At the beginning of his work, he sometimes hid in trees and bushes to hear and notate ceremonies from which he was excluded.[62] After he was included in some events, his sketches were regularly reviewed to make sure he had not violated prohibitions on drawing sacred objects. Paradoxically, Isamitt broke through Mapuche prohibitions on inscribing sacred texts and objects by using earlier inscriptions, specifically the published collections of the German Capuchin missionary, Felix de Augusta. Isamitt combined some of those published texts with his incipient knowledge of Mapuche music to convince a *machi* (shaman) that he had already been entrusted with sacred knowledge by another machi. The machi allowed him to notate some of her songs, an act that did not appear to have any deleterious effects, as she had feared. When Isamitt returned another day with his violin, he was invited for the first time to enter into a thatched-roof home. The reproduction of Mapuche melodies on his violin then led to more trust and intimacy, sharing songs and friendship.

Isamitt's writings in *Aulos* come across as a vivid ethnographic account of intercultural communication, in which he speaks explicitly from his interactive experience. Isamitt did not hide his feelings of being completely entranced on that first day he was invited into a house to hear Mapuche song at close range: "I was peering into a hidden and marvelous grove, the spiritual garden of a people, and the fruit I picked there had a fragrance and a charm capable of creating lasting pleasure." With great emotion, he walked away in the rain, noting "the impression of distancing myself, like someone who has robbed some part of the best spirit of a race."[63] He is honest about his ambivalence, perhaps tied up with the dissimulation that led to his new relationships and access to Mapuche culture. But the passage also conveys a sense of shock in the visceral experience of Mapuche expression in all its social and cultural richness. Isamitt was deeply moved not only by the beauty of Mapuche song, but also by Mapuche ontologies, ways of being that were permeated with singing.[64]

The experience changed the direction of Isamitt's work, as well as his understanding of collection. He had arrived in Mapuche territory to

[62] Isamitt (1932c: 5).
[63] Isamitt (1932c: 8).
[64] The interpretation of this passage as cultural shock comes from Freddy Chávez Cancino, personal communication, June 2022.

collect discrete texts to be incorporated into the national and international paradigms of folklore at the time. The nature of his activity shifted during that first day he was invited to listen in the Mapuche ruca. He did not travel to the congress in Switzerland after all, and instead began to chart his own path of musical documentation and creation.[65] For Isamitt, collection was a form of rescue as well as cultural and political defense. Isamitt knew that the songs he collected were falling out of use following the cultural repression of the Chilean state. Even five years after his first fieldwork, younger Mapuche wrote him to ask for copies of some of the songs he had collected that were no longer remembered. He also recognized Mapuche authorship and tried to protect their work from unauthorized use. Isamitt always used aural transcription in his documentation of Mapuche music. He never made mechanical recordings because his Mapuche interlocutors did not want to be recorded.[66]

Though Isamitt had some supporters in Chile, his work fostered more interest in the international realm. From 1935 to 1941, Isamitt's ethnographic articles, musical compositions, drawings, and paintings based on Mapuche culture were published in the *Boletín Latino Americano de Música*, Lange's music journal based in Uruguay.[67] The first volume included an article by Isamitt about the Mapuche instrument called the trutruka, as well as Isamitt's composition "Wirafun Kawellu (Horses' Gallop), Araucanian Dance" in the musical supplement. When the Pan American Union and the Inter-American Indian Institute (III) launched music projects in the early 1940s, Isamitt's name was circulating as a resource and model for Indigenous music research and composition. Isamitt was one of the "American folklorists" that Lange recommended to Otto Mayer-Serra, the German musicologist who spent most of his career in Spain and Mexico, and who collaborated with the III in Mexico City in the 1940s.[68] In the radio project of the III, discussed in Chapter 2, Isamitt was among the first composers to be contracted to contribute a musical piece. Most composers affiliated with the project were commissioned to write new music using Indigenous themes suggested by the III, but some of Isamitt's existing pieces already captured exactly what the

---

[65] Personal communication with Freddy Chávez Cancino, February 4, 2022.

[66] Personal communication with Freddy Chávez Cancino and Dionis Isamitt Danitz, June 2022.

[67] Isamitt's work appeared in the first five volumes of the *Boletín Latino Americano de Música* between 1935 and 1941.

[68] This is drawn from Palomino's archival research on Lange's correspondence (2020: 162). As discussed in Chapter 2, Otto Mayer-Serra was a German Jewish leftist who spent much of his adult life passing as a Spaniard (Alonso 2019).

project organizers were aiming for—the presentation of Indigenous musical sounds in a score that could be performed by a symphony orchestra. Isamitt was one of the few composers who had conducted his own long-term field-work to learn and document the songs that he used in his compositions.

A radio script featuring the work of Isamitt was preserved in the Inter-American Indian Institute archive.[69] The script was probably written around 1943 by Henrietta Yurchenco in English and then translated to Spanish. As discussed in Chapter 2, Yurchenco brought her radio experience as a folk music producer in New York City to her work with the III in Mexico City between 1942 and 1946. In collaboration with Mexican intellectuals and officials, she produced radio programs promoting the work of the III and carried out extensive recording expeditions of Indigenous music in Mexico and Guatemala during that time.

The III radio script characterizes the Mapuche as the "most progressive and independent" of all the South American tribes and notes their agricul-tural and especially their equestrian skills. The script goes on to describe the ceremonial "Ngillatun" in which Mapuche people "beseech the Supreme Being to send them good weather or thank him for the abundant harvest." According to the script, a key moment arises when "the music of the tra-ditional flutes starts and groups of riders on gaily decorated horses gallop around the multitude describing each time a larger circle more distant from the crowd."[70] Then the announcer says, "Here is the music played for the 'Gallop of the Horses'" and the script provides the instruction, "MUSIC UP WIRAFUN KAWELLU." The music planned for that moment of the broad-cast may have been a rendition of one of Isamitt's transcriptions of Mapuche music. Next, the announcer introduces the music for "'Lonko-perun' or, Chief's Dance," saying, "The melody which you will hear is written for small chamber orchestra and baritone and was taken down by Carlos Isamitt at a wedding."[71]

The script ends with a presentation of Isamitt's piano composition based on the first melody, "Galope de los caballos," probably the same piece as that

[69] Both English and Spanish versions were archived. I quote from the English version, file "Propaganda por Radio, México, 1940–1943," AHIII.

[70] A stunning realization of a contemporary Mapuche Nguillatun filmed in Argentina can be viewed in Marcel Czombos's documentary *Isabel la Criolla*, at 20:55, https://www.youtube.com/watch?v=rMJSsYzFLX4.

[71] Lonko Perún was published in the musical supplement to the fifth volume of the *Boletín Latino Americano de Música*. This and other selected scores of Isamitt are accessible via Freddy Chávez's website: https://www.freddychavezc.com/partituras. It was also republished in Chávez Cancino (2022).

published by the *Boletín Latino Americano de Música* in 1935. The announcer introduces the piece with the following text:

> Two principal elements form its structure: the first, the rhythmical character-istics of the rustic quality of the flute as heard from a great distance, and the second, a song of the medicine women. Mr. Isamitt heard this song, not in its magical contexts, but sung by a young child while tending her flock of sheep, imitating most gracefully the dance as she had seen her parents perform it.

The script illustrates Isamitt's special interest in childhood, as well as his me-ticulous documentation of the contexts in which he heard and transcribed music, including the place and the person who was its source (see Figure 4.2).[72] In the radio script, the distinction between the Indigenous music and the composer's interpretation of it was blurry. Isamitt may have sent transcriptions of the Indigenous music as well as the score for his composi-tion, with plans for the orchestral musicians in Mexico City to perform both for the broadcast. The radio script does not seem finalized and may not have been broadcast or recorded, but it provides evidence of the impact of Isamitt's work in transnational discourses on Indigenous music.[73]

Mapuche people were not directly involved in the III radio broadcasts about their music, but they were involved in other realms of III activities. The Mapuche leaders Venancio Koñwepag and César Kolima were Chilean delegates to the first III congress in 1940 and gave a speech there.[74] Among their proposals was the creation of a library, associated with new Indigenous schools, which would be devoted to Indigenous themes and would include "all the written works about the Araucanian race." They also proposed a center of "scientific studies" devoted to historical research and the collection of Indigenous folklore.[75] At the end of their speech, they expanded from re-gional plans to a continental agenda, including the "creation of Indigenous libraries and Indigenous scientific institutions which would interest Indian

---

[72] Chávez Cancino (2022a).

[73] Yurchenco also discussed Isamitt's work in her 1946 article on Indigenous music documentation, saying that Isamitt's compositions represented neither arrangements nor romantic interpretations, but rather "a creative synthesis of the essence of Araucanian music" (Yurchenco 1946: 322).

[74] See Vergara and Gundermann (2016: 129); Giraudo (2006: 8). I follow the Mapuzugun orthog-raphy provided in a recent reprint of their III presentation (Koñwepag and Kolima [1940] 2017), which was originally published on June 22, 1940 in *El Diario Austral*, a Temuko newspaper in Mapuche territory. Texts of the time listed their names as César Colima and Venancio Coñuepán.

[75] Koñwepag and Kolima ([1940] 2017: 412).

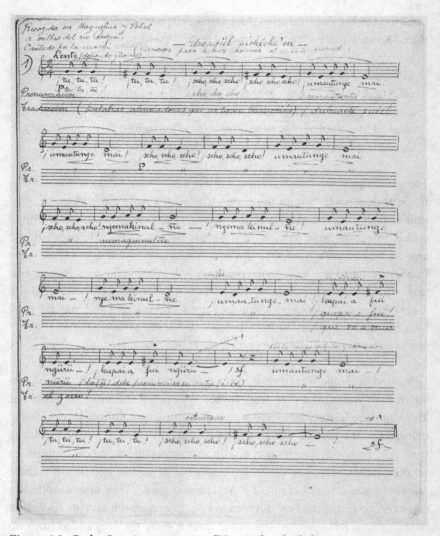

Figure 4.2 Carlos Isamitt manuscript, "Umaq ül pichiche' en, Canción para hacer dormir al niñito querido" (Song for putting a beloved little child to sleep). "Collected in Maquehue and Pelal on the shore of the Quepe river. Sung by the machi Juanita Lemungürü." 1932. *30 Cantos Araucanos de Carlos Isamitt Alarcón*, ed. Freddy Chávez Cancino. Santiago: Fondo para el Fomento de la Música Nacional, 2021 (digital version).

students in the knowledge and study of the historical past of the American peoples, and facilitate exchanges among Indigenous museums of artistic expressions of the past and present."[76] They viewed the III as an "elevated central organization that will use diplomatic means to activate the materialization by different governments of most or all the resolutions approved to benefit the Indian peoples of America."[77] Their vision of international relations as a mechanism for the protection of Indigenous peoples within nation-states was prescient in 1940, prior to the development of contemporary human rights structures.

Koñwepag and Kolima probably realized that their agenda would be an uphill battle in Chile. An immediate challenge was that the Chilean government failed to provide sufficient funds for their trip to the III Congress and left them stranded in Mexico for a time.[78] The Chilean government sent delegates to many of the III congresses, but delayed joining the III until the 1960s and never provided state support to the Instituto Indigenista Chileno, which remained a civil society organization.[79] Nevertheless, the year after the first III congress, a representative from the US Department of Indian Affairs traveled to Mapuche communities to facilitate the discourses of the III in Chile. In the mid-1940s, the official name of the Indigenous-led Araucanian Corporation received the appendage "Movimiento Indigenista de Chile."[80] In 1945, Koñwepag was elected as a regional representative to the Chilean congress, and in 1947 he gave a speech to the Chilean Parliament that drew on his inter-American experiences in 1940, both in Mexico and in the United States, which he had visited after the III congress. Koñwepag quoted from the landmark US Supreme Court case *Worcestor v. Georgia* (1832), which determined that state laws do not have force within Tribal boundaries, and he talked about the 1934 Indian Reorganization Act, closely tied to John Collier's administration, as I discussed in Chapter 2.[81] In practice, US federal Indian law, like the III, had many shortcomings, but what is significant here is the circulation and repurposing of institutional discourses across borders.

---

[76] Koñwepag and Kolima ([1940] 2017: 414).
[77] Koñwepag and Kolima ([1940] 2017: 414).
[78] Vergara and Gundermann (2016: 130).
[79] Vergara and Gundermann (2016) point out that the Instituto Indigenista Chileno, established in 1949, was a nongovernmental entity with limited resources and authority. They also note an antecedent organization formed in 1943 by the German-Chilean academic Hugo Gunckel together with Mapuche leaders and representatives Andrés Chihualilaf, Gregorio Seguel Capitán, Juan Llaimache, Victor Leñán and Juan de Dios Curilem (Vergara and Gundermann 2016: 140).
[80] Vergara and Gundermann (2016: 131).
[81] Crow (2013: 106).

These discourses also demonstrate how influences moved through unofficial channels, notwithstanding the reluctance of the Chilean government to accept III recommendations.[82]

Institutionalizing Musical Folklore

Charles Seeger was involved in the Indigenous music projects of the III, and the III office sent Santa Cruz at least one letter seeking Indigenous music recordings.[83] Though Santa Cruz did not consider Indigenous music to be at the core of Chilean heritage, he was developing interest in supporting systematic field recording in Chile. At the same time that the III music projects were unfolding, Seeger and Santa Cruz were collaborating to transfer recording and copying equipment from the United States to Chile. This was a significant shift from the international recording projects sponsored by the Library of Congress, because the Library of Congress generally required the return of its equipment, which was federal property. The PAU project with Chile was supported by Nelson Rockefeller's Office of Inter-American Affairs and was not subject to this restriction.[84]

The Institute for Research on Musical Folklore was founded in 1943 at the Universidad de Chile, building on a wave of expanding research centers there in the early 1940s, as well as the stimulus of the PAU collaboration.[85] The institute was directed by Eugenio Pereira Salas with a team that included Carlos Isamitt and Filomena Salas, along with the composers Adolfo Allende and Jorge Urrutia Blondel. Santa Cruz often described his wife Filomena Salas as a driving organizational force behind the folkloric initiatives. Though Salas worked primarily behind the scenes, in 1945 she authored an article about the activities of the Institute. She described the "laboratory work"

---

[82] Though Chile sent representatives to all the III congresses, including many Mapuche leaders, Chile was the last country to join the III. Vergara and Gundermann (2016) suggest this late entrance (in the 1960s) reflected the Chilean government's indifference to indigenista movements. The same authors note that Chile declined to sign the International Labor Organization Conventions on Indigenous rights (Conventions 107 and 169) in 1957 and in 1989, respectively.

[83] Gamio to Santa Cruz, November 4, 1942, File "Propaganda por Radio, México, 1940–1943," AHIII.

[84] Based on PAU reports, Pernet (2007: 150–151) notes that the American Council of Learned Societies provided additional funding for the recording equipment, which helped to "circumvent war-time shipping restrictions."

[85] The name of this institute changed over time, which accounts for the different versions of the institute's name mentioned in this chapter. Jorge Cáceres Valencia (1998) describes the expanding cultural initiatives at the Universidad de Chile during this time.

which involved, first of all, "in-depth historical documentation, preparatory to listening and then selection, recording, and archiving of musical forms to distinguish what is sufficiently meritorious to be conserved as musical patrimony." Delving into the past was necessary for the selective process of hearing heritage and conserving it. This work had a reformist and educational aim. In Salas's words, the new institute would "search for the best way to bring to the masses the true traditional and folkloric culture of the past, the only viable pathway, we dare say, to conserve and improve today's popular song which will come to constitute the folklore of tomorrow."[86]

This tightly restricted notion of musical patrimony, however, was challenged by other institutional practices, especially the sponsorship of folkloric performances and the absorptive activity of collection. The new folklore institute sponsored performances and recordings that included nonprofessional musicians, as well as professional musicians who began to conduct their own fieldwork. Margot Loyola was one of these, a left-leaning musical interpreter who forged new paths for folkloric performers, at the same time that her trained voice found sympathetic listeners inside the academic music establishment.[87] Even more radical was Pablo Garrido, a pioneering jazz musician, vanguardist composer, and folklorist who was also an organizer of musicians' unions.[88] Garrido's position at the Universidad de Chile was short-lived precisely because of his political and social commitments, but his multifaceted work opened up alternative visions for organizing music and musicians. Overall, as Juan Eduardo Wolf has written, the institutionalization of folkloric collection and performance had enduring ideological impacts: the development of discourses of authenticity and fieldwork, and the creation of a canon of geographic regions and ethnoracial groups.[89]

In Santa Cruz's collaboration with the Pan American Union in the early 1940s, he was initially interested in studio recording equipment, which would be used for art music recordings, and in new equipment for copying orchestral scores. Folk music could be recorded by inviting musicians to the studio. But as Santa Cruz wrote to Seeger in February of 1942, "It will be necessary to think, also, about portable recording equipment as an indispensable thing. I will see how to buy it. We have met with Carlos Vega, from Argentina, and

---

[86] Salas (1945: 26–27).
[87] Ruiz Zamora (2006).
[88] Donoso Fritz and Ramos Rodillo (2021); Ramos Rodillo and Donoso Fritz (2023); da Costa García (2009); Karmy Bolton (2019); Karmy (2021a, 2021b); Jordán and Salazar (2022).
[89] Wolf (2019: 35). Wolf's work draws attention to a glaring absence in twentieth-century official cartographies of Chilean folklore, that of Afro-descendant music and culture.

Figure 4.3 Isabel Aretz during her fieldwork in Chile, 1941. Film still captured by Claudio Mercado from film recording created by Enrique Thiele. Isabel Aretz Collection, Museo Chileno de Arte Precolombino, Santiago, Chile.

I have felt frank envy for what they are doing there."[90] A portable Presto recorder was part of the PAU donation, but it was damaged en route to Chile; systematic field recording still lagged behind Argentina.

Beginning in 1931, Carlos Vega had developed a music documentation program in Argentina based on regionalist folklore collecting as well as academic paradigms, including the Berlin school of comparative musicology.[91] Vega trained his students—often classical musicians—in fieldwork methods of transcription and recording. Both methodologies were necessary since the unreliability of recording equipment often led to aural transcription as a backup. Curiously, in the letter quoted above, Santa Cruz mentions Vega but not Isabel Aretz, who would become Vega's most famous student in the Americas (see Figure 4.3). Both Vega and Aretz had visited Chile to conduct fieldwork in January of 1941, along with Aretz's first husband Enrique Thiele, who operated the film recording equipment

[90] Santa Cruz to Seeger, February 6, 1942. Seeger Family Collection, LoC Music Division.
[91] Chamosa (2010); Giacosa (2007).

while Aretz made sound recordings. In Santiago, Aretz met with Santa Cruz just before his trip to the United States, recounted at the beginning of this chapter. She also met Isamitt, who listened to her Mapuche recordings, and then she listened to recordings of Isamitt's orchestral compositions based on Mapuche songs. "Buen trabajo," she wrote appreciatively in her logbook.[92] Aretz was also a composer who had studied with Heitor Villa-Lobos, among others, and initially pursued regional musics as an autochthonous source for composition.[93]

From Chile, Aretz continued alone to Bolivia and Peru, developing contacts and making field recordings along the way. She later reflected on the international journey, saying,

> In these travels, my teachers were Araucans and Mapuches, Chinos, Aymaras, and Kollas, Incas and Chancas, whose music was recorded in my spirit, broadening the teachings I had received from illustrious professors, which thus found their own channel in the pathways of our beloved América.[94]

This quote suggests that Aretz recognized the value not only of Indigenous music as an archival object, but also of Indigenous "teachers" who held the knowledge of autochthonous, ancestral generations. Their music was recorded in Aretz's very spirit, as a transformation of her own subjectivity which deepened her identification with "our beloved América."

The reception Aretz received upon returning to Argentina was mixed. As a woman, Aretz's competence was challenged more than that of men. Some expressed doubts about her morality because she had traveled alone in the

---

[92] In Santiago, Aretz wrote in her logbook on Saturday, January 17, 1941: "We went to the university where some musicians were gathered, among them Isamit [sic], to listen to the discs I recorded among the Araucanians. Then I listened to the discs which they had recorded, of the official orchestra with orchestrated Araucanian songs. Good work" (Mercado and Villalobos 2020: 27). Though Aretz's notes do not specify, the "orchestrated Araucanian songs" must have been Isamitt's.

[93] Locatatelli de Pérgamo (2005).

[94] This quotation comes from the documentary film *Voces de la Tierra*. In using the term "Chinos," Aretz was referring to a dance/music performance ritual in central Chile, a significant inclusion of campesino and fishing communities who have maintained these Indigenous practices but are not generally identified as Indigenous (Mercado 2002). See also Izquierdo König's (2018) analysis of the inscription of the *baile chino* as UNESCO intangible heritage. Aretz's original quote in Spanish: "En estos viajes, mis maestros fueron Araucanos y Mapuches, Chinos, Aymaras, y Kollas, Incas y Chancas, cuya música se grabó en mi espíritu, ensanchando las enseñanzas antes recibidas de ilustres maestros, que así encontraron cauce propio en los caminos de nuestra querida América." *Voces de la Tierra*. 1:21:00, https://www.youtube.com/watch?v=e10aAbMkWBc.

countryside and interacted with male musicians.[95] But she was tough and determined, already having successfully entered the male-dominated sphere of art music composition in the 1930s. Aretz continued to build institutional support for her research, both in Argentina and in other Latin American countries. She began working in Venezuela in 1947, sent by the Argentine government, and there she married Luis Felipe Ramón y Rivera, a Venezuelan composer and folklorist who had also studied with Carlos Vega. Together they built an institutional structure for documentary music research that led to an official inter-American entity in 1970, the Instituto Interamericano de Etnomusicología y Folklore (INIDEF). Under Aretz's leadership, INIDEF was a specialized agency of the Organization of American States, which had subsumed the Pan American Union in 1948.

Through INIDEF, Aretz acquired funding to bring students from across Latin America to Venezuela to be trained in documentation, recording, and research methods. The Chilean music scholar Juan Pablo González has aligned Aretz's work with a "renovated inter-Americanism which gained force in Latin America beginning in the 1970s."[96] INIDEF differed from Lange's initiatives by centering the folkloric-popular-ethnic musical spectrum rather than art music; it differed from Seeger's initiatives by grounding the work in Latin American cultural and institutional contexts.[97]

Nevertheless, Latin American solidarities in music research could not be taken for granted in the intimate networks of strong personalities and institutional politics. In a 1953 letter to Seeger, Carlos Vega described a definitive break in his relations with Aretz, who, according to Vega, had taken the collections she made under the auspices of his institute with her to Venezuela.[98] Vega framed the disagreement in both personal and professional terms, but most prominent was a conflict over the ownership and authorship of research and recordings. For her part, Aretz appeared to maintain a public reverence for the pioneering work of her first fieldwork mentor.

[95] Commentary of Mario Silva and María Ester Rodríguez, July 11, 2020, online discussion hosted by Museo Chileno de Arte Precolombino, prior to screening *Voces de la Tierra. Un documental de Isabel Aretz y Mario Silva*, https://www.youtube.com/watch?v=e10aAbMkWBc.

[96] González (2009: 52). Nancy Morris translated Juan Pablo González's use of the word "renovada" as "renewed" (González 2018), but I think the alternative translation, "renovated," is especially meaningful in this context, as it implies transformation and updating more than re-creation.

[97] Aretz was most interested in traditional musics with local and regional roots in oral cultures, though she included mass popular music as well as academic music in her classification systems. See, e.g., Aretz (1977); Aretz (1991: 26–28).

[98] Vega to Seeger, January 3, 1953, Seeger Family Collection, LoC Music Division.

Curiously, the year 1953 was a time of tremendous rupture and reorganization for many of the personal and institutional networks I have been tracing.

Ruptures and Revolutionary Folklore

After World War II, the rise of the Cold War disrupted and reconfigured inter-American exchanges. In 1950, the Spanish-Chilean musicologist Vicente Salas Viu was invited to visit the United States under the auspices of the PAU, but after investing some of his own money into the trip, he was denied a visa by the US government. The reason given was that he had Communist sympathies and advocated "the overthrow by force of the government of the United States," a notion that Seeger and Santa Cruz both found absurd.[99]

Then in January of 1953, Seeger was denied a passport from the US government for travel to an international conference on the grounds of suspicious affiliations. Seeger had participated in the Composers' Collective in New York in the 1930s, which included some Communist Party members.[100] In the early 1950s his son, the folk singer Pete Seeger, was blacklisted and shut out of the music industry along with his enormously popular group, the Weavers.[101] After the passport denial, Charles Seeger felt straightjacketed at the PAU, which led to his retirement. Most devastatingly, later that year his wife Ruth Crawford Seeger, who had been the emotional and economic backbone of the family, was diagnosed with and died of cancer, with their two youngest children still living at home. Charles's meager PAU salary had been crucially supplemented by Ruth's private piano studio and sales of her folk song books. In the Library of Congress Seeger collections and in their biographies, one senses the deep sorrow of losing not only a wife and mother, but also a gifted composer—surpassing Charles—who had just begun to compose again after years of putting her own music on the back burner.[102]

The same year, 1953, Santa Cruz faced different kinds of political shifts in Chile and was subject to accusations of corruption. President Carlos Ibáñez had pledged to combat corruption in state institutions. The president's own

---

[99] Santa Cruz to Seeger, August 16, 1950, Seeger Family Collection, LoC Music Division. Salas Viu's political history merits closer study. He was a refugee from Franco's regime, which might suggest leftist tendencies, though the McCarthyist assessments of communism were greatly exaggerated and distorted in US discourses.

[100] Pescatello (1992: 112).

[101] Corn (2015).

[102] Tick (1997); Pescatello (1992).

Figure 4.4 Carlos Isamitt between Domingo Santa Cruz (left) and
the conductor Armando Carvajal (right). 1933. *Iconografía musical
chilena: investigaciones* / Samuel Claro Valdés [et al.]. 1a. edición.
Santiago: Ediciones UC (Pontificia Universidad Católica de Chile), 1989.

record was dubious; he had controlled Chile as a military dictator from
1925 to 1931. But in 1952, Ibáñez was elected to office with a populist co-
alition that included Mapuche support through an alliance with Venancio
Koñwepag. Based on this alliance, in 1953 Ibáñez acted on Koñwepag's proposal to create a Department of Indigenous Affairs, and Koñwepag became
the first Indigenous person to direct a Chilean national institution.[103]

Though the world of fine arts was a different arena of reform, the new populist orientations made Santa Cruz vulnerable to criticism for his powerful
influence over Chilean arts institutions since 1928 (see Figure 4.4). In 1951,

[103] Crow (2013: 106).

the Chilean press published accusations of financial mismanagement under Santa Cruz's leadership, but he considered these politically motivated. In 1953, more challenges to his leadership emerged. A broad range of organizations representing fine arts, graphic arts, composers, singers, and other professional musicians sent a petition to President Ibáñez calling for investigation. Santa Cruz considered the move to be a conspiracy against him, and he was especially taken aback that Carlos Isamitt, a long-time institutional ally, did not come to his defense. Santa Cruz wrote in his memoir, "What did the visual arts have to do with our case? And how had they recruited Carlos Isamitt, who as a result was also responsible for the enormities of the denunciations?"[104]

As a result of the petition, the Consejo Universitario called for a review of the Instituto de Extensión Musical, which included performance and research branches with a national purview, directed by Santa Cruz. The review was concerned with the coordination of university services and the need for a system to evaluate conflicts of interest. The review also recommended more transparent procedures for prizes, and the incorporation of more popular (working-class) labor into the institutions. Santa Cruz's reflections in his memoir were defiant and dismissive of all the charges, and he considered the point about popular labor to be nonsensical. But the momentum of the challenge was beyond his control. The political pressure forced Santa Cruz into early retirement, at least for a time.[105]

The year 1953 was also a pivotal time in the creation of new pathways for folkloric research through the work of Violeta Parra, which took place on the fringes or entirely outside of institutions. Violeta Parra had grown up in a musical family in southern Chile near Temuco, then moved to Santiago in 1934 at the age of eighteen, following her studious elder brother, Nicanor Parra. As a singer and guitarist she played a wide repertoire, at different times specializing in rancheras and corridos (popularized by Mexican cinema), Spanish folk music (inspired by the arrival of Spanish musicians at the end of the Spanish Civil War), and Chilean cuecas and tonadas.[106]

Toward the end of the year 1952, Violeta discovered the lettered world of folkloric inscription through her brother Nicanor, after he had returned from studies abroad and was launching a dual career as a physicist and poet.

---

[104] Santa Cruz (2008: 863, 886).
[105] Santa Cruz later returned to work in the same position, from which he fully retired in 1968 to devote himself to composing music and writing his massive memoir.
[106] Herrero (2017: 64,79,91); Verba (2017).

Figure 4.5 Violeta Parra taking notes during fieldwork with Don Emilio Lobos in Santa Rita de Pirque, Puente Alto, Chile. From the book *Violeta Parra. Cantos Folklóricos Chilenos. Colección Arte y Fotografía.* 2013. Photographs by Sergio Larraín and Sergio Bravo. CEIBO Ediciones.

Violeta was also writing poetry, and their conversations led to Nicanor showing her a collection of "vulgar poetry" that Rodolfo Lenz had published in 1909. It was a revelation, because it reminded Violeta of the songs she had grown up with in southern Chile, the songs of drunks and farmers and religious processions.[107] She came to the conclusion that the popular classes were the true sources of Chilean music and culture and that their music was under threat as the result of urban migration and new technologies of communication. Parra began to conduct research almost immediately, collecting songs from elderly singers she knew in Santiago and following their recommendations to rural areas. She was an excellent musician with a gift for deep listening, though she had not learned to read or write conventional musical notation. In the beginning, she wrote lyrics by hand in a notebook, and used her own invented symbols for musical patterns (see Figure 4.5). Parra's inscriptions, combined with her acute musical ear and absorptive memory,

---

[107] Herrero (2017: 110–111) draws the story from an interview by Leónidas Morales with Nicanor Parra, who recalled Violeta's exclamation, "Pero si esas son las canciones de los borrachos, pues!" An English translation of the original interview is in Morales (2017: 43).

were the first part of her preservation system. But for Parra, preservation could not be confined to written inscriptions. Preservation also required performance, which entailed her own aesthetic transformations. Gradually Parra's preservationist projects merged with her creative projects, and she used folk materials as the core elements for new compositions with her own lyrics.[108]

Violeta Parra had already begun to collect songs with this sensibility of creative preservation before she entered institutional networks. On July 12, 1953, she broke into a new sphere of influence when Nicanor took her to Pablo Neruda's forty-ninth birthday party and she played old campesino songs as well as her own compositions. Margot Loyola heard about Parra's performance at the party, which was unlike anything performed in the professional folk music circuit. Parra intentionally emulated the aesthetics of campesino singers by voicing a straight tone with a sandy texture that iconized the earthy contexts of rural Chile. Though they were aware of each other before, Loyola and Parra finally met in person in September of 1953, and Loyola began to introduce Parra to the institutional networks that could bring her songs to a larger audience.

Violeta went to great effort to acquire a recording device through solicitations to various entities. Finally, in 1955 she made a public request, via a magazine interview, directed at the Universidad de Chile: "I consider that an organization like the Universidad de Chile should provide me with a recorder. I have worked very hard to overcome the shyness of these singers and convince them to show me their songs. It would be even more valuable to record the songs directly and conserve their voices, styles, and themes as a musical archive."[109] The public pressure worked; the Universidad de Chile provided Violeta with a magnetic tape recorder imported from Poland (see Figure 4.6). As part of the agreement, she deposited the recordings in the Institute of Folkloric Research at the Universidad de Chile.[110]

Parra was passionate about her documentary work, but making field recordings was not easy. Rural singers tended to be hesitant to sing for the tape recorder, either because it was unfamiliar or because they could hear that it distorted the sound of their voices.[111] Gonzalo Montero argues that Parra's writings demonstrate a consciousness that the recorder activated

---

[108] For more discussion of these processes, see Torres Alvarado (2004).
[109] Quoted in Herrero (2017: 106).
[110] Herrero (2017: 174).
[111] Montero (2018: 136).

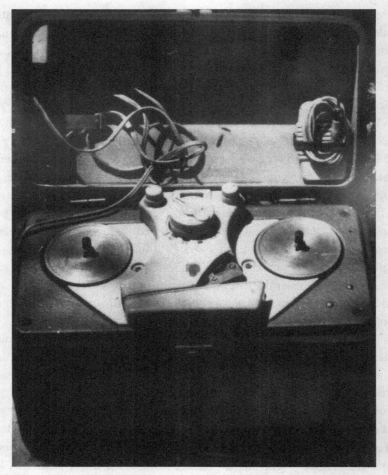

Figure 4.6 Violeta Parra's first field recorder. From the book *Violeta Parra. Cantos Folklóricos Chilenos. Colección Arte y Fotografía* (2013). Photographs by Sergio Larraín and Sergio Bravo. CEIBO Ediciones.

unequal power dynamics, which she sometimes used to her advantage in recording reluctant performers.[112]

Museums and archives contributed to Parra's concerns about preservation as well as representation of Chilean music and arts. In Chile, Violeta recorded rural music performed by peasant and working-class singers to be deposited in

[112] Montero (2018: 136–137).

Chilean archives. When she traveled to Europe later in 1955, Violeta's singing of peasant songs became the object of sound archive collections. She performed Chilean peasant songs on recordings for the sound archive of the Musée de l'Homme in Paris. In defense of her work without pay, she replied, "France is a museum; they will conserve these songs forever."[113] In London she was recorded for the BBC archives and for the personal archive of Alan Lomax, the pioneering folk music recordist from the United States, whom she met in the BBC offices.[114] There was a complicated relationship between Chilean patrimony and foreign collections. Many Europeans perceived Parra's performances of Chilean folk music to be representative of Indigenous culture, and this may have contributed to her interest in documenting and preserving Indigenous music in Chile. Parra also sometimes claimed Indigenous ancestry or a desire for it, though she would not have been considered Indigenous in Chile.[115]

Fernando Rios has meticulously traced the development of the stylized Andean music performed in Paris beginning in the 1950s and its impact on Violeta Parra and her children, Isabel and Ángel Parra, who had their own professional music careers.[116] It was in Paris that Violeta Parra began to play the Andean quena and charango, in addition to the Venezuelan cuatro. Rios focuses on representations of Andean music in the transnational Latin American folk music scene. Some of Parra's later songs had clear Mapuche referents, such as "Arauco tiene una pena (Levántate, Huenchullán)" (1962) and "El guillatún" (1967).[117]

After the literary scholar Paula Miranda published a book about Parra's poetry in 2013, she began to search archives for evidence of Parra's relations with Mapuche communities. In 2014, while reviewing collections in the sound archive of the Institute of Musical Research at the Universidad de Chile, Miranda encountered four field recordings that Parra had made in Mapuche territory in 1957 and 1958. Parra was affiliated with the Universidad de Concepción around this time, from approximately November 1957 to July 1958, but she apparently made the Mapuche recordings independently. Miranda worked together with the Mapuche linguist Elisa Loncón and the literary scholar Allison Ramay to trace the sources and social contexts of these recordings. Loncón, a native speaker of Mapuzugun, contributed

---

[113] Herrero (2017: 208).
[114] Herrero (2017: 215); Escobar-Mundaca (2022).
[115] Herrero (2017: 425–426).
[116] See Rios (2008).
[117] See Crow (2013: 130–135).

transcriptions, translations, and detailed cultural knowledge about the meanings of the songs recorded.

The resulting book, *Violeta Parra en el Wallmapu: Su encuentro con el canto Mapuche*, demonstrates the constant potential for uptake and resignification of archival sources.[118] Tracing the histories of these recordings entailed a search for origins, a process that is often spurred by encounters with old sound recordings. Perhaps most significantly, it was a project of reconnecting archival sources with the descendants of the Mapuche singers who were recorded. Those descendants considered Parra's song "Gracias a la vida" (Thanks to Life) to express Mapuche culture most profoundly. The authors link Mapuche concepts of communication and socialization to the following strophe of "Gracias a la vida":

> Gracias a la vida que me ha dado tanto
> Me ha dado el sonido y el abecedario
> Con él las palabras que pienso y declaro
> Madre, amigo, hermano y luz alumbrando
> La ruta del alma del que estoy amando.
> Thanks to life which has given me so much
> It has given me sound and the letters of the alphabet
> With it the words that I think and speak
> Mother, friend, brother and shining light
> The route of the soul of the one I love.

"Gracias a la vida" evokes the act of close listening to all kinds of sounds and beings, the balance of forces and elements in the world, the unity of the cosmos and the individual, the pendulum of joy and sorrow, the specificity and universality of life—all under the recurring theme of profound gratitude, so often a prominent focus of Indigenous poetics and relationalities. Likewise, Mapuche ontologies of speech and song, the word that is taught and the word that is heard, weave together "community, histories, identities, and memories, illuminating the souls of those we love."[119] In her sand-textured voice, Parra sang the lyrics slowly, with the fatigue of someone who had walked "beaches and deserts, mountains and plains" to arrive

---

[118] Miranda, Loncón, and Ramay (2017); Miranda (2017).

[119] Miranda, Loncón, and Ramay (2017: 48). "Este sentido es lo que impacta más profundamente a Violeta Parra en su creación: el de una palabra que teje comunidad, historias, identidades, recuerdos y que alumbra el alma de aquellos que amamos, como lo expresa en 'Gracias a la vida.'"

at "your house, your street, your patio." The bright, metallic strums of the Andean charango ripple in the foreground, with soft percussion in the background. "Gracias a la vida" undoubtedly emerged from a lifetime of Parra's experiences within and across national and cultural borders, but Mapuche listeners recognized something of their own in the song's essence.

Recuperations

Less than a year after the 1973 coup which initiated a brutal military dictatorship in Chile, Santa Cruz wrote a letter to Seeger to convey his view of political and artistic developments. Like many conservative Chileans, Santa Cruz initially supported the coup as a means of resisting the social reforms which were upending the established structures of arts, economics, and society. In the letter, after relaying his analysis of events, Santa Cruz nostalgically turns his attention to the archiving projects of the 1940s, hoping to recuperate lost collections. He says he is going to write to Carleton Sprague Smith to see if there is still a microfilm of his score for the *Cantata de los Ríos de Chile* which he deposited in the New York Public Library in 1942.[120] During the political unrest in Chile, he writes, "the savages appear to have burned it." Santa Cruz also wants to know who replaced Harold Spivacke at the Library of Congress, so he can write and ask about the acetate discs of Chilean art music that Filomena Salas had deposited there in 1941. "It is interesting," he writes, "because they are the first recordings made here of that type, us forcing the RCA [to make them]."[121] Here is the familiar sense of authenticity and primordiality of first recordings, but instead of field recordings like those of Aretz, these were studio recordings of Chilean art music. Still, some contained echoes of popular, folkloric, and Indigenous sounds.[122]

[120] See Merino (1979: 23) for discussion of Santa Cruz's *Cantata a los Ríos de Chile*, composed in 1941.

[121] Santa Cruz to Seeger, June 10, 1974, Seeger Family Collection, LoC Music Division.

[122] During her solo visit to the United States in December 1941, Filomena Salas brought recordings from the Universidad de Chile which were copied for their dissemination in the United States through her lectures and library deposits. According to a letter from Santa Cruz to Seeger at the time, the discs included Allende's "Escenas Campesinas," Leng's "Fantasía para piano y orquesta," and Bisquertt's "Nochebuena." Santa Cruz said that two other works would arrive separately: Isamitt's "Friso Araucano" and Santa Cruz's own "Suite para cuerdas." (Santa Cruz to Seeger, December 7, 1941, Seeger Family Collection, LoC Music Division.) The Library of Congress collection that appears to have resulted from this exchange is titled "Chilean Folk Music and Art Music" (LCCN 2014655377). Other recordings were probably added later to the original 1941 collection. This collection includes two of Isamitt's "Cantos Araucanos" for voice and piano. The orchestral "Friso Araucano" may have been deposited at the same time (it has an undated Library of Congress card

The micro-histories embedded in archives show that collections are not neutral, fixed repositories of knowledge. They are created through social and political relationships. In discussing the histories of collectors in this chapter, I have emphasized individual contributions to shifting paradigms of collection in the context of institutional networks. This should not be taken as an idealization of the heroics of collecting. Chilean music collectors were complicated figures with their own struggles and limitations. Institutional discourses shifted over time and were often subject to repurposing by authorized as well as unauthorized actors. The legacies of individuals and institutions are continually reshaped by debates about musical canons, rights to culture, representations of indigeneity, and the material sources of history.

In recent years, Carlos Isamitt's works have gained more attention through the concerted efforts of his son, Dionis Isamitt Danitz, and Freddy Chávez Cancino, who has become the curator of the family archive. Isamitt died in 1974, the year after the right-wing coup set the country on the path of a long military dictatorship. The family kept Isamitt's archive close, bound up with their love for its creator. Isamitt was a prolific producer of works but not an organizer. Dionis prepared the first catalog of his father's compositions before his passing. When Freddy Chávez Cancino began to work through Isamitt's archive, in close dialogue with Dionis, he decided to start with the music, to resurrect compositions from a fixed format on yellowed staff paper and "make them sound." This was Freddy's instinct as a music professor, composer, and multi-instrumentalist who began playing the accordion professionally in folk music groups at the age of twelve. Isamitt's Mapuche documentation also had cultural resonance for Freddy, whose grandmother was likely a Mapuche descendant.

Freddy and Dionis want performances of Isamitt's compositions to engage with the cultural depth of his work rather than rushing through a token inclusion. When they have the opportunity, they work with performers during rehearsal so that the Indigenous aesthetic is not sublimated by classical technique, especially in vocal style. As Freddy prepared new scores and a critical edition of Isamitt's 30 Cantos Araucanos, he relied on Dionis to make decisions such as choosing between alternate versions, or the placement of dynamic markings. For Dionis, his father's acts of preservation and performance were bound up in the logic of Indigenous relationality, reciprocity, and love.

catalog record), but the recording has not yet surfaced. If "Friso Araucano" was deposited in 1941, it would constitute the earliest recording of that work. Correspondence suggests that the original was sent to Washington to be copied in late 1941. In Chile, the earliest extant recording of Friso Araucano is from 1946 (Freddy Chávez Cancino, personal communication).

Dionis spent long periods during his childhood accompanying his father on fieldwork trips and established his own close relations with Mapuche friends who continued to visit him after Carlos Isamitt's passing. Dionis embodies an aural archive of preferred performance practices for his father's music, which he applies to the work of recuperation.[123] This recuperative work is a massive project stretching across creative media, including visual art as well as music and writings, and across the networks of a long life of friendships.[124] Because Carlos Isamitt was not especially attached to the products of his creativity, he sometimes gave away originals without keeping copies.

"¿Conoces a Carleton Sprague Smith?" Dionis asked me toward the end of our first visit, trilling the name as it would be pronounced in Spanish.[125] Carleton Sprague Smith, the well-connected music librarian and cultural diplomat, met Isamitt while visiting Chile during his 1940 Latin American tour.[126] Dionis wondered if his father had sent Smith a solo piano sonata which no longer existed in the family archive. I was struck by the recurrence of Smith's name in efforts to track down scattered musical works, following the networks of 1940s cultural diplomacy. I wrote to Jessica Wood, the assistant curator of music and recorded sound at the New York Public Library for the Performing Arts, where Carleton Sprague Smith's papers are archived. Wood promptly located three published and two unpublished scores of Isamitt, but the solo piano sonata wasn't there.

Neither US nor Chilean institutions managed to preserve all their collections, all the time. On both sides, even "dominant" institutions had uneven funding and varying archival protocols. At the Universidad de Chile, Rodrigo Torres has noted that the key actors in the 1940s accumulated archival materials but did not focus on organizing them.[127] In today's institutional context, the impressive digital collections based at the Universidad de Chile and the Biblioteca Nacional are evidence of the passion and professionalism surrounding musical and historical research in Chile.[128] Still, ongoing

[123] In a different cultural context, see Alex Chávez's theorization of an embodied aural archive (Chávez 2017: 234–235).

[124] Dionis's mother, Beatriz Danitz, was also a prolific visual artist whose works can be found in national and international museums.

[125] In English: "Do you know of Carleton Sprague Smith?"

[126] Smith (1940: 178). See also Shepard (2006).

[127] Personal communication, June 2022.

[128] These include the *Revista Musical Chilena* at the Universidad de Chile, and the online platform Memoria Chilena at the Biblioteca Nacional. Thematically focused digital archive projects are also launched through graduate and post-graduate research funded by the cultural branches

struggles over social, political, and economic hierarchies often play out in public institutions. The Biblioteca Nacional was on strike during my visit in June 2022. Across civil society, massive protests in 2019 led to a process of drafting a new constitution with the aim of replacing the constitution that had been created under the dictatorship. The Mapuche scholar Elisa Loncón, coauthor of *Violeta Parra en el Wallmapu*, headed the constitutional convention. Cultural recovery is ever more tied up with representation and political struggle.

A range of Chilean researchers are engaged in projects of Indigenous cultural recuperation through archives. Jorge Pavez Ojeda and his collaborators have framed the publication of documents from official archives as a project of declassification, where historical records and access to them constitute political power.[129] In unofficial circuits of knowledge, cultural recuperation sometimes entails bringing together institutional collections and private family collections to uncover Indigenous research contributions. With this approach, Laura Jordán and Andrea Salazar have recovered the 1940s collaboration between Juan de Dios Curilem Millanguir (1912–1985), considered the first Mapuche musicologist, and Pablo Garrido (1905–1982), mentioned earlier in this chapter for his work in folklore, jazz, and musicians' unions.[130]

Margarita Canio Llanquinao and Gabriel Pozo Menares have explored the documentary collections of the German anthropologist Robert Lehmann-Nitsche (1872–1938) held by German archives. As a museum director in Argentina, Lehmann-Nitsche made sound recordings and transcriptions of the speech and songs of Mapuche people who were forcibly relocated to Buenos Aires at the turn of the twentieth century. In 2010, Canio—a native speaker of Mapuzugun—and Pozo began studying Lehmann-Nitsche's collections archived in Germany, resulting in a 2013 book titled *Historia y conocimiento oral mapuche: Sobrevivientes de la "Campaña del Desierto" y "Ocupación de la Araucanía (1899–1926).*[131] The twenty-four Mapuche individuals whose voices were recorded by Lehmann-Nitsche are listed

---

of the Chilean government. See, for example Eileen Karmy Bolton's website "Memoria Musical de Valparaíso," http://memoriamusicalvalpo.cl/.

[129] Menard and Pavez (2005); Pavez Ojeda (2015).
[130] Jordán and Salazar (2022).
[131] In English: *Mapuche Oral History and Knowledge: Survivors of the "Desert Campaign" and "Occupation of the Araucanía" (1899–1926)* (Canio Llanquinao and Pozo Menares 2013). The Ibero-American Institute in Berlin held unpublished works of Lehmann-Nitsche, and the Ethnological Museum of Berlin (heir to the Berlin Phonogram Archive) held wax cylinder recordings made by Lehmann-Nitsche in Argentina (Canio Llanquinao and Pozo Menares 2014: 71).

as coauthors of the book. The texts (almost 600 pages) are printed in dual columns on each page: Mapuzugun on the left and Spanish translations on the right. At the end of the book is an annex of color images, set off from the page in a three-dimensional visual effect, which puts the archive in the hands of the reader. The largest number of photographs are portraits of individual Mapuche people who contributed to Lehmann-Nitsche's research, as well as a few group photographs of extended families who were being held in Buenos Aires. They are clear, close-up images, many of them named, a vivid portrayal of Mapuche life in transition. The visceral recognition of Mapuche people—their images, stories, and voices—underscores their status as living survivors. The recuperative work of Canio and Pozo makes these voices audible again.

The documentation of Aretz's 1941 trip to Chile has also taken on a life of its own in overlapping networks of recuperation. In 1997, after the passing of her husband, Luis Felipe Ramón y Rivera, Aretz moved from Venezuela back to Argentina, where she had grown up and launched her career. She brought some of her earliest collections with her. (One wonders if these were the collections Vega was so concerned about in 1953.) Mario Silva, a music teacher and ethnographer of Indigenous music, began to work on organizing and restoring the audio and visual materials, a labor of love which he felt was urgent to undertake while Aretz still had a strong, clear mind and voice. In 1999 they completed a documentary film titled *Voces de la Tierra* [Voices of the Land]: *Mapuches, Aymaras, Incas*, based on Aretz's travels through Chile, Bolivia, and Peru from 1941 to 1942. After Aretz's passing in 2005, Silva made the monumental decision to repatriate the documentary materials to the countries in which they were collected. This required more organizational and technical labor, along with the development of institutional relationships. The first repatriation project involved Chile, where Silva already had contact with a museum professional, Claudio Mercado. Mercado was himself a documentary ethnomusicologist long committed to sharing archival materials with source communities. He considered the 1941 collection to be a "patrimonial treasure."[132] In an online conversation about the project hosted by the museum, Silva and his wife, María Ester Rodríguez, commented on the gendered aspects of Aretz's work and reception. Silva used the metaphor of "weaving" when he described Aretz's careful handling

[132] Online presentation, July 11, 2020. Museo del Arte Precolombino, https://www.youtube.com/watch?v=e10aAbMkWBc.

of the thread of material emerging from the disc as it was stripped away by the cutting needle—a creative, gendered metaphor that contrasts with the masculinized metaphors often used for recording technology (male and female connectors, virgin discs, fetishization of microphones, etc.).[133]

In 2018, the Argentine filmmaker Marcel Czombos released a film called *Isabel la criolla*, which follows the repatriation of Aretz's documentary materials and the travels of Silva and Mercado to the places where Aretz made recordings in 1941. Naming Aretz "la criolla" evokes her strong identification with, and search for, autochthonous Latin American culture. Her family ancestry was German, but she was born in América (thus, criolla), and she was driven to document and promote distinctively Latin American musics. While most documentarists of her time focused on national collections, Aretz was concerned with transnational collections and the recognition of commonalities as well as differences across borders. The film is about mediation, memory, and the passing of time; about the continuance of Indigenous cultural practices; and about the mourning of relationships that have passed from the mundane world to the world of memory and mediation, especially the teacher-student relationship between Aretz and Silva.

Like many of the narratives in this chapter, the film *Isabel la criolla* shows how collections are intimately bound up with the subjectivities of collectors. Collections are also bound up with different kinds of longing for the past, or for cultural alterity itself, in different temporalities and ontologies. The film raises questions about the tension between the search for Indigenous origins and the testimony of Indigenous "survivance"—Vizenor's term for the self-determination and continuance of Indigenous peoples.[134] At different moments of the journey to revisit Aretz's recording sites in the film, literal and figurative signs of Indigenous resistance disrupt the temporal narratives entailed by searching for the past. The tension is manifest in the very name of the cultural institution where Aretz's recordings were repatriated, the Chilean Museum of Pre-Columbian Art. Yet the collection description makes clear that the intended audience includes not only researchers interested in the past, but also the living descendants of the people who were recorded.[135]

---

[133] See Locatatelli de Pérgamo (2005) for another discussion of Aretz's handling of the disc material.

[134] Vizenor (2008).

[135] Mercado and Villalobos (2020: 9). For recent work focused on contemporary Mapuche music and related cultural practices, see Bacigalupo (2013, 2016); Cárcamo-Huechante (2013); Díaz Collao (2020); Ñanculef Huaiquinao, Cuyanao/Waikil, and Díaz-Collao (2022); Pérez de Arce ([2007] 2020); Rekedal (2015); Rekedal (2022); Velásquez Arce (2017); and the works of the

Roughly at the midway point of the film, we see a contemporary shot of a man in a blue t-shirt, standing at the edge of a sonorous, swiftly moving river.[136] His straight black hair falls to his shoulders, which support a circular instrument that appeared in the historic footage from 1941. We hear the man's voice while the scene shows him watching and listening to the river, with the occasional trill of bird calls in the soundscape. The man identifies himself as Ramón Cayumil Pillén, and he says (in Spanish),

> We are [engaged] in the interesting work of rescuing and reinterpreting history from a Mapuche perspective. And especially because we are here in this current condition after the state of Chile stripped us of our territory, of all our property (*bienes*). And that is the part of history that is not told, and we try to recuperate it and tell it again.[137]

Then he goes on to describe and demonstrate the musical instruments that are central to Mapuche culture. As he explains their use and cosmological significance, the film alternates between the contemporary view of Ramón Cayumil Pillén and views of Aretz's 1941 footage, showing Mapuche people of that time playing the same instruments. It is a powerful reminder that musical instruments and voices are not confined to collections, recordings, drawings, or other inscriptions. They are a living force in the recuperation of Indigenous histories and ontologies.

Mapuche intellectual/political collective Comunidad de Historia Mapuche / Centro de Estudios e Investigaciones Mapuche, among others.

[136] The segment begins at 28:02 in the film as it appears on Youtube: https://www.youtube.com/watch?v=rMJSsYzFLX4.

[137] "Estamos en un trabajo interesante de rescatar, reinterpretar la historia desde una perspectiva propia Mapuche. Y especialmente porque aquí estamos en esta condición actual después que el estado de Chile nos despoja de nuestro territorio, de todos nuestros bienes. Y esa es la parte de la historia que no se cuenta, y nosotros intentamos de recuperarla y volver a contarla."

Epilogue

On April 8, 1941, on the campus of the University of Oklahoma, the second broadcast of the Indians for Indians radio show featured Chief Yellowfish of the Comanche Nation. The show would become immensely popular in the following decades, with some 75,000 listeners from many different Tribes who had been removed to Indian Territory in the nineteenth century. The announcements and small talk were mostly in English, but stories and especially songs were shared in Native languages. During that second broadcast, Chief Yellowfish gave an eyewitness account, in the Comanche language, of the Second Battle of Adobe Walls (1874) in the Texas panhandle, where he had fought against Anglo buffalo hunters.[1] The broadcast was apparently not recorded; if it was, the recording did not survive. But the host Don Whistler made note of Chief Yellowfish's appearance in his logbook, and later recordings of the Indians for Indians show referred to the story that Yellowfish had narrated. Whistler mentioned that Yellowfish had "told us the Indian side of the story of the Battle of Adobe Walls."[2]

Rather than trying to pry into the details of Yellowfish's story, I am interested in this mediated memory as Indigenous historical narrative. Colonial ideas about Indigenous orality are remarkably persistent in contemporary discourse, and still intertwined with antiquated ideologies of race and culture. These ideas are prominent in S. C. Gwynne's award-winning, bestselling book published in 2010, titled *Empire of the Summer Moon: Quanah Parker and the Rise and Fall of the Comanches, the Most Powerful Indian Tribe in American History*. The book synthesizes archival sources, popular histories from the late nineteenth and early twentieth centuries, and borrowings from academic scholarship in a gripping narrative modeled on investigative journalism with novelistic flourishes. Gwynne reproduces the assumptions of nineteenth-century sociocultural evolutionism which put peoples of the world on a scale of development from the most primitive to the

[1] Ortega (2019: 6, 32).
[2] Garrett-Davis (2018: 262).

Indigenous Audibilities. Amanda Minks, Oxford University Press. © Oxford University Press 2024.
DOI: 10.1093/oso/9780197532485.003.0006

most civilized.[3] Sociocultural evolutionism was an ideology of racialization through temporalization (again, the projection of Indigenous peoples into the past), which justified colonial conquest. Even when Gwynne presents Comanches as agents of history as they gained power through their military horsemanship, he erases their ability to tell their own histories. For example, discussing a battle that took place in south Texas in 1840, Gwynne writes: "The Texans considered the battle [of Plum Creek] a major victory. Whether it was or not remains, to this day, very hard to tell, mainly because, as usual, the Indians never offered their own version of events."[4] It becomes clear, a few pages later, that Gwynne equates history with specific genres of writing that are commonly privileged in dominant archives and dominant history: "Plains Indians did not write letters or journals or record their legal proceedings, or even keep copies of treaties—history meant nothing to them."[5] Even a cursory study of the cultural practices of regional Tribes would have highlighted other genres for recording historical events, such as pictographic calendars drawn on hides, cloth, and paper. Engagement with Tribal oral histories would also have provided "their own versions of events."

This is part of the broader significance of that broadcast in 1941, when Yellowfish was telling "the Indian side of the story" for an audience of cultural insiders. The host Don Whistler was also involved in institutional projects of historic preservation and archiving, as I discussed in Chapter 1. Especially after World War II, Native communities in Oklahoma engaged in practices of cultural revival, which often explored history and memory through oral and written sources, as well as embodied performance and material arts.[6] Yellowfish's son-in-law Chief Albert Attocknie and their descendants contributed to keeping old stories and songs alive during their frequent appearances on the Indians for Indians radio show. In the 1950s,

[3] The following passage is but one example of Gwynne's antiquated and problematic use of sociocultural evolutionism: "What explains such a radical difference in the moral systems of the Comanches and the whites they confronted? Part of it has to do with the relative progress of civilizations in the Americas compared to the rest of the world . . . The Americas, isolated and in any case without the benefit of the horse or the ox, could never close the time gap. They were three or four millennia behind the Europeans and the Asians, and the arrival in Columbus in 1492 guaranteed they would never catch up . . . Thus the fateful clash between settlers from the culture of Aristotle, St. Paul, Da Vinci, Luther, and Newton and aboriginal horsemen from the buffalo plains happened as though in a time warp—as though the former were looking backward thousands of years at premoral, pre-Christian, low-barbarian versions of themselves" (Gwynne 2010: 45–46).

[4] Gwynne (2010: 99).

[5] Gwynne (2010: 103).

[6] See, for example, McKenzie-Jones's discussion of 1950s practices of cultural revitalization in his biography of Ponca activist Clyde Warrior (McKenzie-Jones 2015: 33–38).

Albert Attocknie's son, Francis Joseph (Joe) Attocknie, took on the work of inscribing Comanche oral narratives from his immediate ancestors, which were published posthumously in 2016 as *The Life of Ten Bears: Comanche Historical Narratives.*

Attocknie addressed his collection of narratives to Comanche children and grandchildren, and he dedicated them to Comanche elders. He emphasized the importance of *listening* to history when he noted, "the elders of the Comanche Tribe may want to compare our account of Comanche history with any accounts or stories that may have reached their own ears in their own lifetime."[7] In the preface, Attocknie reviewed the multiple kinds of Comanche historical recordings, and the importance of cross-generational storytelling and listening:

> Although there were Comanche pictographic recordings of important or time-marking events in the history of the Comanche Tribe, the greatest and most reliable source of Comanche history was the enjoyable, time-passing evening sessions of storytelling by wise, ancient, and loving grandfathers and grandmothers.
>
> Those story sessions entertained as well as taught. Sometimes there would be more than one person holding the session; a visiting ancient one might collaborate or add bits here and there, or just audibly agree to the account as it unwound and held spellbound its listeners, both young and adult. Repetition never bored the enthralled listeners. In fact, the young, especially, often asked for repeats of favorite accounts of certain events or stories. These stories, too, often had musical tones as the storyteller interspersed the accounts with an appropriate song that had a place in the telling of an account.
>
> Such an historically conscious storyteller was Querherbitty, granddaughter of Ten Bears. Querherbitty's talent for telling stories was inherited by her son, Albert Attocknie, who passed on to his own grandchildren the stories of the Comanche people as he had learned them from his own parents and other reliable Comanche older people.[8]

We can surmise that Joe Attocknie heard some of these stories directly from his grandmother, Querherbitty, who passed away in 1928 when Joe was

---

[7] Attocknie (2016), dedication page.
[8] Attocknie (2016: 5–6).

about sixteen, as well as from his father Albert Attocknie. The text above emphasizes the aurality, the pleasure, and the familial love embedded in stories and songs as they unfolded in close gatherings of tellers, singers, and listeners.

The way Attocknie's book came to publication is also a rich "archive story."[9] The book's editor, Thomas Kavanagh, describes meeting Joe Attocknie at the Smithsonian Institution's 1970 Festival of American Folklife, where Attocknie was demonstrating the making of traditional flutes. After that encounter, Kavanagh went to visit the Attocknies in Oklahoma and began to develop research projects related to their interests in Comanche histories. He heard references to a historical work that Joe Attocknie had written, but sadly the manuscript had been lost when it was in the trunk of a car that was stolen. In 1987, about three years after Attocknie's death, Kavanagh was visiting the National Anthropological Archives (NAA) in Washington, DC, and, as he later wrote, "the archivist James Glenn showed me a pile of unaccessioned papers and asked me if I knew what they might be." Kavanagh recognized the papers as the missing manuscript. It turned out that Attocknie had shared the manuscript with Herman Viola in the NAA in 1974; Viola had made a "security copy" while Attocknie continued to work on it. Upon this discovery, Kavanagh made copies for Attocknie's family and for himself, and left the "original copy" in the archives. Kavanagh "continued consulting with the Attocknie family and with others in the Comanche community" as he edited the manuscript for publication.[10]

The story of Attocknie's book brings out yet again the intertwined practices of voicing, listening, and writing as people make sense of their own cultural pasts for present and future generations. This kind of Indigenous historical narrative is overshadowed by approaches to history that pursue a narrow range of archival documents and present them as transparent sources of evidence. In this book I have employed a reflexivity around archival sources and an ethnography of the constitution of archives, both physical and conceptual. Archival collections are constituted by particular formats and forces that mediate voices and stories. These include different modes of inscription—handwritten and typed oral histories, sound recordings, folkloric publications, and interpersonal letters. Bringing these different formats

---

[9] Burton (2005).
[10] Kavanagh (2016: xii–xiii).

explicitly into the frame of analysis helps to challenge the hegemonic authority of the written record in archival research.

The inter-American networks which I have traced from the 1940s were limited in many ways, with non-Indigenous people most often taking leadership roles. Nevertheless, each case study shows how certain actors were grappling with decolonial thought and strategic interventions, challenging the limitations of institutions. There are many small and large counterhegemonic roles throughout the book, but the key actors I have emphasized include Don Whistler in the Indian Pioneer history project, Henrietta Yurchenco in the Inter-American Indian Institute, Pablo Antonio Cuadra in Nicaraguan writings, and Carlos Isamitt along with Violeta Parra with their literally creative approaches to collecting in Chile. These actors pushed back against the ideologies of their time to stretch, even if only a little bit, the frameworks of Indigenous authenticity which justified institutional investments in collections. Their collecting practices were bound up with listening practices. In forging relations across the activities of listening, voicing, and writing, their subjectivities became deeply embedded in their collecting labor. Both personal struggles and political struggles formed areas of repression, sites of memory outside the institutionally authorized archive. But these areas of repression, as well as the multivocal collections themselves, provide resources for cultural recuperation in the present and the future. Heritage discourses are not always about collections and they are not always about the past, but past collections are a valuable resource for critical analysis as well as cultural labor related to struggles over identity, difference, and belonging.[11]

The nuances of these histories, and the intertwining of personal and professional stories, reveal the heterogeneity of institutional projects of collecting. Critiques of the "colonial archive" have helped to raise awareness about the power structures shaping collections, but an overly generalized approach limits recognition of the multiple voices and actors that have coproduced archives. An overemphasis on colonial collecting runs the risk of evacuating Indigenous agency. Indigenous voices and their historical agency have been embedded in archives all along, but to hear them, archival sources need to be reconnected across collections and between collections and community.[12]

---

[11] Bigenho, Stobart, and Mújica Angulo (2018) argue that contemporary Latin American discourses on heritage, especially intangible heritage, are built around cultural alterity more than on representations of the past. Their intervention makes evident the variable uses of heritage discourse in specific cultural and political contexts. My analysis in this book has focused on past discourses about Indigenous culture and heritage, which is a different point of departure.

[12] Bruchac (2018); Glass, Berman, and Hatoum (2017).

In discourses on heritage and archives, there is a tension between openings and closures. US institutions (among others) increasingly recognize the harm that has been inflicted by the unrestrained circulation of Indigenous knowledge. These institutions are entering a broad international movement to implement new standards and platforms for Indigenous cultural collections which involve paradigms of cultural sovereignty, repatriation, collaborative curation, and regulated access.[13] Fewer critics have drawn attention to the stockpiling of Latin American archival collections in the United States since the nineteenth century. When these collections are held by US institutions, they are generally out of reach for Latin American students and scholars, except for the few who manage to acquire the economic and bureaucratic capital for international travel to US archives. In some cases, collections may be restricted due to the sensitivity of Indigenous cultural materials, which should always be managed with care and consultation. But all too often, the logic of public access in US archives means that collections are available to people with certain modes of power, such as academic or journalistic researchers.[14] The term "open access" can also obscure the inequities that are built into the production of knowledge and technology, and the real access to knowledge/power, at all levels.

Another challenge for collections is the sheer mass of dusty, disintegrating stuff, the cultural material often neglected in heritage institutions until an archivist happens to pull an item off a shelf, or a researcher requests it on a call slip, and then (maybe) figures out what it is, and why it matters. Obviously, people with cultural knowledge about these items will more quickly ascertain their nature. As Margaret Bruchac has written, tracing the social relations around collections can help establish provenance for Indigenous cultural property.[15] Institutions close to heritage communities are well positioned for making community connections and facilitating return and/or repatriation. Given the ever-increasing mediation of personal and professional communication, institutions located farther away should also be able to make these connections. Yet Native cultural institutions are still often left to go searching for their materials in distant archives and museums in order to tell their own histories.

Multilateral exchange of ideas about paradigms of access and restriction could pave the way to new approaches. More US institutions could benefit

---

[13] See Gray (1986, 1997); Christen (2011); Fox (2013); Anderson and Christen (2019); Gunderson et al. (2019).

[14] See Simpson (2007); Christen (2011).

[15] Bruchac (2018: 183–188).

from models such as that of Chile, with targeted support for thematic projects that combine research, digitization, and digital access to materials drawn from public as well as private collections. On the one hand, given the history of imperialist accumulation, US institutions have an ethical mandate to develop modes of access to their Latin Americanist collections, by Latin Americans. On the other hand, Latin American institutions with strong discourses of public patrimony could benefit from more negotiation of the boundaries between Indigenous patrimony and public patrimony, following international guidelines such as the UN Declaration on the Rights of Indigenous Peoples. Cross-border collaborations between institutions could also help resolve issues around intellectual property, which often determine the potential for online digital collections. These are not quick or easy projects, but they are worth undertaking to improve access to archival materials from their places of origin, and to safeguard collections for the future (thinking especially of the benefits of carefully placed copies during times of climate change).

In our highly globalized world, a hemispheric gaze (or ear) cannot capture all the networks that put people, things, and sounds in contact and in motion. But regional borderlands still matter, and networks (especially media networks) create new kinds of borders, new juxtapositions and negotiations of difference and belonging.[16] Public discourses often neglect the overlapping layers of colonialism and imperialism that have shaped the pathways of Indigenous and Afro-descendent peoples in the Americas, the historical conditions that have led to radical disparities in wealth and health and to forced migration at different moments, including the "time of now," in Walter Benjamin's words.[17] The submersion of these histories has been a key mechanism for the subjugation of these peoples.

Dominant heritage discourses try to fix history and memory in place, constricting their essence, mobility, and impact. As Alex Chávez has shown, embodied aural memory is central to the experiences of those who live in motion and yet remain connected to particular places and people.[18] Even for Derrida, the externality of the archive is less clear when he considers inscriptions that may be engraved upon and attached to bodies, as well as new technologies that augment and archive memory.[19] The traces of lives and voices cannot be contained by the material archive as a site of power and institutional governance.

[16] Tahmahkera (2022); Mendoza-Denton (2016).
[17] Benjamin ([1935] 1968: 263).
[18] Chávez (2017: 235).
[19] Derrida (1995).

Kimberly G. Wieser, a poet/scholar of the borderlands, has a poem called "Texas Traces," which ends with these verses:

> We still pray down here,
> respect those spirits,
> los antepasados,
> and the ancestors of those
> who traversed the Red River.
> Those old Comanches.
> Kiowas,
> Lipans,
> Wichitas,
> Caddos,
> Tonkawas,
> Tehuacanas,
> Huacos,
> those old ones on the coast,
> by Annette's house
> and my mom's,
> those Karankawas
> and others whose names
> white man's story
> has erased
> from even our memory,
> we still remember them anyway.
> Nameless, they are still family.
>
> With language unremembered,
> we utter cries calling them back.[20]

These memories are not determined by history or "white man's story." They are not determined by language or by naming—though the enunciation of Tribal names, each on a separate line, is important. There are still many other modalities of heritage that facilitate echoes of something shared, something remembered, something heard across temporalities.

---

[20] Wieser (2019).

References

Archives

Chile

Biblioteca Nacional, Memoria Chilena (digital collection)

Mexico

AHIII Historical Archive of the Instituto Indigenista Interamericano, Centro de Documentación Manuel Gamio, PUIC-UNAM (Universidad Nacional Autónoma de México), Mexico City. While this is currently the institutional access point, I consulted the AHIII documents via Espinosa Velasco and Cruz González (2002).

CENART Centro Nacional de las Artes (CENART), Biblioteca de las Artes; Fondo Henrietta Yurchenco, Mexico City

Nicaragua

IHNCA Instituto de Historia de Nicaragua y Centroamérica, Universidad Centroamericana, Managua, Nicaragua

United States

BLAC Benson Latin American Collection, University of Texas, Austin
CML   Columbus Memorial Library, Organization of American States, Washington, DC
LoC   Library of Congress, Washington, DC
OHS   Oklahoma Historical Society, Oklahoma City, Oklahoma
WHC   Western History Collections, University of Oklahoma Libraries

Publications and Presentations

al Attar, Mohsen, Nicole Aylwin, and Rosemary Coombe. 2009. "Indigenous Cultural Heritage Rights in International Human Rights Law." In *Protection of First Nations Cultural Heritage: Laws, Policy, and Reform*, ed. Catherine Bell and Robert Paterson, 311–342. Vancouver: UBC Press.

Allende, Humberto. 1931. "Chilean Folk Music." *Bulletin of the Pan American Union* 65(9): 917–924.

Alonso, Diego. 2019. "From the People to the People: The Reception of Hanns Eisler's Critical Theory of Music in Spain through the Writings of Otto Mayer-Serra." *Musicologica Austriaca: Journal for Austrian Music Studies*, 1–26.

Alonso Bolaños, Marina. 2008. *La 'Invención' de la Música Indígena de México.* Buenos Aires: Editorial Sb.

Alvarado Martínez, Enrique. 2010. *La UCA: una historia a través de la Historia.* Managua: Universidad Centroamericana.

Álvarez Lejarza, Emilio. 1971. "El problema del indio en Nicaragua." *Revista Conservadora* 26(127): 38–43.

Ananías, Nayive. 2021. Roundtable, "Patrimonio y Género," Pontificia Universidad Católica de Chile, Semana de la Musicología, October 28, 2021.

Anderson, Jane, and Kimberly Christen. 2019. "Decolonizing Attribution: Traditions of Exclusion." *Journal of Radical Librarianship* 5(June): 113–152.

Anderson, Jane, and Haidy Geismar, eds. 2017. *The Routledge Companion to Cultural Property.* New York: Routledge.

Anderson, Mark. 2009. *Black and Indigenous: Garifuna Activism and Consumer Culture in Honduras.* Minneapolis: University of Minnesota Press.

Aplin, Thomas Christopher. 2010. "Fort Sill Apache Cosmopolitans: Southwestern Music, Experience, and Identity in the Southern Plains." PhD diss., UCLA.

Arellano, Jorge Eduardo. 1969. *El movimiento de Vanguardia de Nicaragua: Gérmenes, desarrollo, significado 1927–1932.* Managua: Colección Revista Conservadora de Pensamiento Centroamericano.

Arellano, Jorge Eduardo. [1966] 1986. *Panorama de la literatura nicaragüense,* 5th ed. Managua: Editorial Nueva Nicaragua.

Arellano, Jorge Eduardo. 1992. "El *Cuaderno del Taller San Lucas:* archivo perdurable de la identidad cultural de Nicaragua." *América: Cahiers du CRICCAL* 9–10: 99–117.

Arellano, Jorge Eduardo. 1997. *Pablo Antonio Cuadra: Aproximaciones a su Vida y Obra.* Managua: Academia Nicaragüense de la Lengua.

Arrellano, Jorge Eduardo, 2017. "Los Dones de don Dionisio de la Quadra." *El Nuevo Diario,* April 8.

Aretz, Isabel. 1977. *Qué es el folklore.* Caracas: Instituto Interamericano de Etnomusicología y Folklore.

Aretz, Isabel. 1991. *Historia de la Etnomusicología en América Latina.* Caracas: Fundación de Etnomusicología y Folklore, Consejo Nacional de la Cultura, and Organization of American States.

Attocknie, Francis Joseph. 2016. *The Life of Ten Bears: Comanche Historical Narratives.* Ed. Thomas W. Kavanagh. Lincoln: University of Nebraska Press.

Bacigalupo, Ana Mariella. 2013. "Mapuche Struggles to Obliterate Dominant History: Mythohistory, Spiritual Agency, and Shamanic Historical Consciousness in Southern Chile." *Identities: Global Studies in Culture and Power* 20(1): 77–95.

Bacigalupo, Ana Mariella. 2016. *Thunder Shaman: Making History with Mapuche Spirits in Patagonia.* Austin: University of Texas Press.

Bakhtin, Mikhail. 1981. *The Dialogic Imagination: Four Essays.* Edited by Michael Holquist, trans. Caryl Emerson and Michael Holquist. Austin: University of Texas Press.

Barr, Juliana. 2009. *Peace Came in the Form of a Woman: Indians and Spaniards in the Texas Borderlands.* Chapel Hill: University of North Carolina Press.

Barr, Juliana. 2017. "There's No Such Thing as 'Prehistory': What the Longue Durée of Caddo and Pueblo History Tells Us about Colonial America." *William and Mary Quarterly* 74(2): 203–240.

Barrera Narvaez, Alfredo. 1997. *Salvador Cardenal Argüello, Vida y Obra.* Managua: Fondo Editorial, Instituto Nicaragüense de Cultura.

Barros, Felipe. 2013. *Música, etnografia e arquivo nos anos 40: Luiz Heitor Corrêa de Azevedo e suas viagens a Goiás (1942), Ceará (1943) e Minas Gerais (1944).* Rio de Janeiro: Editora Mulifoco.

Bartis, Peter. 1982. "A History of the Archive of Folk Song at the Library of Congress: The First Fifty Years." PhD diss., University of Pennsylvania.

Bauman, Richard. 1977. *Verbal Art as Performance.* Prospect Heights, IL: Waveland.

Bauman, Richard, and Charles Briggs. 1990. "Poetics and Performance as Critical Perspectives on Language and Social Life." *Annual Review of Anthropology* 19: 59–88.

Bauman, Richard, and Charles Briggs. 2003. *Voices of Modernity: Language Ideologies and the Politics of Inequality.* Cambridge: Cambridge University Press.

Baumgartner, Alice. 2020. *South to Freedom: Runaway Slaves to Mexico and the Road to the Civil War.* New York: Basic Books.

Bendaña, Alejandro. 2016. *Sandino: Patria y Libertad.* Managua: Anamá Ediciones.

Bendix, Regina. 1997. *In Search of Authenticity: The Formation of Folklore Studies.* Madison: University of Wisconsin Press.

Benjamin, Walter. [1935] 1968. *Illuminations,* ed. Hannah Arendt, trans. Harry Zohn. New York: Shocken Books.

Bigenho, Michelle, Henry Stobart, and Richard Mújica Angulo. 2018. "From *Indigenismo* to *Patrimonialismo:* An Introduction to the Special Issue on Music and Cultural Heritage Making in Latin America." *Trans: Revista Transcultural de Música* 21–22: 1–21.

Biondi, Michala. 2004. "Gilbert Chase Papers, 1920–1992." Finding Aid. New York: New York Public Library for the Performing Arts.

Birenbaum Quintero, Michael. 2018. *Rites, Rights and Rhythms: A Genealogy of Musical Meaning in Colombia's Black Pacific.* New York: Oxford University Press.

Bitrán Goren, Yael. 2018. "Henrietta Yurchenco: Ethnomusicology Pioneer in Mexico and Guatemala." *Oxford Research Encyclopedia, Latin American History,* 1–20. Oxford: Oxford University Press.

Blackhawk, Ned. 2006. *Violence over the Land: Indians and Empires in the Early American West.* Cambridge, MA: Harvard University Press.

Boggs, Ralph Stanley. 1943. "El folklore, definición, ciencia, arte." *El Cuaderno del Taller San Lucas* 3:85–92.

Born, Georgina, and David Hesmondhalgh. 2000. "Introduction: On Difference, Representation, and Appropriation in Music." In *Western Music and its Others,* ed. Born and Hesmondhalgh, 1–58. Berkeley: University of California Press.

Brady, Erika. 1999. *A Spiral Way: How the Phonograph Changed Ethnography.* Jackson: University Press of Mississippi.

Bravo, Carlos A. 1944. "A la Costa Atlántica entre las nubes." *El Cuaderno del Taller San Lucas* 4: 33–40.

Briggs, Charles. 1986. *Learning How to Ask: A Sociolinguistic Appraisal of the Role of the Interview in Social Science Research.* Cambridge: Cambridge University Press.

Bronfman, Alejandra. 2016. *Isles of Noise: Sonic Media in the Caribbean.* Chapel Hill: University of North Carolina Press.

Brooks, James. 2001. *Captives and Cousins: Slavery, Kinship, and Community in the Southwest Borderlands.* Chapel Hill: University of North Carolina Press.

Browner, Tara. 1995. "Transposing Cultures: The Appropriation of Native North American Musics, 1890–1990." PhD diss., University of Michigan.

Browner, Tara. 1997. "'Breathing the Indian Spirit': Thoughts on Musical Borrowing and the 'Indianist' Movement in American Music." *American Music* 15(3): 265–284.

Bruchac, Margaret. 2018. *Savage Kin: Indigenous Informants and American Anthropologists.* Tucson: University of Arizona Press.

Bulletin of the Pan American Union (no author given). 1934. "Latin American Music at the Pan American Union." *Bulletin of the Pan American Union* 68(8): 561–563.

Burton, Antoinette, ed. 2005. *Archive Stories: Facts, Fictions, and the Writing of History.* Durham, NC: Duke University Press.

Cáceres Valencia, Jorge. 1988. *La Universidad de Chile y su aporte a la cultura tradicional chilena, 1933–1953.* Florida, Chile: Fondo Nacional de Desarrollo Cultural y las Artes.

Cage, John. 1942. "Chávez and the Chicago Drouth." *Modern Music* 19(2): 185–186.

Campbell, Jennifer. 2012. "Creating Something Out of Nothing: The Office of Inter-American Affairs Music Committee (1940–1941) and the Inception of a Policy for Musical Diplomacy." *Diplomatic History* 36(1): 29–39.

Canio Llanquinao, Margarita, and Gabriel Pozo Menares. 2013. *Historia y conocimiento oral mapuche: Sobrevivientes de la "Campaña del Desierto" y "Ocupación de la Araucanía" (1899–1926).* Santiago: Consejo Nacional de la Cultura y las Artes.

Canio Llanquinao, Margarita, and Gabriel Pozo Menares. 2014. "Regina y Juan Salva: primeras grabaciones de cantos mapuches en soporte cilindros de fonógrafo (1905 y 1907)." *Revista Musical Chilena* 68(222): 70–88.

Cárcamo-Huechante, Luis E. 2013. "Indigenous Interference: Mapuche Use of Radio in Times of Acoustic Colonialism." *Latin American Research Review* 48(Special Issue): 50–68.

Cardoso, Leonardo. 2019. *Sound-Politics in São Paulo.* New York: Oxford University Press.

Carvalho-Neto, Paulo de. 1976. "Rodolfo Lenz (1863–1938): Un precursor del Folklore en América Latina." *Folklore Americano* 21(June): 33–62.

Carter, Robert A. 2000. *Buffalo Bill Cody: The Man Behind the Legend.* New York: Wiley.

Castillo, Argelia. 2003. "Da Yurchenco conferencias en México: refleja la música lo íntimo y lo social." *Reforma* (November 10). Sección Cultura, p. 2C.

Castro Pantoja, Daniel. 2018. "Antagonism, Europhilia, and Identity: Guillermo Uribe Holguín and the Politics of National Music in Early Twentieth-Century Colombia." PhD diss., University of California, Riverside.

CENIDIM. 2016. *CENIDIM: 40 años construyendo la memoria musical de México.* México: Secretaría de la Cultura, Instituto Nacional de Bellas Artes y Literatura, Centro Nacional de Investigación, Documentación e Información Musical Carlos Chávez.

Chamorro Escalante, Jorge Arturo. 1991. "Sones de la guerra: Purépecha Music and its Audience Responses as Audible Symbols of Rivalry and Emotion in Northern Michoacán, Mexico." PhD diss., University of Texas, Austin.

Chamosa, Oscar. 2010. *The Argentine Folklore Movement: Sugar Elites, Criollo Workers, and the Politics of Cultural Nationalism, 1900–1955.* Tucson: University of Arizona Press.

Chávez, Alex E. 2017. *Sounds of Crossing: Music, Migration, and the Aural Poetics of Huapango Arribeño.* Durham, NC: Duke University Press.

Chávez Cancino, Freddy. 2019. Presentation, Conferencia del Libro "Cantos Araucanos de Carlos Isamitt." https://www.youtube.com/watch?v=UY1C6HBxJaw).

Chávez Cancino, Freddy, ed. 2021. *Los Treinta Cantos Araucanos.* Digital version. Santiago: Fondo para el Fomento de la Música Nacional. https://www.freddychavezc.com.

Chávez Cancino, Freddy. 2022a. "El caballo de Troya: la edición crítica de *Los treinta cantos araucanos* de Carlos Isamitt Alarcón." *Revista Musical Chilena* 76(238): 9–45.

Chávez Cancino, Freddy, ed. 2022b. *Carlos Isamitt y sus investigaciones en las comunidades araucanas: Escritos académicos (1932–1949)*. Santiago: Fondo de la Cultura y Artes.

Chocano, Rodrigo. 2019. "Producing African-descent: Afro-Peruvian Music, Intangible Heritage, Authenticity and Bureaucracy in a Latin American Music Compilation." *International Journal of Heritage Studies* 25(8): 763–779.

Chocano, Rodrigo. 2022. "Musical Sustainability vis-à-vis Intangible Cultural Heritage: Safeguarding and Incentives in the Feast of the Virgin of Candelaria, Puno, Perú." *Ethnomusicology Forum* 31(2): 283–303.

Chocano, Rodrigo. 2023. "Strategic Skepticism: The Politics of Grassroots Participation in an Afro-Andean Nomination to the UNESCO Intangible Cultural Heritage Representative List." *Journal of American Folklore* 136(541): 249–273.

Christen, Kimberly. 2011. "Opening Archives: Respectful Repatriation." *The American Archivist* 74(1): 185–210.

Christen, Kimberly, and Jane Anderson. 2019. "Toward Slow Archives." *Archival Science* 19(June): 87–116.

Clark, Stanley. 1953. "Grant Foreman." *The Chronicles of Oklahoma* 31 (Autumn): 226–242.

Collier, John. 1941. "Nuevos conceptos sobre la unidad indígena." *América Indígena* 1(1): 11–15.

Collier, John. 1963. *From Every Zenith: A Memoir*. Denver: Sage Books.

Cobb, Amanda. 2000. *Listening to Our Grandmothers' Stories: The Bloomfield Academy for Chickasaw Females, 1852–1949*. Lincoln: University of Nebraska Press.

Cobb-Greetham, Amanda. 2022. "Foreword." In *And Still the Waters Run: The Betrayal of the Five Civilized Tribes*, by Angie Debo, ix–xxxviii. Princeton, NJ: Princeton University Press.

Comité Editorial. 1966. "Entrevista: Carlos Isamitt, el hombre, el artista y el investigador." *Revista Musical Chilena* 20(97): 5–13.

Comité Editorial. 1967. "Andrés Sas (1900–1967)." *Revista Musical Chilena* 21(101): 123.

Coombe, Rosemary. 1998. *The Cultural Life of Intellectual Properties: Authorship, Appropriation and the Law*. Durham, NC: Duke University Press.

Coombe, Rosemary. 2009. "First Nations Intangible Cultural Heritage Concerns: Prospects for Protection of Traditional Knowledge and Traditional Cultural Expressions in International Law." In *Protection of First Nations Cultural Heritage: Law, Policy, and Reform*, ed. Catherine Bell and Robert Paterson, 247–277. Vancouver: UBC Press.

Corn, David. 2015. "Pete Seeger's FBI File Reveals How the Folk Legend First Became a Target of the Feds." *Mother Jones*, December 18.

Cramer, Gisela, and Ursula Prutsch. 2006. "Nelson A. Rockefeller's Office of Inter-American Affairs (1940–1946) and Record Group 229." *Hispanic American Historical Review* 86(4): 785–806.

Cramer, Gisela, and Ursula Prutsch, eds. 2012. *¡Américas unidas! Nelson A. Rockefeller's Office of Inter-American Affairs (1940–46)*. Madrid: Iberoamericano.

Crandall, Maurice. 2019. *These People Have Always Been a Republic: Indigenous Electorates in the U.S.–Mexico Borderlands, 1598–1912*. Chapel Hill: University of North Carolina Press.

Crow, Joanna. 2013. *The Mapuche in Modern Chile: A Cultural History*. Gainesville: University Press of Florida.

Cuadra, Manolo. 1937. *Itinerario de Little Corn Island*. Managua: Editorial Novedades.

Cuadra, Pablo Antonio. 1951. "El indio al pie de la letra." *El Cuaderno del Taller San Lucas* 5: 25–41.

Cuadra, Pablo Antonio. 1954. "La herencia del indio en el nicaragüense." *Nicaragua Indígena* 2: 10–18.

da Costa Garcia, Tânia. 2009. "Canción popular, nacionalismo, consumo y política en Chile entre los años 40 y 60." *Revista Musical Chilena* 63(212): 11–28.

Darío, Rubén. 1954a. "Folklore de América Central: representaciones y bailes populares en Nicaragua." *Nicaragua Indígena* 2(2): 5–9.

Darío, Rubén. 1954b. "Estética de los primitivos nicaragüenses." *Nicaragua Indígena* 2(3): 19–26.

Davis, Susan. 2010. "Ben Botkin's FBI File." *Journal of American Folklore* 122(487): 3–30.

Dawson, Alexander. 1998. "From Models for the Nation to Model Citizens: Indigenismo and the 'Revindication of the Mexican Indian, 1920–1940." *Journal of Latin American Studies* 30(2): 279–308.

Dawson, Alexander. 2004. *Indian and Nation in Revolutionary Mexico.* Tucson: University of Arizona Press.

de la Cadena, Marisol. 2005. "The Production of Other Knowledges and its Tensions: From Andeanist Anthropology to Interculturalidad?" *Journal of the World Anthropology Network* 1: 13–33.

de la Cadena, Marisol. 2014. "El racismo silencioso y la superioridad de los intelectuales en el Perú." In *Racismo y Etnicidad*, ed. Christine Hünefeldt, Cecilia Méndez, and Marisol de la Cadena, 54–97. Lima: Ministerio de la Cultura/Dirección Desconcentrada de Cultura de Cusco.

De la Peña, Guillermo. 1996. "Nacionales y extranjeros en la historia de la antropología mexicana." In *La historia de la antropología en México: Fuentes y transmisión.* Ed. Mechthild Rutsch, 41–81. Mexico City: Universidad Iberoamericana, INI, Plaza y Valdés, S. A. de C. V.

Delay, Brian. 2008. *War of a Thousand Deserts: Indian Raids and the U.S.–Mexican War.* New Haven, CT: Yale University Press.

Delgado Aburto, Leonel. 2002. *Márgenes recorridos: Apuntes sobre procesos culturales y literatura nicaragüense del siglo XX.* Managua: IHNCA.

Delpar, Helen. 1992. *The Tremendous Vogue of Things Mexican: Cultural Relations between the United States and Mexico, 1920–1935.* Tuscaloosa: University of Alabama Press.

Dent, Alexander. 2009. *River of Tears: Country Music, Memory, and Modernity in Brazil.* Durham, NC: Duke University Press.

Derrida, Jacques. 1995. *Archive Fever: A Freudian Impression.* Trans. Eric Prenowitz. Chicago: University of Chicago Press.

Derrida, Jacques. 2002. "Archive Fever (Transcription of Derrida Seminar)." In *Refiguring the Archive*, ed. Carolyn Hamilton, Verne Harris, Michèle Pickover, Graeme Reed, Razia Saleh, and Jane Taylor, 38–80. Dordrecht: Kluwer Academic Publishers.

Díaz Collao, Leonardo. 2020. "Música, sonido y práctica ritual mapuche: etnografía de una *machi*." PhD diss., Universidad de Valladolid.

Díaz Navarrete, Wenceslao, ed. 2013. *Pájaro libro como soy: Cartas de Wanda Morla Lynch.* Santiago: Ediciones Universidad Católica de Chile.

Donoso Fritz, Karen y Ignacio Ramos Rodillo. 2021. "La cueca según Pablo Garrido: Entre el compromiso político-cultural y un decreto dictatorial (1928–1979)." *Revista NEUMA* 14(1): 56–83.

"Editorial." 1941. *América Indígena* 1(1): 5–6.

"Editorial." 1947. *Nicaragua Indígena* 1(3): 2.

"Editorial de 'Novedades,'" 1957. *Nicaragua Indígena* 2(13–14): 3–5.

Escobar-Mundaca, Alejandro. 2022. "'Así Canta Violeta Parra': ¿un programa radial [pionero] antes de las 'Radio Ballads' británicas?" Presentation, I Encuentro de las Músicas Tradicionales y Folclóricas, Universidad Mayor, Chile, June 17.

Espinosa Velasco, Guillermo, and Lilia Cruz González, eds. 2002. *La música y el Instituto Indigenista Interamericano, 1940–1947. Índice y facsímil de documentos; artículos de H. Yurchenco y notas del Boletín Indigenista.* México: Instituto Indigenista Interamericano. CD edition.

Faudree, Paja. 2013. *Singing for the Dead: The Politics of Indigenous Revival in Mexico.* Durham, NC: Duke University Press.

Feld, Steven. 1984. "Communication, Music, and Speech about Music." *Yearbook for Traditional Music* 16: 1–18.

Feld, Steven. 2015a. "Listening to Histories of Listening: Collaborative Experiments in Acoustemology with Nii Otoo Annan." In *Musical Listening in the Age of Technological Reproduction,* ed. Gianmario Borio, 91–106. New York: Routledge.

Feld, Steven. 2015b. "Acoustemology." In *Keywords in Sound,* ed. David Novak and Matt Sakakeeny, 12–21. Durham, NC: Duke University Press.

Feld, Steven, and Don Brenneis. 2004. "Doing Anthropology in Sound." *American Ethnologist* 31(4): 461–474.

Fernández Bravo, Álvaro. 2009. "Redes latinoamericanas en los años cuarenta: la revista *Sur* y el mundo tropical." In *Episodios en la formación de redes culturales en América Latina,* ed. Álvaro Fernández Bravo and Claudio Maíz, 113–135. Buenos Aires: Prometeo.

Fonoteca Nacional, CENIDIM, PUIC (2015). *Propuesta para la inscripción en el registro Memoria del Mundo de México 2015: Documentos sonoros de Henrietta Yurchenco. Grabaciones históricas de música de pueblos indígenas de México y Guatemala.* México: Fonoteca Nacional; Centro Nacional de Investigación, Documentación e Información Musical "Carlos Chávez"; Secretaría de Cultura; Programa Universitario de Estudios de la Diversidad Cultural y la Interculturalidad de la Universidad Nacional Autónoma de México. Documento interno.

Foucault, Michel. 1972. *The Archaeology of Knowledge, and the Discourse on Language.* New York: Pantheon.

Fox, Aaron. 2013. "Repatriation as Reanimation through Reciprocity." *The Cambridge History of World Music,* ed. Philip Bohlman, 522–554. Cambridge: Cambridge University Press.

Fox, Aaron. 2017. "The Archive of the Archive: the Secret History of the Laura Boulton Collection." In *The Routledge Companion to Cultural Property,* ed. Jane Anderson and Haidy Geismar, 194–211. New York: Routledge.

Fox, Claire F. 2013. *Making Art Panamerican: Cultural Policy and the Cold War.* Minneapolis: University of Minnesota Press.

Francis, Hartwell, Tanya Clement, Gena Peone, Brian Carpenter, and Kristen Suagee-Beauduy. 2016. "Accessing Sound at Libraries, Archives, and Museums." In *Indigenous Notions of Ownership and Libraries, Archives and Museums,* ed. Camille Callison, Loriene Roy, and Gretchen Alice LeCheminant, 344–368. Berlin: DeGruyter.

Freeland, Jane. 1995. "'Why Go to School to Learn Miskitu?': Changing Constructs of Bilingualism, Education, and Literacy among the Miskitu of Nicaragua's Atlantic Coast." *International Journal of Education and Development* 15(2): 245–261.

Gamio, Manuel. 1916. *Forjando Patria (Pro nacionalismo).* México: Porrúa.

Gamio, Manuel. 1942. "Calificación de características culturales de los grupos indígenas." *América Indígena* 2(4): 17–22.

Gamio de Alba, Margarita. 1957. "La mujer misquito de Nicaragua." *Nicaragua Indígena* 2(13–14): 53–60.

García Canclini, Nestor. [1990] 1995. *Hybrid Cultures: Strategies for Entering and Leaving Modernity*. Minneapolis: University of Minnesota Press.

García Sudo, Alejandro. 2019. "Cuando la Banda de la Marina Estadounidense tocaba el compás panamericano: esbozo de los albores del intercambio musical en el sistema interamericano (1924–1933). *Revista de Historia de América* 156(January–June): 351–370.

Garrett-Davis, Josh. 2018. "The Intertribal Drum of Radio: The *Indians for Indians Hour* and Native American Media, 1941–1951." *Western Historical Quarterly* 49(3): 249–273.

Garrett-Davis, Josh. 2020. "Resounding Voices: Native Americans and Sound Media, 1890–1970." PhD diss., Princeton University.

Garrett-Davis, Josh. 2021. "American Indian Soundchiefs: Cutting Records in Indigenous Sonic Networks." *Resonance: The Journal of Sound and Culture* 1(4): 394–411.

Garrett-Davis, Josh. Forthcoming. *Resounding Voices: A History of Native American Sound Media*. New Haven, CT: Yale University Press.

Gayle, Caleb. 2022. *We Refuse to Forget: A True Story of Black Creeks, American Identity, and Power*. New York: Riverhead Books.

Geismar, Haidy. 2013. *Treasured Possessions: Indigenous Interventions into Cultural and Intellectual Property*. Durham, NC: Duke University Press.

Geismar, Haidy. 2015. "Anthropology and Heritage Regimes." *Annual Review of Anthropology* 44: 71–85.

Giacona, Christina. Forthcoming. "Revival, Collections, and the Rediscovered Compositions of Jack Frederick Kilpatrick." PhD diss., University of Oklahoma.

Giacosa, Santiago Manuel. 2007. "Carlos Vega, a cuarenta años de su muerte (1966–2006)." *Temas de Historia Argentina y Americana* 10(January–June): 31–68.

Giannachi, Gabriella. 2016. *Archive Everything: Mapping the Everyday*. Cambridge, MA: MIT Press.

Giraudo, Laura. 2006. "El Instituto Indigenista Interamericano y la participación indígena (1940–1998)." *América Indígena* 62(3): 6–34.

Giraudo, Laura. 2012. "Neither 'Scientific' nor 'Colonialist': The Ambiguous Course of Inter-American Indigenismo in the 1940s." *Latin American Perspectives* 39(5): 12–32.

Giraudo, Laura. 2013. Grant proposal RE-INTERINDI: "Los reversos del indigenismo: socio-historia de las categorías étnico-raciales y sus usos en las sociedades latinoamericanas." Ministerio de Economía y Competitividad, Secretaría de Estado de Investigación, Desarrollo e Innovación, España, HAR2013-41596-P, 2014–2017.

Giraudo, Laura. 2022. "Lecturas inéditas desde la música, la etnología y el periodismo: tres mujeres en el campo indigenista a mediados del siglo XX." In *Intrépidas: Entre Europa y las Américas: Cultura, Arte y Política en Equidad*, ed. Esmeralda Broullón, 167–198. Madrid: Plaza y Valdés.

Giraudo, Laura, and Emilio J. Gallardo-Saborido. 2022. "Staging *indianización*/Staging *indigenismo*: Artistic Expression, Representation of the 'Indian' and the Inter-American *Indigenista* Movement." *Latin American and Caribbean Ethnic Studies* 17(4): 389–398.

Giraudo, Laura, and Stephen E. Lewis. 2012. "Pan-American *Indigenismo* (1940–1970): New Approaches to an Ongoing Debate." *Latin American Perspectives* 39(5): 3–11.

Giraudo, Laura, and Juan Martín-Sánchez, eds. 2011. *La Ambivalente Historia del Indigenismo: Campo Interamericano y Trayectorias Nacionales, 1940-1970*. Lima: Instituto de Estudios Peruanos.

Giraudo, Laura, and Juan Martín-Sánchez. 2016. "'Soy indígena e indigenista': Repensando el indigenismo desde la participación de algunos, no tan pocos, indígenas." In *Protagonismo Ameríndio, de ontem e hoje*, ed. María Cristina Dos Santos and Guilherme Galhegos Felippe, 257-294. Jundiaí, Brasil: Paco Editorial.

Gitelman, Lisa. 1999. *Scripts, Grooves, and Writing Machines: Representing Technology in the Edison Era*. Stanford, CA: Stanford University Press.

Glass, Aaron, Judith Berman, and Rainer Hatoum. 2017. "Reassembling *The Social Organization*: Collaboration and Digital Media in (Re)making Boas's 1897 Book." *Museum Worlds: Advances in Research* 5(1): 108-132.

Gobat, Michel. 2013. "The Invention of Latin America: A Transnational History of Anti-Imperialism, Democracy, and Race." *American Historical Review* 118(5): 1345-1375.

Goett, Jennifer. 2006. "Diasporic Identities, Autochthonous Rights: Race, Gender, and the Cultural Politics of Creole Land Rights in Nicaragua." PhD diss., University of Texas.

Goett, Jennifer. 2017. *Black Autonomy: Race, Gender, and Afro-Nicaraguan Activism*. Stanford, CA: Stanford University Press.

Gómez, Juan Pablo. 2015. *Autoridad/Cuerpo/Nación: Batallas culturales en Nicaragua (1930-1943)*. Managua: Instituto de Historia de Nicaragua y Centroamérica-Universidad Centroamericana.

González, Juan Pablo. 2009. "Musicología y América Latina: Una relación posible." *Revista Argentina de Musicología* 10(January): 43-72.

González, Juan Pablo. 2018. *Thinking about Music from Latin America: Issues and Questions*. Translated by Nancy Morris. Lanham, MD: Lexington Books.

González Echevarría, Roberto. [1990] 1998. *Myth and Archive: A Theory of Latin American Narrative*. Durham, NC: Duke University Press.

Gonzalez, Moises, and Enrique Lamadrid. 2019. *Nación Genízara: Ethnogenesis, Place, and Identity in New Mexico*. Albuquerque: University of New Mexico Press.

Gordillo, Bernard. 2019. "Luis A. Delgadillo and the Cultural Occupation of Nicaragua under U.S.-American Intervention." PhD diss., University of California, Riverside.

Gordillo Brockmann, Bernard. 2020a. "The Raja's Nicaraguan Dream: Exoticism, Commemoration, and Nostalgia in Luis A. Delgadillo's 'Romance Oriental.'" *Diagonal: an Ibero-American Music Review* 5(1) : 22-41.

Gordillo Brockmann, Bernard. 2020b. "Musical Cosmopolitanism in Central America: In Search of an Obituary of Alejandro Cousin (ca. 1835-1910)." *Ensayos. Historia y Teoría del Arte* 24(38): 61-75.

Gordillo, Bernard. 2021. "Vatican II, Liberation Theology, and Vernacular Masses for the Family of God in Central America." *Yale Journal of Music & Religion* 7(1): 53-91.

Gordillo, Bernard. Forthcoming. *Canto de Marte: Art Music, Popular Culture, and U.S. Intervention in Nicaragua*. New York: Oxford University Press.

Gordon, Edmund. 1998. *Disparate Diasporas: Identity and Politics in an African Nicaraguan Community*. Austin: University of Texas Press.

Gottfried, Jessica. 2017. "Music and Folklore Research in the Departamento de Bellas Artes, 1926-1946." *Oxford Research Encyclopedia, Latin American History*, 1-19.

Gottfried Hesketh, Jessica. 2010. "Tras los pasos de Roberto Téllez Girón: Sierra Norte de Puebla 1938-2009." In *Tras los pasos de Roberto Téllez Girón Olace*, by Jessica Gottfried

Hesketh, and Ricardo Téllez Girón López, 33–78. Puebla: Consejo Nacional para la Cultura y las Artes.

Gottfried Hesketh, Jessica, and Ricardo Téllez Girón López. 2010. *Tras los pasos de Roberto Téllez Girón Olace*. Puebla: Consejo Nacional para la Cultura y las Artes.

Gough, Peter. 2015. *Sounds of the New Deal: The Federal Music Project in the West*. Urbana: University of Illinois Press.

Gould, Jeffrey. 1990. *To Lead as Equals: Rural Protest and Political Consciousness in Chinandega, Nicaragua, 1912–1979*. Chapel Hill: University of North Carolina Press.

Gould, Jeffrey. 1998. *To Die in This Way: Nicaraguan Indians and the Myth of Mestizaje, 1860–1965*. Durham, NC: Duke University Press.

Gray, Judith. 1986. "Early Ethnographic Recordings in Today's Indian Communities: Federal Agencies and the Federal Cylinder Project." In *Songs of Indian Territory: Native American Music Traditions of Oklahoma*, ed. Willie Smyth, 49–55. Oklahoma City: Center of the American Indian.

Gray, Judith. 1997. "Returning Music to the Makers: The Library of Congress, American Indians, and the Federal Cylinder Project." *Cultural Survival Quarterly Magazine* 20(Winter): 42–44.

Gray, Lila Ellen. 2020. "Listening for Affect: Musical Ethnography and the Challenge of/to Affect." *Culture, Theory and Critique* 61(2–3): 319–337.

Gray, Robin. 2015. "Ts'msyen Revolution: The Poetics and Politics of Reclaiming." PhD diss., University of Massachusetts, Amherst.

Gray, Robin. 2019. "Repatriation and Decolonization: Thoughts on Ownership, Access, and Control." In *Oxford Handbook of Musical Repatriation*, ed. Frank Gunderson, Robert C. Lancefield, and Bret Woods, 723–738. New York: Oxford.

Green, Raina, and John Troutman. 2000. "'By the Waters of the Minnehaha': Music and Dance, Pageants and Princesses." In *Away from Home: American Indian Boarding School Experiences, 1879–2000*, ed. Margaret L. Archuleta, Brenda J. Child, and K. Tsianina Lomawaima, 60–83. Phoenix: The Heard Museum.

Gunderson, Frank, Robert Lancefield, and Bret Woods, eds. 2019. *The Oxford Handbook of Musical Repatriation*. New York: Oxford University Press.

Gwynne, S. C. 2010. *Empire of the Summer Moon: Quanah Parker and the Rise and Fall of the Comanches, the Most Powerful Indian Tribe in American History*. New York: Scribner.

Hale, Charles. 1994. *Resistance and Contradiction: Miskitu Indians and the Nicaraguan State, 1894–1987*. Stanford, CA: Stanford University Press.

Hamalainen, Pekka. 2008. *The Comanche Empire*. New Haven, CT: Yale University Press.

Hamilton, Carolyn, Verne Harris, and Graeme Reid. 2002. "Introduction." In *Refiguring the Archive*, ed. Carolyn Hamilton, Verne Harris, Michèle Pickover, Graeme Reed, Razia Saleh, and Jane Taylor, 7–17. Dordrecht: Kluwer Academic Publishers.

Hanneman, C. G. 2000. "Baffles, Bridges, and Bermuda: Oklahoma Indians and the Civilian Conservation Corps-Indian Division." *The Chronicles of Oklahoma* 77(4): 428–449.

Harrison, Rodney. 2013. *Heritage: Critical Approaches*. New York: Routledge.

Hawley, Susan. 1997. "Protestantism and Indigenous Mobilisation: The Moravian Church among the Miskitu Indians of Nicaragua." *Journal of Latin American Studies* 29(1): 111–129.

Hayes, Joy Elizabeth. 2000. *Radio Nation: Communication, Popular Culture, and Nationalism in Mexico, 1920–1950*. Tucson: University of Arizona Press.

Herndon, Marcia, and Norma McLeod, eds. 1980. *The Ethnography of Musical Performance*. Norwood, PA: Norwood Editions.

Herrera, Eduardo. 2017. "The Rockefeller Foundation and Latin American Music in the 1960s: The Creation of Indiana University's LAMC and Di Tella Institute's CLAEM." *American Music* 35(1): 51–74.

Herrera, Eduardo. 2020. *Elite Art Worlds: Philanthropy, Latin Americanism, and Avant-Garde Music*. New York: Oxford University Press.

Herrero, Victor. 2017. *Después de vivir un siglo, Violeta Parra, una biografía*. Santiago: Lumen.

Hess, Carol. 2013a. *Representing the Good Neighbor: Music, Difference, and the Pan American Dream*. Oxford: Oxford University Press.

Hess, Carol. 2013b. "Copland in Argentina: Pan Americanist Politics, Folklore, and the Crisis in Modern Music." *Journal of the American Musicological Society* 66(1): 191–250.

Hess, Carol. 2017. "Walt Disney's Saludos Amigos: Hollywood and the Propaganda of Authenticity." In *The Tide Was Always High: The Music of Latin America in Los Angeles*, ed. Josh Kun, 105–123. Berkeley: University of California Press.

Hirsch, Jerrold. 2003. *Portrait of America: A Cultural History of the Federal Writers' Project*. Chapel Hill: University of North Carolina Press.

Hirsch, Jerrold. 2013. "Theorizing Regionalism and Folklore from the Left: B. A. Botkin, the Oklahoma Years, 1921–1939." In *Regionalists on the Left*, ed. Michael C. Steiner, 135–156. Norman: Oklahoma University Press.

Hochman, Brian. 2014. *Savage Preservation: The Ethnographic Origins of Modern Media Technology*. Minneapolis: University of Minnesota Press.

Hodges, Donald. 1986. *Intellectual Foundations of the Nicaraguan Revolution*. Austin: University of Texas Press.

Hooker, Juliet. 2005. "'Beloved Enemies': Race and Official Mestizo Nationalism in Nicaragua." *Latin American Research Review* 40(3): 14–39.

Isamitt, Carlos. 1932a. "Apuntes sobre nuestro folklore nacional." *Aulos* 1(1): 8–9.

Isamitt, Carlos. 1932b. "Apuntes sobre nuestro folklore musical." *Aulos* 1(2): 4–6.

Isamitt, Carlos. 1932c. "Apuntes sobre nuestro folklore musical." *Aulos* 1(3): 3–8.

Isamitt, Carlos. 1933. "Apuntes sobre nuestro folklore musical." *Aulos* 1(6): 6–9.

Izquierdo König, José Manuel. 2011a. "Aproximación a una recuperación histórica: compositores excluidos, músicas perdidas, transiciones estilísticas y descripciones sinfónicas a comienzos del siglo XX chileno." *Revista Resonancias* 15(28): 33–47.

Izquierdo, König, José Manuel. 2011b. "Prólogo." In *Palabra de Soro*, ed. Roberto Doniez Soro, 15–19. Viña del Mar: Ediciones Altazor.

Izquierdo König, José Manuel. 2018. "Bailes chinos: Problemáticas institucionales y estéticas en torno a una declaratoria de patrimonio inmaterial UNESCO ." *Trans: Revista Transcultural de la Música* 21–22(June): 1–20.

Jacoby, Karl. 2008. *Shadows at Dawn: An Apache Massacre and the Violence of History*. New York: Penguin.

Jacoby, Karl. 2016. *The Strange Career of William Ellis, the Texas Slave who Became a Mexican Millionaire*. New York: Norton.

Jacoby, Sally, and Elinor Ochs. 1995. "Co-Construction: An Introduction." *Research on Language and Social Interaction* 18(3): 171–183.

Jordán, Laura, and Andrea Salazar. 2022. *Trafülkantun: Cantos cruzados entre Garrido y Curilem*. Santiago: Ariadna Ediciones.

Karmy, Eileen. 2021a. *Música y trabajo: Organizaciones gremiales de músicos en Chile, 1893–1940*. Santiago: Ariadna Ediciones.

Karmy, Eileen. 2021b. "Pablo Garrido y su defensa de los derechos laborales de los músicos en Chile (1932–1940)." *Revista Musical Chilena* 75(236): 98–118.

Karmy Bolton, Eileen. 2019. "The Path to Trade Unionism: Musical Work in Chile (1893–1940)." PhD diss., University of Glasgow.

Kavanagh, Thomas. 2016. "Introduction." In *The Life of Ten Bears: Comanche Historical Narratives*, collected by Francis Joseph Attocknie, vii–xix. Lincoln: University of Nebraska Press.

Kelly, Lawrence. 1983. *The Assault on Assimilation: John Collier and the Origins of Indian Policy Reform*. Albuquerque: University of New Mexico Press.

Kheshti, Roshanak. 2015. *Modernity's Ear: Listening to Race and Gender in World Music*. New York: NYU Press.

Kirshenblatt-Gimblett, Barbara. 2004. "Intangible Heritage as Metacultural Production." *Museum International* 56(1–2): 52–65.

Koñwepag, Venancio, and César Kolima. [1940] 2017. "El problema indígena de Chile." *Anales de la Universidad de Chile* 13: 407–414.

LaBarre, Weston. 1975. *The Peyote Cult*. 4th ed. Hamden, CT: Archon Books.

Landau, Greg. 1999. "Guitarra Armada: The Role of Music in the Nicaraguan Revolution." PhD diss., University of California, San Diego.

Lange, Francisco Curt. 1936. "Sistemas de investigación folclórica y el empleo del acervo folklórico en la música artística." *Boletín Latino Americano de Música* 2(April): 143–156.

La Gaceta Diario Oficial (Nicaragua). 1942. 46(34): 301.

La Vere, David. 1998. *Life among the Texas Indians: The WPA Narratives*. College Station: Texas A&M University Press.

Leckie, Shirley. 2000. *Angie Debo: Pioneering Historian*. Norman: University of Oklahoma Press.

León Villagra, Mariana, and Ignacio Ramos Rodillo. 2011. "Sonidos de un Chile profundo: Hacia un análisis crítico del Archivo Sonoro de Música Tradicional Chilena en relación a la conformación del folklore en Chile." *Revista Musical Chilena* 65(215): 23–39.

Levy, David W. 2015. *The University of Oklahoma, A History, Volume 2, 1917–1950*. Norman: University of Oklahoma Press.

Locatatelli de Pérgamo, Ana María. 2005. "Recordando à Isabel Aretz (13/4/1909–01/06/2005)." *Latin American Music Review* 26(20): 158–163.

López, Rick A. 2010. *Crafting Mexico: Intellectuals, Artisans, and the State after the Revolution*. Durham, NC: Duke University Press.

López Hernández, Haydeé. 2022. "Art, Folklore, and Industry: Popular Arts and Indigenismo in Mexico, 1920–1946." *Latin American and Caribbean Ethnic Studies* 17(4): 495–518.

Loughlin, Patricia. 2005. *Hidden Treasures of the American West: Muriel H. Wright, Angie Debo, and Alice Marriott*. Albuquerque: University of New Mexico Press.

Luker, Morgan. 2016. *The Tango Machine: Musical Culture in the Age of Expediency*. Chicago: University of Chicago Press.

Luker, Morgan. 2022. "Matrix Listening; or, What and How We Can Learn from Historical Sound Recordings." *Ethnomusicology* 66(2): 290–318.

Madrid, Alejandro. 2009. *Sounds of the Modern Nation: Music, Culture and Ideas in Post-Revolutionary Mexico*. Philadelphia: Temple University Press.

Madrid, Alejandro. 2011a. "Transnational Musical Encounters at the U.S.–Mexico Border: An Introduction." In *Transnational Encounters: Music and Performance at the U.S. Mexico Border*, ed. Alejandro Madrid, 1–16. New York: Oxford University Press.

Madrid, Alejandro. 2011b. "Transnational Identity, the Singing of Spirituals, and the Performance of Blackness among Mascogos." In *Transnational Encounters: Music and Performance at the U.S. Mexico Border*, ed. Alejandro Madrid, 171–190. New York: Oxford University Press.

Mallon, Florencia E. 2010. "La 'doble columna' y la 'doble conciencia' en la obra de Manuel Manquilef." *Revista de Antropología* 21(10): 59–80.

Mark, Joan. 1988. *A Stranger in Her Native Land: Alice Fletcher and the American Indians*. Lincoln: University of Nebraska Press.

Martí, José. 2002. *Selected Writings*. Edited and translated by Esther Allen. New York: Penguin.

Masquiarán Díaz, Nicolás. 2011. "La construcción de la institucionalidad musical en Concepción, 1934–1963." Masters thesis, University of Chile.

Matamoros Mercado, Ruth Herenia. 2008. "A Nation Beyond Borders: Transnational Identity and Land Rights Struggles among the Miskitu of Honduras and Nicaragua." Masters thesis, University of Texas at Austin.

Mbembe, Achille. 2002. "The Power of the Archive and its Limits." In *Refiguring the Archive*, ed. Carolyn Hamilton, Verne Harris, Michèle Pickover, Graeme Reed, Razia Saleh, and Jane Taylor, 19–26. Dordrecht: Kluwer Academic Publishers.

McAllester, David. 1949. *Peyote Music*. New York: Viking.

McDonald, William F. 1969. *Federal Relief Administration and the Arts*. Columbus: Ohio State University Press.

McKenzie-Jones, Paul. 2015. *Clyde Warrior: Tradition, Community, and Red Power*. Norman: University of Oklahoma Press.

Mejía Sánchez, Ernesto. 1946. *Romances y Corridos Nicaragüenses*. Mexico City: Imprenta Universitaria.

Menard, André, and Jorge Pavez. 2005. "Documentos de la Federación Araucana y del Comité Ejecutivo de la Araucanía de Chile." *Anales de Desclasificación* 1(1): 51–109.

Mendoza, Zoila S. 2008. *Creating Our Own: Folklore, Performance, and Identity in Cuzco, Peru*. Durham, NC: Duke University Press.

Mendoza-Denton, Norma. 2016. "Norteño and Sureño Gangs, Hip hop, and Ethnicity on YouTube: Localism in California through Spanish Accent Variation." In *Raciolinguistics: How Language Shapes Our Ideas about Race*, ed. H. S. Alim, J. R. Rickford, and A. F. Ball, 135–150. Oxford: Oxford University Press.

Mercado, Claudio. 2002. "Ritualidades en conflicto: los bailes chinos y la Iglesia Católica en Chile Central." *Revista Musical Chilena* 56(197): 39–76.

Mercado, Claudio, and Pablo Villalobos. 2020. "Colección Isabel Aretz." Museo Chileno de Arte Precolombino.

Merida, Carlos. [1937] 1968. *Modern Mexican Artists*. Originally published by Frances Toor Studios. Freeport, NY: Books for Libraries Press.

Meringer, Eric Rodrigo. 2010. "The Local Politics of Indigenous Self-Representation: Intraethnic Political Division among Nicaragua's Miskito People during the Sandinista Era." *The Oral History Review* 37(1): 1–17.

Merino, Luis. 1979. "Presencia del Creador Domingo Santa Cruz en la Historia de la Música Chilena." *Revista Musical Chilena* 33(146–147): 15–79.

Merino, Luis. 1983. "Nuevas Luces sobre Acario Cotapos." *Revista Musical Chilena* 37(159): 3–49.

Merino, Luis. 2000. "Juan Orrego-Salas a los Ochenta Años." *Latin American Music Review* 21(1): 3–8.

Meyn, Susan Labry. 2001. *More Than Curiosities: A Grassroots History of the Indian Arts and Crafts Board and its Precursors, 1920–1942*. Lanham, MD: Lexington Books.

Miles, Tia. 2005. *Ties That Bind: The Story of an Afro-Cherokee Family in Slavery and Freedom*. Berkeley: University of California Press.

Minks, Amanda. 2013. *Voices of Play: Miskitu Children's Speech and Song on the Atlantic Coast of Nicaragua*. Tucson: University of Arizona Press.

Minks, Amanda. 2014. "Reading Nicaraguan Folklore through Inter-American Indigenismo, 1940–1970." *Latin American and Caribbean Ethnic Studies* 9 (3): 197–221.

Minks, Amanda. 2020a. "Inter-American Mediations: Charles Seeger, Domingo Santa Cruz, and the Politics of International Musical Exchange." *Latin American Music Review* 41(1): 93–119.

Minks, Amanda. 2020b. "Auralidad e interculturalidad en la Vanguardia nicaragüense." *Trans: Revista Transcultural de Música* 24(December): 1–19.

Minks, Amanda. 2022. "Henrietta Yurchenco, música indígena e indigenismo interamericano en la década de 1940." *Latin American Caribbean and Ethnic Studies* 17(4): 423–444.

Minks, Amanda, and Ana María Ochoa Gautier. 2021. "Music, Language, Aurality: Latin American and Caribbean Resoundings." *Annual Review of Anthropology* 50: 23–39.

Minks, Amanda, Daniel Swan, and Joshua Nelson. 2018. "Community Archiving of Native American Music." NEH Humanities Collections and Reference Resources White Paper, grant number PW-234685-16.

Miranda, Carolina. 2016. "Las cartas privadas de Wanda Morla Lynch: Entre género discursivo y fuente documental." *Logos: Revista de Lingüística, Filosofía y Literatura* 26(2): 148–162.

Miranda, Paula. 2017. "Violeta Parra, Creative Researcher." In *Violeta Parra, Life and Work*, ed. Lorna Dillon, 83–104. Woodbridge, UK: Tamesis.

Miranda, Paula, Elisa Loncón, and Allison Ramay. 2017. *Violeta Parra en el Wallmapu: Su encuentro con el canto Mapuche*. Santiago: Pehuén Editores.

Monte, Antonio, and Juan Pablo Gómez. 2020. "Autoritarismo, violencia y élites en Nicaragua. Reflexiones sobre la crisis (2018–2019)." *Anuario de Estudios Centroamericanos* (Universidad de Costa Rica) 46: 1–29.

Montero, Gonzalo. 2018. "'Entre campo y grabación': Violeta Parra y las tecnologías migrantes." *Studies in Latin American Popular Culture* 36: 128–144.

Moore, Chauncey, and Ethel Moore. 1966. *Ballads and Folk Songs of the Southwest*. Norman: University of Oklahoma Press.

Morales, Leónidas. 2017. "Violeta Parra: The Genesis of her Art." In *Violeta Parra: Life and Work*, ed. Lorna Dillon. Woodbridge, UK: Tamesis.

Morgan, Anne Hodges. 1986. "Introduction." In *The WPA Guide to 1930s Oklahoma*, vii–xviii. Lawrence: University Press of Kansas.

Moses, L. G. 2002. *The Indian Man: A Biography of James Mooney*. Lincoln: University of Nebraska Press.

Ñanculef Huaiquinao, Juan. 2022, Jaime Cuyanao (Waikil), and Leonardo Díaz-Collao. 2022. *Allkütuayiñ: Introducción a la música mapuche*. Santiago: Ministerio de las Culturas, las Artes y el Patrimonio and International Council for Traditional Music—Chile.

Novak, David. 2011. "The Sublime Frequencies of New Old Media." *Public Culture* 23(365): 603–634.

Novak, David. 2013. *Japanoise: Music at the Edge of Circulation*. Durham, NC: Duke University Press.

Ochoa Gautier, Ana María. 2006. "Sonic Transculturation, Epistemologies of Purification and the Aural Public Sphere in Latin America." *Social Identities* 12(6): 803–825.

Ochoa Gautier, Ana María. 2014. *Aurality: Listening and Knowledge in 19th Century Colombia*. Durham, NC: Duke University Press.

Ochs, Elinor. 2004. "Narrative Lessons." In *Companion to Linguistic Anthropology*, edited by Alessandro Duranti, 269–89. Hoboken, NJ: Blackwell.

Offen, Karl. 2010. "Race and Place in Colonial Mosquitia." In *Blacks and Blackness in Central America: Between Race and Place*, ed. Lowell Gudmundson and Justin Wolfe, 92–129. Durham, NC: Duke University Press.

Ortega, Lina. 2019. *The Indians for Indians Radio Show*. Norman: University of Oklahoma Libraries.

Ospina Romero, Sergio Daniel. 2019. "Recording Studios on Tour: The Expeditions of the Victor Talking Machine Company through Latin America, 1903–1926." PhD diss., Cornell University.

Palomino, Pablo. 2015. "Nationalist, Hemispheric, and Global: 'Latin American Music' and the Music Division of the Pan American Union, 1939–1947." *Nuevo Mundo— Mundos Nuevos* (June).

Palomino, Pablo. 2020. *The Invention of Latin American Music: A Transnational History*. New York: Oxford University Press.

Paraskevaídis, Graciela. 2004. "Edgard Varèse and His Relationships with Latin American Musicians and Intellectuals of His Time." *Contemporary Music Review* 23(2): 3–17.

Parker, Dorothy. 1994. *Singing an Indian Song: A Biography of D'Arcy McNickle*. Lincoln: University of Nebraska Press.

Pavez Ojeda, Jorge. 2015. *Laboratorios etnográficos: Los archivos de la antropología en Chile (1880–1980)*. Santiago: Alberto Hurtado.

Peña Queralt, Pilar. 2010. "La revolución ilustrada de la música chilena 1960–1973: Una aproximación al problema del arte." Master's thesis, Universidad de Chile.

Pereira Salas, Eugenio. 1943. *Notes on the History of Music Exchange between the Americas before 1940*. Washington, DC: Music Division, Pan American Union.

Pérez de Arce, José. [2007] 2020. *Música mapuche*. Santiago: Ocho Libros.

Pernet, Corinne. 2007. "'For the Genuine Culture of the Americas': Musical Folklore, Popular Arts, and the Cultural Politics of Pan Americanism, 1933–1950." In *Decentering America*, ed. J. Gienow-Hecht, 132–68. New York: Bergahn.

Pernet, Corinne. 2004. "The Popular Fronts and Folklore: Chilean Cultural Institutions, Nationalism and Pan-Americanism, 1936–1948." In *North Americanization of Latin America? Culture, Gender, and Nation in the Americas*, ed. Hans Joachim Köbug and Stefan Rinke, 254–276. Stuttgart: Verlag Hans-Dieter Heinz Akademischer Verlag.

Pescatello, Ann. 1992. *Charles Seeger: A Life in American Music*. Pittsburgh: University of Pittsburgh Press.

Petrusich, Amanda. 2014. *Do Not Sell at Any Price: The Wild, Obsessive Hunt for the World's Rarest 78rpm Records*. New York: Simon and Schuster.

Phelan, Andrew. 2015. *Unfinished, Unknown or Unseen: The Life of Emilio Amero (1901–1976) with Examples of His Graphic Designs, Illustrations, Photographs and Films.* Norman, OK: Quail Creek Editions.

Philp, Kenneth. 1977. *John Collier's Crusade for Indian Reform, 1920–1954.* Tucson: University of Arizona Press.

Pineda, Baron. 2001. "The Chinese Creoles of Nicaragua: Identity, Economy, and Revolution in a Caribbean Port City." *Journal of Asian American Studies* 4(3): 209–233.

Pineda, Baron. 2006. *Shipwrecked Identities: Navigating Race on Nicaragua's Mosquito Coast.* New Brunswick, NJ: Rutgers University Press.

Pisani, Michael V. 2005. *Imagining Native America in Music.* New Haven, CT: Yale University Press.

Pomian, Krzysztof. 1990. *Collectors and Curiosities: Paris and Venice, 1500–1800.* Trans. Elizabeth Wiles-Portier. Cambridge: Polity Press.

Poveda, Juan Carlos. 2019. "HELLO FRIENDS, CANTEMOS: La música en las representaciones de lo latinoamericano en largometrajes de ficción hollywoodenses durante el período de la Política del buen vecino (1933–1945)." PhD diss., Universidad de Chile.

Poveda Viera, Juan Carlos. 2021. "Música y propaganda en dos filmes animados producidos por Disney durante la Segunda Guerra Mundial." *Revista Musical Chilena* 75(236): 119–142.

Povinelli, Elizabeth. 2011. *Economies of Abandonment: Social Belonging and Endurance in Late Liberalism.* Durham, NC: Duke University Press.

Quiroa, Néstor. 2017. "Friar Francisco Ximénez and the *Popol Vuh*: From Religious Treatise to Digital Sacred Book." *Ethnohistory* 64(2): 241–270.

Rama, Angel. [1984] 1996. *The Lettered City.* Durham, NC: Duke University Press.

Rama, Angel. [1982] 2012. *Writing across Cultures: Narrative Transculturation in Latin America.* Trans. David Frye. Durham, NC: Duke University Press.

Ramírez, Sergio. 2007. *Tambor Olvidado.* San José: Santillana de Costa Rica.

Ramos, Alcida Rita. 1998. *Indigenism: Ethnic Politics in Brazil.* Madison: University of Wisconsin Press.

Ramos, Julio. [1989] 2001. *Divergent Modernities: Culture and Politics in Nineteenth Century Latin America.* Durham, NC: Duke University Press.

Ramos Rodillo, Ignacio, and Karen Donoso Fritz. 2023. "La función social del folclor: crítica, investigación y política cultural durante la trayectoria inicial de Pablo Garrido—Chile, 1928–1944." *Revista Musical Chilena* 77(239): 61–82.

Ramsey, Jarold. 1992. "Francis LaFlesche's 'The Song of Flying Crow' and the Limits of Ethnography." *boundary 2*, 19(3): 180–196.

Reed, Trevor. 2019. "Reclaiming Ownership of the Indigenous Voice: The Hopi Music Repatriation Project." In *Oxford Handbook of Musical Repatriation*, ed. Frank Gunderson, Robert C. Lancefield, and Bret Woods, 627–654. New York: Oxford University Press.

Regnier, Amanda, Patrick Livingood, and Scott Hammerstedt. 2013. "The Last of WPA Archaeology in Oklahoma: The Clement and McDonald Sites." In *Shovel Ready: Archaeology and Roosevelt's New Deal for America*, ed. Bernard K. Means, 110–126. Tuscaloosa: University of Alabama Press.

Rekedal, Jacob. 2015. "Warrior Spirit: From Invasion to Fusion Music in the Mapuche Territory of Southern Chile." PhD diss., University of California Riverside.

Rekedal, Jacob, organizer. 2022. "Collaborative Knowledge Production in the Territories of the Southern Cone." In *Dialogues: Towards Decolonizing Music and Dance Studies*, ed. Tan Sooi Beng and Marcia Ostashewski. International Council of Traditional Music. https://ictmdialogues.org/

Repp, Diana. 2005. "The Doris Duke American Indian Oral History Program: Gathering the 'Raw Material of History.'" *Journal of the Southwest* 47(1): 11–28.

Reynolds, Andrew. 2016. "Postcards, Autographs, and *Modernismo*: Rubén Darío on Popular Collecting and Textual Practices." In *Collecting from the Margins: Material Culture in a Latin American Context*, ed. María Mercedes Andrade, 93–114. Lewisburg, PA: Bucknell University Press.

Rhea, John M. 2016. *A Field of Their Own: Women and American Indian History, 1830–1941*. Norman: University of Oklahoma Press.

Rios, Fernando. 2008. "*La Flûte Indienne*: The Early History of Andean Folkloric-Popular Music in France and its Impact on *Nueva Canción*." *Latin American Music Review* 29(2): 145–189.

Rios, Fernando. 2020. *Panpipes and Ponchos: Musical Folklorization and the Rise of the Andean Conjunto Tradition in La Paz, Bolivia*. New York: Oxford University Press.

Roberts, Alaina. 2021. *I've Been Here All the While: Black Freedom on Native Land*. Philadelphia: University of Pennsylvania Press.

Robinson, Dylan. 2020. *Hungry Listening: Resonant Theory for Indigenous Sound Studies*. Minneapolis: University of Minnesota Press.

Rodriguez, Alberto, and Rene Torres. 2016. "John Lomax's Southern States Recording Expedition: *Brownsville, Texas, 1939*." *Journal of Texas Music History* 16: 8–21.

Romero, Raúl. 2017. "Nationalisms and Anti-*Indigenismos*: Rudolph Holzmann and his Contribution to a 'Peruvian' Music." In *Sound, Image, and National Imaginary in the Construction of Latin/o American Identities*, 91–105. Lanham, MD: Lexington Books.

Romero Vargas, Germán. 1993. "La población de origen africano en Nicaragua." In *Presencia Africana en Centroamérica*, ed. Luz María Martínez Montiel, 151–198. Mexico City: Consejo Nacional para la Cultural y las Artes.

Root, Deane L. 1972. "The Pan American Association of Composers (1928–1934). *Anuario Interamericano de Investigación Musical* 8: 49–70.

Rosemblatt, Karin Alejandra. 2018. *The Science and Politics of Race in Mexico and the United States, 1910–1950*. Chapel Hill: University of North Carolina Press.

Roy, Thomas. 2007. "Yí:sàum: Parker McKenzie's Double Vision of Kiowa Culture and Language." PhD diss., University of Oklahoma.

Rozental, Sandra. 2017. "On the Nature of Patrimonio: Cultural Property in Mexican Contexts." In *The Routledge Companion to Cultural Property*, ed. Jane Anderson and Haidy Geismar, 237–257. New York: Routledge.

Rozental, Sandra, John F. Collins, and Jason Ramsey. 2016. "Matters of Patrimony: Anthropological Theory and the Materiality of Replication in Contemporary Latin America." *Journal of Latin American and Caribbean Anthropology* 21(1): 7–18.

Ruiz Zamora, Agustín. 2006. "Margot Loyola y Violeta Parra: Convergencias y divergencias en el paradigma interpretativo de la Nueva Canción chilena." *Cátedra de Artes* 3: 41–58.

Saavedra, Leonora. 1999. "The American Composer in the 1930s: The Social Thought of Seeger and Chávez." In *Understanding Charles Seeger, Pioneer in American Musicology*, ed. Bell Yung and Helen Rees, 29–63. Urbana: University of Illinois Press.

Saavedra. Leonora. 2015a. "Carlos Chávez and the Myth of the Aztec Rennaissance." In *Carlos Chávez and his World*, ed. Leonora Saavedra, 134–164. Princeton, NJ: Princeton University Press.

Saavedra, Leonora. 2015b. "Carlos Chávez's Polysemic Style: Constructing the National, Seeking the Cosmopolitan." *Journal of the American Musicological Society* 68(1): 99–149.

Sachs, Joel. 2012. *Henry Cowell: A Man Made of Music*. New York: Oxford.

Salas, Filomena. 1945. "El Instituto de Investigaciones del Folklore Musical." *Revista Musical Chilena* 1(3): 19–27.

Salas Viu, Vicente. 1967. "Carlos Lavín y la musicología en Chile." *Revista Musical Chilena* 21(99): 8–14.

Salvatore, Ricardo. 2005. "Library Accumulation and the Emergence of Latin American Studies." *Comparative American Studies* 3(4): 415–436.

Salvatore, Ricardo. 2014. "Progress and Backwardness in Book Accumulation: Bancroft, Basadre, and Their Libraries." *Comparative Studies in Society and History* 56(4): 995–1026.

Samuels, David, Louise Meintjes, Ana María Ochoa, and Thomas Porcello. 2010. "Soundscapes: Toward a Sounded Anthropology." *Annual Review of Anthropology* 39: 329–345.

Sanders, Douglas. 1977. "The Formation of the World Council of Indigenous Peoples." IWGIA Document ISSN 0105–4503. Copenhagen: International Working Group for Indigenous Affairs.

Sandoval Valdívia, Elba. 1957. "Los Miskitos: Costumbres y Folklore." *Nicaragua Indígena* 2(15): 17–28.

Sandoval Valdívia, Elba. 1999. "Nicaragua: Funerales y otros ritos mískitos." In *Nuestra Cosmovisión: Creencias, Prácticas y Rituales*, ed. Giselle Chang Vargas, 359–365. Libro 2, Serie Culturas Populares Centroamericanas. San José, Costa Rica: Coordinación Educativa y Cultural Centroamericana (CECC), Secretaría General, UNESCO.

Sanjinés, Javier. [2009] 2013. *Embers of the Past: Essays in Times of Decolonization*. Durham, NC: Duke University Press.

Santa Cruz, Domingo. 1932. "Una conferencia de Carlos Isamitt sobre música araucana." *Aulos* 1(1): 22–23.

Santa Cruz, Domingo. 1950. "Mis Recuerdos Sobre la Sociedad Bach." *Revista Musical Chilena* 6(40): 8–62.

Santa Cruz, Domingo. 2008. *Mi vida en la música: Contribución al estudio de la vida musical Chilena durante el siglo XX*. Santiago: Gobierno de Chile, Consejo Nacional de la Cultura y las Artes, Consejo National del Libro y la Lectura.

Schell, William. 2001. *Intimate Outsiders: The American Colony in Mexico City, 1876–1911*. Lanham, MD: SR Books.

Scruggs, T. M. 1994. "The Nicaraguan Baile de la Marimba and the Empowerment of Identity." PhD diss., University of Texas at Austin.

Scruggs, T. M. 1999. "Let's Enjoy as Nicaraguans": The Use of Music in the Construction of a Nicaraguan National Consciousness. *Ethnomusicology* 43(2): 297–321.

Scruggs, T. M. 2002. "Socially Conscious Music Forming the Social Conscience: Nicaraguan Música Testimonial and the Creation of a Revolutionary Moment." In *From Tejano to Tango. Latin American Popular Music*, edited by Walter Aaron Clark, 41–69. New York: Routledge.

Seeger, Anthony. 2009. "Lessons Learned from the ICTM (NGO) Evaluation of Nominations for the UNESCO *Masterpieces of the Oral and Intangible Heritage of*

Humanity, 2001–5." In *Intangible Heritage*, ed. Laurajane Smith and Natsuko Akagawa, 112–128. New York: Routledge.

Serrano, Leopoldo. 1955. "Crónica Folklórica de las Festividades de San Sebastián de Diriamba." *Nicaragua Indígena* 2(5–6): 41–63.

Shepard, John. 2006. "The Legacy of Carleton Sprague Smith: Pan American Holdings in the Music Division of the New York Public Library for the Performing Arts." *Notes*, Second Series, 62(3): 621–662.

Simpson, Audra. 2007. "On the Logic of Discernment." *American Quarterly* 59(2): 479–491.

Skilton, Charles. 1919. "Realism in Indian Music." In *Studies in Musical Education History and Aesthetics. Papers and Proceedings of the Music Teachers' National Association*, 106–114. Hartford, CT: Music Teachers National Association.

Slonimsky, Nicolas. 1945. *Music of Latin America*. New York: Thomas Y. Crowell.

Smith, Carleton Sprague. 1940. *Musical Tour through South America, June–October, 1940*. New York: Conference on Inter-American Relations in the Field of Music.

Smith, Laurajane. 2006. *Uses of Heritage*. New York: Routledge.

Smith, Laurajane, and Natsuko Akagawa. 2009. "Introduction." In *Intangible Heritage*, ed. Laurajane Smith and Natsuko Akagawa, 1–10. New York: Routledge.

Snyder, Michael. 2017. *John Joseph Mathews: Life of an Osage Writer*. Norman: University of Oklahoma Press.

Solís, Eudoro. 1959. "Informe del Gobierno de Nicaragua al IV Congreso Indigenista Interamericano." *Nicaragua Indígena* 3(26): 23–34.

Solís Cuadra, Pedro Xavier. 2001. *El movimiento de Vanguardia de Nicaragua: Análisis y antología*. Managua: Fundación Vida.

Solís Cuadra, Pedro Xavier. 2008. *Pablo Antonio Cuadra: Intinerario*. Managua: Academia Nicaragüense de la Lengua.

Spencer-Espinosa, Christian, Antonieta Contreras, and Gabriel Rammsy. 2019. "Historia, Producción y Continuidad de la Sociedad de Folklore Chileno." *Recial* 10(16): 1–24.

Steedman, Carolyn. 2002. *Dust: The Archive and Cultural History*. New Brunswick, NJ: Rutgers University Press.

Stefano, Michelle, and Peter Davis, eds. 2017. *The Routledge Companion to Intangible Cultural Heritage*. New York: Routledge.

Sterne, Jonathan. 2003. *The Audible Past: Cultural Origins of Sound Reproduction*. Durham, NC: Duke University Press.

Stewart, Omer C. 1987. *Peyote Religion, A History*. Norman: University of Oklahoma Press.

Stoler, Ann. 2009. *Along the Archival Grain: Epistemic Anxieties and Colonial Common Sense*. Princeton, NJ: Princeton University Press.

Sturm, Circe. 2002. *Blood Politics: Race, Culture, and Identity in the Cherokee Nation of Oklahoma*. Berkeley: University of California Press.

Sullivan, John Jeremiah. 2014. "The Ballad of Geeshie and Elvie: On the Trail of the Phantom Women who Changed American Music and then Vanished without a Trace." *New York Times Magazine*, April 13.

Swan, Daniel. 1990. "West Moon-East Moon: An Ethnohistory of the Peyote Religion among the Osage Indians, 1898–1930." PhD diss., University of Oklahoma.

Swan, Daniel. 1999. *Peyote Religious Art: Symbols of Faith and Belief*. Jackson: University Press of Mississippi.

Szwed, John. 2010. *Alan Lomax: The Man Who Recorded the World*. New York: Viking Penguin.

Tahmahkera, Dustin. 2022. *Cinematic Comanches: The Lone Ranger in the Media Borderlands*. Lincoln: University of Nebraska Press.

Taussig, Michael. 1993. *Mimesis and Alterity: A Particular History of the Senses*. New York: Routledge.

Tercero, Dorothy M. 1940. "The First Inter-American Congress on Indian Life, Pátzcuaro, Michoacán, Mexico, April 14–24, 1940." *Bulletin of the Pan-American Union* 74(10): 702–712.

Tick, Judith. 1997. *Ruth Crawford Seeger: A Composer's Search for American Music*. New York: Oxford University Press.

Tone-Pah-Hote, Jenny. 2019. *Crafting an Indigenous Nation: Kiowa Expressive Culture in the Progressive Era*. Chapel Hill: University of North Carolina Press.

Torres Alvarado, Rodrigo. 2004. "Cantar la diferencia. Violeta Parra y la canción chilena." *Revista Musical Chilena* 58(201): 53–73.

Troutman, John. 2009. *Indian Blues: American Indians and the Politics of Music, 1879–1934*. Norman: University of Oklahoma Press.

Trujillo, Michael. 2008. "Oñate's Foot: Remembering and Dismembering in Northern New Mexico." *Aztlán: A Journal of Chicano Studies* 33(2): 91–119.

Tucker, Joshua. 2013. *Gentleman Troubadours and Andean Pop Stars: Huayno Music, Media Work, and Ethnic Imaginaries in Urban Peru*. Chicago: University of Chicago Press.

Turner, Hannah. 2020. *Cataloguing Culture: Legacies of Colonialism in Museum Documentation*. Vancouver: UBC Press.

Urtecho, Isidro. [1906] 1968. "Costumbres de los indios mosquitos." *Revista Conservadora* 18(88): 45–49.

"'Vanishing Race' Gaining Rapidly." July 8, 1941. *El Reno Daily Tribune* 50(111): 6.

Vaughan, Mary Kay. 1997. *Cultural Politics in Revolution: Teachers, Peasants, and Schools in Mexico, 1930–1940*. Tucson: University of Arizona Press.

Velásquez Arce, José Alberto. 2017. "Patrimonio musical mapuche, su presencia en la comunidad y en la escuela. Consideraciones culturales necesarias para la enseñanza en el aula de música." PhD diss., Universitat Autònoma de Barcelona.

Vera, Alejandro. 2014. "Music, Eurocentrism and Identity: The Myth of the Discovery of America in Chilean Music History." *Advances in Historical Studies* 3(5): 298–312.

Vera Malhue, Fernanda Carolina. 2015. "¿Músicos sin pasado? Construcción conceptual en la historiografía musical chilena." Masters thesis, Universidad de Chile.

Verba, Ericka. 2017. "Back in the Days When She Sang Mexican Songs on the Radio . . . Before Violeta Parra was Violeta Parra." In *Violeta Parra: Life and Work*, ed. Lorna Dillon, 63–82. Woodbridge, UK: Tamesis.

Vergara, Jorge Iván, and Hans Gundermann. 2016. "Chile y el Instituto Indigenista Interamericano, 1940–1993. Una visión de conjunto." *Chungara, Revista de Antropología Chilena* 48(1): 127–144.

"Visitors from Hispanic America." 1941. *Hispanic American Historical Review* 21(2): 352–353.

Vizenor, Gerald. 2008. *Survivance: Narratives of Native Presence*. Lincoln: University of Nebraska Press.

Watland, Charles D. 1965. *Poet Errant: A Biography of Rubén Darío*. New York: Philosophical Library.

Webster, Anthony. 1999. "Sam Kenoi's Coyote Stories: Poetics and Rhetoric in Some Chiricahua Apache Narratives." *American Indian Culture and Research Journal* 23(1): 137–163.

Weidman, Amanda. 2014. "Anthropology and Voice." *Annual Review of Anthropology* 43: 37–51.

Weld, Kristin. 2014. *Paper Cadavers: The Archives of Dictatorship in Guatemala*. Durham, NC: Duke University Press.

Wheelock Román, Jaime. 1974. *Raíces indígenas de la lucha anticolonialista en Nicaragua*. Mexico: Siglo Veintuno Editores.

Whisnant, David E. 1995. *Rascally Signs in Sacred Places: The Politics of Culture in Nicaragua*. Chapel Hill: University of North Carolina Press.

White, Steven. 1993. *Modern Nicaraguan Poetry: Dialogues with France and the United States*. Lewisburg, PA: Bucknell University Press.

Wieser, Kimberly. 2019. *Texas . . . To Get Horses*. Harrah: That Painted Horse Press.

Williams, Raymond. 1977. *Marxism and Literature*. New York: Oxford University Press.

Wolkowicz, Vera. 2022. *Inca Music Reimagined: Indigenist Discourses in Latin American Art Music*. New York: Oxford University Press.

Wolf, Juan Eduardo. 2019. *Styling Blackness in Chile: Music and Dance in the African Diaspora*. Bloomington: Indiana University Press.

Wolfe, Justin. 2007. *The Everyday Nation-State: Community and Ethnicity in 19th-Century Nicaragua*. Lincoln: University of Nebraska Press.

Wunderlich, Volker. 1995. *Sandino: Una biografía política*. Managua: Editorial Nueva Nicaragua.

Yarbrough, Fay. 2008. *Race and the Cherokee Nation: Sovereignty in the Nineteenth Century*. Philadelphia: University of Pennsylvania Press.

Yúdice, George. 2003. *The Expediency of Culture: Uses of Culture in the Global Era*. Durham, NC: Duke University Press.

Yurchenco, Henrietta. 1943. "La música indígena en Chiapas, México." *América Indígena* 3 (4): 305–311.

Yurchenco, Henrietta. 1946. "La recopilación de música indígena." *América Indígena* 6(4): 321–331.

Yurchenco, Henrietta. 2002. *Around the World in 80 Years: A Memoir*. Point Richmond, CA: Music Research Institute Press.

Zambrano, Helga. 2020. "Modern, Mechanical Sounds Signal Ambivalence and Alarm: A Sound Reading of Three Short Stories and an Essay by Rubén Darío." *Trans: Revista Transcultural de la Música* 24(December): 1–19.

Zambrano, Helga. 2021. "The Sonic Archive of Twentieth-Century Nicaraguan Literature: Sound, Music, Technology, and Listening in Selected Works by Rubén Darío and Sergio Ramírez." PhD diss., University of California Los Angeles.

Zúñiga, Ariel. 2008. *Emilio Amero: Un Modernista Liminal/A Liminal Modernist*. [Mexico]: Albedrío.

Index